A BILLY GRAHAM CENTER MONOGRAPH

Health, Healing and God's Kingdom

New Pathways to Christian
Health Ministry in Africa

A BILLY GRAHAM CENTER MONOGRAPH

Health, Healing and God's Kingdom

New Pathways to Christian Health Ministry in Africa

W. Meredith Long

regnum

First published 2000 by
Regnum Books International
in association with Paternoster Publishing, PO Box 300, Carlisle, CA3 0QS, UK
and PO Box 1047, Waynesboro, GA 30830-2047, USA
and
the Billy Graham Center
Wheaton College, Wheaton, IL 60107-5593, USA

Regnum Books International

PO Box 70, Oxford, OX2 6HB, UK

17951 Cowan, Irvine, California, 92714 USA

José Marmol 1734, 1602 Florida, Buenos Aires, Argentina

PO Box 76, Akropong-Akuapem, Ghana

Post Bag number 21, Vasant Kunj, New Delhi 110057, India

c/o Dr Hwa Yung, Seminaria Theologi Malaysia,
PO Box 175, 70720 Seremban, Malaysia

04 03 02 01 00   7 6 5 4 3 2 1

British Library Cataloguing in Publication Data
A catalogue record for this book is available from the British Library.

ISBN (Regnum) 1-870345-36-3
ISBN (Billy Graham Center) 1-879089-34-3

Typeset by Reesprint,
Radley, Oxfordshire, OX14 3AJ, UK

Printed and bound by R.R. Donnelly and Co.,
Harrisonburg, VA, USA

Dedication

TO

My mother, Evelyn, who was ending her life well while I was writing this book, setting an example of courage and faith in dying; and to my father, Carlton, who throughout my life has demonstrated Christ's love, grace, and compassion in joyful and humble service.

AND TO

Marcy Lesesne and her parents, Hank and Jean. To Marcy for showing how life can be lived fully in the face of disability and to her parents for their lives of Christlike healing ministry to Marcy, to our family, and to thousands of others throughout the world.

Contents

Section 2
Discovering New Models for Health Care

Preface

> The truth was that all I heard about them (eldil or angelic-like spirits)
> served to connect two things which one's mind tends to keep separate, and
> that connecting gave one a sort of shock. We tend to think ... in two dis-
> tinct categories which we label "scientific" and "supernatural" respectively.
> (When thinking of eldil) the distinction between the natural and the
> supernatural, in fact, broke down; and when it had done so, one realized
> how great a comfort it had been – how it erased the burden of intolerable
> strangeness which the universe imposes on us by dividing it into the halves
> and encouraging the mind never to think of both in the same context.
> What price we may have paid for this comfort in the way of false security
> and accepted confusion of thought is another matter (Lewis 1965).

Christian health workers in Africa often feel some of the same discomfort
as the hero of C.S. Lewis' *Perelandra* as he anticipated meeting creatures
that fell somewhere in the gap between the natural and supernatural categories of his dualistic worldview. Western-trained clinicians in Africa
administer scientific medicine to peoples who believe that their experience of health and disease is intimately bound with a world of spiritual
relationships.

The fit is often an uncomfortable one. Christian doctors may be overwhelmed by traditional cures that, from a scientific perspective, delay
effective treatment of disease and injury or even increase the harmfulness
of the disease. African patients, on the other hand, wonder why Christian
doctors take a secular approach to healing, separating their medical treatment from their spiritual ministry.

When I first began my involvement in international health work twenty years ago, I felt I must persuade others to accept my scientific views on health and disease. Traditional beliefs and practices were almost invariably barriers to be overcome as we taught about germ theory, infection, and vaccination. And our efforts met with much success. Medical and health interventions that emerged from science have brought tremendous improvement in health and the treatment of disease. Immunizations, modern medicine, surgical interventions, access to clean water, and good sanitation have saved many lives and brought many into God's kingdom.

The longer I worked overseas, however, and particularly during my last seven years in Africa, I came to realize that scientific medicine was limited in what it could accomplish, and that some of these limitations lay in the nature of science itself. The limitations of scientific medicine will persist because science has no tools to intervene in the immaterial aspects of God's created order.

Many Africans, even Christians, still go to their traditional healers to answer the questions that scientific medicine cannot. "Who among my living or dead relatives have I offended to cause this disease or injury? Am I being punished for my wrongdoing or am I the victim of another's hatred or curse? How may I make things right with God, the ancestral or created spirits, or with those who have become my enemies so that I may escape the ill health that has befallen me and my family?"

Even among Christians who belong to churches that deny the presence of the spirit world, or who acknowledge its presence but teach that it is an evil that Christians must avoid, the last areas of life to fall under God's control are those traditional beliefs regarding disease, injury, and death. The rapid growth of indigenous churches throughout Africa is due in large part to their willingness to embrace both tradition and Christianity, even when the teachings of the two seem to conflict with one another.

We have often attributed these behaviors to a lack of spiritual maturity and the power of evil superstition. Only recently have we begun to examine ourselves and ask, "Do African traditions of health and healing address an aspect of our nature as God's creatures that scientific medicine is ill equipped even to examine? What may they know about health and healing that has been excised from our understanding by bio-medicine?"

In this book I try to answer some of these questions by bringing convergence of three streams of thought concerning health and healing — biblical teaching, African tradition, and medical and public health theory and practice. By exploring biblically holistic models of health and healing ministry in Africa I hope to ease the "burden of intolerable strangeness" that confronts those who daily interact with people who have woven the material and immaterial worlds into a single fabric of thought and practice.

I also pray that this book will stimulate reflection that ends in the transformation of Christian health and healing ministries in Africa. I join with those who are pointing in a new direction and offer some unique tools and insights to help Christian workers who wish to follow a pathway of biblically integrated health ministry that will bring many more into God's kingdom. I cannot, however, describe the road itself. It is a road that we must make by walking it. The boundaries are not yet clear and each culture represents a new terrain that the road must transverse. We must walk the road with Christ and with one another, guided by God as he reveals his will in Christ and the Bible, and moving together in community.

Acknowledgments

I wish to acknowledge those who contributed to this book. First, thanks to the Billy Graham Center of Wheaton College which provided the resources to end the first twenty years of my international health ministry with this reflective pause. Thanks to the advisory committee of scholars that helped to shape my thoughts and sharpen them; Dr. Evvy Campbell, Dr. Muriel Elmer, Dr. Scott Moreau, Dr. Robert Stickney, and Dr. Ken Gill. I express appreciation particularly to Dr. Richard Schultz for several readings of the portions of the manuscript related to Old Testament teaching. Thanks also to my colleagues at MAP International and now at World Relief who have helped to shape my vision and provided support to express it in continued ministry.

I am deeply thankful to my African friends and colleagues who have patiently taught and counseled me, rejoicing whenever I leapt to the obvious (to them). I hope that I have honored their instruction in this book.

I wish to thank my family for bearing with me through what must have seemed an interminable time. Particularly I thank my wife Kendra who encouraged me with her cheerfulness and appreciation through what may have seemed at times a second dissertation. The name given to her by my Kenyan colleagues was "Mother of Light" and she has been that to me for 30 years.

Finally, thanks to Byron Klaus and Dotsey Welliver who helped edit this manuscript. Like most authors what I intend to say is so clear to me that I lose sight of what I *did* say. God bless editors.

I wish to express a special appreciation also for the African proverbs scattered throughout this book. They were gleaned from *African Proverbs: Collections, Studies, Bibliographies,* ed. Stan Nussbaum. Compact Disk #3, 20:21 Library. Colorado Springs, CO: Global Mapping International, 1996.

Meredith Long

Section I

African Shadows of *Shalom*

Chapter 1

Health and Disease:
Rediscovering *Shalom*

◆ ◆ ◆

Daudi came into the clinic and I immediately saw that he had not improved since his previous visit. As a younger man Daudi had been full of boundless energy and as he aged, he had retained his vigor and love of life. The last-born son, he had been a herdsboy for his father's cattle. But he was extraordinarily gifted. He won fame in wars against neighboring tribes and now was the richest man in the region with numerous wives and children. People in the region said that he had the heart of a god because he had been so successful.

But today he was listless. When I asked him a question, he paused for several seconds before answering as though he hadn't heard me. When he did answer, he spoke softly and without energy or passion. Normally he stood straight but now he stooped over like a very old man. He complained of severe back pain. He could not sleep because of the pain, and at times his heart would begin racing even when there had been no exertion. He had two or three infected abrasions that I had treated earlier but that were not healing properly. I was uncertain how to proceed. He was slowly dying before my eyes and I could not discover why.

◆ ◆ ◆

I have sometimes used this case study with Christian health workers in Africa to open a workshop or discussion. "Suppose you were Daudi's physician. What would you do next? Do you have any tentative diagnoses to offer?" Most respond that additional diagnostic work would be the most appropriate step. Others offer a tentative diagnosis, often suggesting conditions such as chronic fatigue syndrome. I then continue to tell them the case study.

◆ ◆ ◆

I continued to probe and Daudi told me more. Like many rich men, he had extensive obligations to others in his clan and the wider community. As a generous man, he had provided for many. Most had returned gratitude but more recently some had turned against him, betraying his confidences and despising his gifts even as they received them. He suspected that some of them had joined with his enemies to plot evil against him. They constantly spoke evil about him. His sickness had compounded the effectiveness of their words and as he weakened, even more of his friends began to avoid him. They suspected that the gods had finally turned against him. Some were simply waiting to see if he would retain his wealth and power and others genuinely felt that, if they remained too close, they too would be included in Daudi's suffering.

Daudi could think of no specific evil he had done against those who had turned against him. Nevertheless, he felt that they were probably right; the gods had turned against him either because of some unknown sinful deed or some other trespass that he chose not to share with me. He felt that his only recourse to regain divine favor and his health was to repent and offer a sacrifice.

I felt out of my depth. I suspected that there was an underlying organic problem but had little to offer. I sent him away with some medicines that might relieve his pain and clear up some of the stubborn infection but knew that I had not adequately addressed his problem.

What happened to Daudi? He recovered, lived to a good old age, and died quietly. He selected the son of one of his most beautiful wives as his heir. His son managed the estate wisely and became richer and more powerful than his father.

◆ ◆ ◆

By the time I complete my account, some of the health care workers have thought of similar cases that they have faced. If they wish to know the reference for this case study, I tell them it's Psalm 38. Daudi, of course, is King David.

Psalm 38

O Lord, do not rebuke me in your anger or discipline me in your wrath. For your arrows have pierced me, and your hand has come down upon me. Because of your wrath there is no health in my body; my bones have no soundness because of my sin. My guilt has overwhelmed me like a burden too heavy to bear.

My wounds fester and are loathsome because of my sinful folly. I am bowed down and brought very low; all day long I go about in mourning. My back is filled with searing pain; there is no health in my body. I am feeble and utterly crushed; I groan in anguish of heart.

All my longings lie open before you, O Lord; my sighing is not hidden from you. My heart pounds, my strength fails me; even the light has gone from my eyes. My friends and companions avoid me because of my wounds; my neighbors stay far away. Those who seek my life set their traps, those who would harm me talk of my ruin; all day long they plot deception.

I am like a deaf man, who cannot hear, like a mute, who cannot open his mouth; I have become like a man who does not hear, whose mouth can offer no reply. I will wait for you, O Lord; you will answer, O Lord my God. For I said, "Do not let them gloat or exalt themselves over me when my foot slips."

For I am about to fall, and my pain is ever with me. I confess my iniquity; I am troubled by my sin. Many are those who are my vigorous enemies; those who hate me without reason are numerous. Those who repay my good with evil slander me when I seek what is good.

O Lord, do not forsake me; be not far from me, O my God. Come quickly to help me, O Lord my Savior.

The imaginary meeting of a medical doctor and a stricken David sounds strange but, for health workers in Africa, there is a ring of familiarity. Traditional perspectives on health, disease, and healing in Africa more strongly parallel certain aspects of King David's worldview than that of the biomedically trained clinician.

When most Christian health care workers evaluate traditional African practices concerning health, disease, and healing, they use criteria drawn from their medical and health training. As a result, their evaluation never penetrates below the level of practice and into the values and worldviews of those to whom they are ministering (Fountain 1989). In the first section of this book, I will bounce back and forth between biblical perspectives on health and healing and the traditional beliefs and practices in Africa. By exploring biblical teachings as the starting point for evaluating

African experience, I hope to build new understandings of health and healing. Working from a biblical basis of understanding, Christian health workers in African cultures will be better able to identify traditional beliefs and practices that may be affirmed, those that may be transformed by Christ to new meanings, and those that must be combated. In the second section, I bring these ideas together with medical and public health perspectives to challenge men and women in health-related ministry in Africa to new paths of healing and preventive ministry.

SUFFERING, SIN, AND PUNISHMENT: THE OLD COVENANT

David's struggle with his illness has lost none of its currency. Even if David lived today and had access to the best of scientific medicine, his healing would still require more than identifying the proper antibiotic. Prevention of his condition would still encompass more than teaching antiseptic technique for the care of wounds to a cadre of volunteer health workers. Neither of these responses would be wrong, but both would be incomplete. Neither would address the root cause of David's problem and neither, alone, would transform David's understanding of himself and his relationship to his God.

When David wrote this psalm, his world was falling apart.

* *David was alienated from his God.* The God who had made covenants of peace and blessing with Noah, Abraham, and David himself had turned upon David with terrible intensity. Though God had wounded David, he was also David's only hope of restoration. For David to flee from God would be impossible. But he could not approach God with confidence. His ceremonial uncleanness because of his sores prevented his worship in the tabernacle. David pleaded with God to rescue him even as he feared he would be forsaken. He suffered the silence of God as he awaited his answer.

* *David was alienated from others.* Because David was ceremonially unclean, his friends could not touch him but they also abandoned him, not even coming near. In a downward spiral, his enemies' slander tormented David even as his torment empowered their slander. David's enemies told others, "God has withdrawn his favor. Otherwise David would not be near death." Some of those David thought had been his friends, who had enjoyed his hospitality and favor, joined his enemies in setting traps for his ruin.

- *David was alienated from the good gifts of God's creation.* He could no longer observe the restoring cycles of life. He was deprived of the creative joy of work as well as the comfort of rest. There was nothing in the created world that brought joy to David; he was cut off from the grace of the ordinary.

David's inner struggle was a mirror image of the terrible turmoil of his outer world. Physically he suffered. He described the symptoms vividly – searing pain, fatigue, festering wounds, and weakness. Emotionally and spiritually he suffered. Hope struggled with fear; guilt struggled with grace. David's world extended no further than his own pain and guilt. His sickness was a progressive dying.

Sin, Disease, and Punishment

Like any of us, David struggled with the question of why this was happening. His worldview allowed him only one answer. He was stricken because he had sinned and violated the provisions of God's covenants. Before the coming of Christ, God's relationship to his people was structured by the covenants that he made with them.[1]

Obedience to God's covenants brought his blessings; disobedience brought punishment. David, like those around him, assumed that severe, incurable, and untimely illness or injury represented God's punishment of sin.[2] In disease, God's breath of life (Genesis 2:7) became bated. For the people of God's covenants, serious, untimely disease foreshadowed death. The root word for sickness *(hlh)* signified a sapping of the vital energy of life given by God (Wolff 1981). It was a diminution of his presence. When a person was seriously ill, God was distant.

Before Moses died, he warned the Israelites that God would curse them if they disobeyed his covenants. Individual sickness was part of the curse.

> However, if you do not obey the Lord your God and do not carefully follow all of his commands and decrees I am giving you today, all these curses will come upon you and overtake you… The Lord will plague you with diseases until he has destroyed you from the land you are entering to possess. The Lord will strike you with wasting disease, with fever and inflammation, with scorching heat and drought, with blight and mildew, which will plague you until you perish…The Lord will afflict you with the boils of Egypt and with tumors, festering sores and the itch, from which you

cannot be cured. The Lord will afflict you with madness, blindness and confusion of mind...The Lord will afflict your knees and legs with painful boils that cannot be cured, spreading from the soles of your feet to the top of your head (Deuteronomy 28:15, 21–22, 27–28, 35).

God also punished the community and nation that was unfaithful to him and broke his covenants. Moses warned that if the nation of Israel turned away from Yahweh (their Lord God), he would destroy the peace, prosperity, and eventually the very identity of the community. Moses described a vividly horrific vision for the disobedient nation.

The sky over your head will be bronze, the ground beneath you iron. The Lord will turn the rain of your country into dust and powder, it will come down from the skies until you are ruined. The Lord will cause you to be defeated before your enemies. You will come at them from one direction but flee from them in seven, and you will become a thing of horror to all the kingdoms on earth...

Your sons and daughters will be given to another nation, and you will wear out your eyes watching for them day after day, powerless to lift a hand. A people that you do not know will eat what your land and labor produce, and you will have nothing but cruel oppression all your days...

Because of the suffering that your enemy will inflict on you during the siege, you will eat the fruit of the womb, the flesh of the sons and daughters the Lord your God has given you. Even the most gentle and sensitive man among you will have no compassion on his own brother or the wife he loves or his surviving children, and he will not give to one of them any of the flesh of his children that he is eating...The most gentle and sensitive woman among you – so sensitive and gentle that she would not venture to touch the ground with the sole of her foot – will begrudge the husband she loves and her own son or daughter the afterbirth from her womb and the children she bears. For she intends to eat them secretly during the siege and in the distress that your enemy will inflict on you in your cities (Deuteronomy 28: 23–25, 32–33, 53–57).

Brown (1995, 79–80) summarized the perspective on sickness and calamity captured in these verses.

Destructive maladies are a curse! Painful, wasting diseases are terrible afflictions, *not* divine blessings. Health is good; illness is bad. Debilitating sickness and devastating plagues are signs of God's anger, not his pleasure. *In fact, nowhere in the Bible does God ever promise sickness, disease, or calamity as blessings for his obedient children. Nowhere in the Bible is sickness, in and of itself, described as a good thing.*

SUFFERING, SIN, AND GRACE: THE NEW COVENANT

◆ ◆ ◆

When I asked my mother to read an early draft of the first part of this chapter, neither of us knew that she had only a month left to live, though she had battled cancer for several years. After reading it, my mother gave it back to me and said that she did not like the content. The implications of the Law were too severe. Did she suffer from cancer because of her sin? Was it God's punishment for some transgression? She had no problem in recognizing that cancer was neither a good thing nor a blessing but was it, for that reason, a curse of God upon her? She rejected the conclusions that David and his fellow Israelites (and many Africans) accepted.

◆ ◆ ◆

Questions concerning disease and catastrophe are ultimately personal, and the implications of the Law are severely disturbing to a person suffering from a serious disease. When we began our work with AIDS and African churches, we encountered some pastors who had no interest in ministering to those affected by AIDS because they felt AIDS sufferers were only receiving what they deserved. The assumption that illness and misfortune represent a just punishment of God leads to victim-blaming and may lessen compassion (Hilton 1996). Those who believe that misfortune and disease are invariably a punishment from God are not equipped to handle suffering, either their own or that of others.

Echoes of the Old Covenant in the New

In his anguish of soul, David believed that the suffering he wrote about in Psalm 38 was retribution for his sin. Jesus' disciples expressed this traditional perspective when they falsely assumed that the man who had been born blind was suffering punishment for his own or his parents' sins (John 9). The theme of retribution does not disappear from the New Testament. Jesus appealed to the strength of this belief when he cited his restoration of the paralytic as proof of his authority to forgive sins (Matthew 9:1–8). The illness and death of Herod (Acts 12:19–23), the sudden deaths of Ananias and Sapphira (Acts 5:1–11), and the illness and death of Corinthians who refused to honor the Lord's table at communion (1 Corinthians 11:27–32) as well as the catastrophic events in the prophecies in Revelation are all attributed to God's punishment for sin. The idea of retributive suffering lies at the heart of the atonement as well. Christ had to suffer because of the sins of the world that he bore.

Additionally, throughout his teachings, Jesus affirmed the principle that good and evil actions have good and evil consequences. Paul is more explicit in restating the biblical principle that people reap what they sow (Galatians 6:7). Though neither one applies this principle of naturally occurring consequences specifically to illness and death, their listeners and readers would recognize that ill health was among the possible consequences of sinful living.

Other themes regarding suffering that begin to emerge in the Old Testament (Kaiser 1982), however, find fuller expression in the story of the gospel and teaching of the early followers of Christ.

- People may suffer for doing what is right (1 Peter 3: 14–17; Matthew 5:10–12) but this suffering is usually limited to outside persecution, not to illness or injury unless it is a consequence of the persecution (Brown 1995).
- People may suffer with or on behalf of others. As Jesus suffered on behalf of others, so his followers are sometimes called to suffer for others. Having compassion (suffering with) for others, however, rarely takes the form of a voluntarily contracted disease or injury.
- People may suffer so that God is glorified. Jesus stated that the man born blind suffered so that "the work of God might be displayed in his life" (John 9:3). Whether or not Paul's "thorn in the flesh" (2 Cor. 12:7–10) was a chronic illness or disability, it illustrated a more basic biblical teaching that God's strength becomes most effective in weakness, including perhaps, the weakness that accompanies illness.
- People may suffer because of God's discipline (Heb. 12:1–12). Though God's discipline is described as hard and painful, the writer of the Hebrews did not specifically mention illness and injury.

The teachings of Jesus and the new covenant expand the concept of suffering beyond punishment for sin, but it does not take away the problem of asking why. How may I apply the additional insights of the New Testament to my mother's struggle with cancer, for instance?

- My mother certainly used the occasion of her cancer to witness to the goodness of God. Her courage in facing suffering, her cheerful and indomitable spirit, and her unwavering faith in God's goodness toward her demonstrated God's glory. But did God cause her death by cancer in order to be glorified? Would he not have brought greater glory to himself by healing her?

- Or perhaps my mother's death was the result of reaping what she had sowed? Her first bout with cancer came at a time of inner conflict in her own life. The complicating conditions of diabetes and hypertension may have been aggravated by her lack of exercise as she became older. But this seems unnecessarily harsh. Many others live a far less healthy life style than my mom did and live longer.

- Or perhaps the cancer represented God's punishment for some inner sin that she hid from us or that persisted when she failed to respond as God desired to his discipline? To those who knew her, this seems unlikely, but this question is basically unanswerable. If other people chose to attribute her death to God's punishment for sin that only he and my mother knew, we could make no more of a convincing counter-argument to them than Job made to his accusers.

- Or perhaps she was simply fated to repeat a family pattern. The Bible is silent on the question of heredity. My mother's mother suffered from hypertension and eventually succumbed to cancer at about the same age as my mother.

However I may choose to attribute Mom's suffering, I ultimately come back to the conclusion that illness and injury are the "common lot of humanity," and usually unrelated to suffering for the faith. Jesus never said, "Blessed are the sick" (Brown 1995, 232–233). Her death was in God's hands and in his timing. As in most deaths and serious disease and injury, we cannot answer the "whys" with the assurance of being correct, even with the additional insights of New Testament teaching.

The major differences between the Old and New Testaments may best be captured in contrasting a contractual agreement with a family relationship. The emphasis of the Old Testament was upon the contract between God and his people. The covenantal contracts specified the rewards for keeping the contract and the consequences of breaking it. God enforced the contract. When a contract is concluded between two parties, the underlying assumption is that both will keep its provisions. In practice, the covenantal contracts of the Old Testament were far more often broken than kept. "For the most part, Israel suffered God's wrath. Many were smitten; relatively few were healed" (Brown 1995, 210). In Old Testament thought, my mother's sickness would have represented God's enforcement of her intentionally or unintentionally breaching his contract with her.

Her relationship to God would therefore be ambivalent. The God of blessing and healing would also be for her the God of curses and judgement. David reflected that deep ambivalence in his lament, recognizing that his only hope of restoration and healing lay with the God who had grievously and fearfully wounded him. The history of God's people in the Old Testament was inexorably bound to these two expressions of God's character – the fearsome, righteous judge who punished disobedience and cursed the offenders, and the merciful, loving healer who blessed obedience and restored the repentant person, family, and nation.

Health, Healing and the Kingdom of God

The ministry of Jesus began with the understanding that he would fulfill God's contracts that men and women had permanently broken. The thrust of the gospels is upon healing and not judgement. Early in Jesus' ministry he declared his purpose in the synagogue of his hometown of Nazareth. He read from Isaiah:

> The Spirit of the Lord is on me, because he has anointed me to preach good news to the poor. He has sent me to proclaim freedom for the prisoners and recovery of sight for the blind, to release the oppressed, to proclaim the year of the Lord's favor (Lk. 4:18–19).

Jesus stopped in mid-sentence. The passage from Isaiah continues, "and the day of vengeance of our God" (Isa. 61:2). Jesus came to offer forgiveness and healing, to proclaim God's grace and not his judgement (Brown 1995, 210–211).

Because my mother had accepted Jesus' invitation of grace, had been adopted into his family, and become part of his kingdom, the provisions of covenantal contracts became relatively insignificant in coping with her illness. The contracts had not been annulled but had been covered in grace. Unlike David, my mother did not fear alienation from the family of God. God's healing promises for her have now been fulfilled.

> ... no one understands that the righteous are taken away to be spared from evil. Those who walk uprightly enter into peace; they find rest as they lie in death (Isa. 57:1b–2).

> Now the dwelling of God is with men, and he will live with them. They will be his people, and God himself will be with them and be their God. He will wipe every tear from their eyes. There will be no more death or mourning

or crying or pain, for the old order of things has passed away (Rev. 21:3–4).

But within the "old order of things," illness, injury, and death still feel alien to us, as though they should not be a part of living. Our intuition that illness, injury, and death do not belong is itself God-given. God created us for fullness of life in all of its dimensions. We will not experience complete fullness of health until God redeems all his creation, but we are able to experience the blessings of shalom even within a fallen world.

GOD'S BLESSING OF SHALOM

When our Israeli neighbors in Kenya greeted one another, they did not simply wish each other a good day. Like the Hebrew people for many generations before them, they blessed one another with "*shalom.*" In greeting one another with this blessing, they were saying, "May you and your family and community experience 'well-being, prosperity, and bodily health.' May you be 'at ease, satisfied, and fulfilled' in all of your relationships" (Nel 1997). It is an individual greeting but it recognizes that individual well-being is impossible outside the context of community and divine relationships (Harris 1970).

Our experience of shalom depends upon God's grace and our obedience. Righteousness and shalom are so intimately related that the psalmist said they kiss one another in the company of love and faithfulness (Ps. 85:10). In his farewell speech to the people he had led for forty years, Moses set a choice before them. They could choose life or death, blessings or curses, shalom or destruction. Just as David's sickness affected every aspect of his being, so the blessings of God's peace encompass all of life.

> If you fully obey the Lord your God and carefully follow all his commands I give you today, the Lord your God will set you high above all the nations on earth. All these blessings will come upon you and accompany you if you obey the Lord your God:
> You will be blessed in the city and blessed in the country. The fruit of your womb will be blessed, and the crops of your land and the young of your livestock – the calves of your herds and the lambs of your flocks. Your basket and your kneading trough will be blessed. You will be blessed when you come in and blessed when you go out.
> The Lord will grant that the enemies who rise up against you will be defeated before you. They will come at you from one direction but flee

from you in seven. The Lord will send a blessing on your barns and on everything you put your hand to. The Lord your God will bless you in the land he is giving you.

The Lord will establish you as his holy people, as he promised you on oath, if you keep the commands of the Lord your God and walk in his ways. Then all the peoples on earth will see that you are called by the name of the Lord and they will fear you. The Lord will grant you abundant prosperity – in the fruit of your womb, the young of your livestock and the crops of your ground – in the land he swore to your forefathers to give you.

The Lord will open the heavens, the storehouse of his bounty, to send rain on your land in season and to bless all the work of your hands. You will lend to many nations but will borrow from none. The Lord will make you the head, not the tail. If you pay attention to the commands of the Lord your God that I give you this day and carefully follow them, you will always be at the top, never at the bottom. Do not turn aside from any of the commands I give you today, to the right or to the left, following other gods and serving them (Deut. 28:1–14).

In illness, David's entire world fell apart. In shalom, or health, our relationships to God, one another, and the environment are at peace.

- Shalom is experienced in a right relationship to God. God is the author and giver of shalom. From the Aaronic blessing (Num. 6:24–26) it is evident that God blesses, guards, and treats graciously those to whom he gives his peace (Nel 1997). Shalom is rooted in relationship to God, and maintained only by his power (Brueggemann 1976).
- Shalom is experienced communally. We truly experience shalom only in community with one another (Brueggemann 1976). The well-being of the individual Hebrew in Moses' blessing cannot be separated from his blessing on the entire community; the well-being of one member of Christ's body cannot be separated from the corporate well-being of the church. Our experience of shalom depends not only on our individual peace but peace between peoples as well. As anyone who has worked in a war zone recognizes, individual well-being depends upon the peace and security of the nation in relationship to surrounding peoples. Shalom expresses "the social or communal relations between friends, parties, and nations." It signifies a treaty of peace between peoples (Nel 1997). The experience of shalom also depends upon the equitable distribution of wealth within the nation and community. God promised that the Hebrew people would prosper together if they kept his commands.

- Finally, we fully experience shalom only within the context of a family.[3] The ability to bear children is one of the blessings of God specified in his covenant of shalom. In Israel, the man who fathered no offspring was greatly shamed. The greatest punishment of God was not to destroy a man but to end his entire house. Barrenness was also a curse for the woman. Hagar despised Sarah for her barrenness (Gen. 16:4) just as Hannah's rival provoked her to tears (1 Sam. 1:6–7). Though both of these women were loved dearly by their husbands, they felt great shame.

- Shalom is experienced in a right relationship to the environment. God's blessings of shalom require a creative, productive dominion over God's creation. Productivity also requires God's work in maintaining the cycles of night and day, cold and heat, rain and dryness. Finally, it requires equity in the distribution of the wealth that is derived from the created world. Many diseases and injuries spring from an imbalance in our relationship to God's created order in choosing what we eat and drink, our patterns of exposure to harmful substances, our hygiene and sanitation, and our honoring of the cycles of work and rest that God established.

God's blessings of shalom embraced the full range of relationships that defined fullness of life for individual Israelites as well as the entire nation. *In this book, I will use the biblical construct of shalom to describe the fullness of life and relationship that constitutes good health in all of its dimensions* (Atkins 1990).

In the remainder of this first section, I examine biblical and African perspectives on health, disease, and healing by focusing on the key relationships that enable us to experience shalom. In the succeeding chapters I examine how relationships to God, community, and the environment influence health from biblical and African perspectives. In the concluding chapters of this section, I examine healing practices in the Bible and in Africa.

Notes

1   The covenant of creation, made with Adam and Eve (Genesis 1–3) and renewed with Noah following the flood (Genesis 8–9) established the nature of God's relationship to the created order, including the men and women he created in his image (Dumbrell 1984). These passages also reveal how the

essential nature of that relationship was marred by disobedience.

In the covenants of identification, God chose to identify himself with a particular people. He established personal covenants first with Abraham and later with David. His promises to establish the descendants of Abraham as a great nation and the line of David in an eternal kingdom were unilateral (McComiskey 1985). The initiation of the covenant with Abraham was implicitly contingent upon his obedience to God's command. Whether or not the individual descendants of Abraham and David received the blessings of the covenants was also contingent upon their identification with the God of their fathers.

In the covenant of law made at Mt. Sinai, God specified how individual and national obedience to standards of worship and behavior result in blessing and how disobedience brings destruction. The covenants were rooted in the relationship of God to his creatures. God stood alone on the one side of each of these covenants. He initiated each covenant and was himself the guarantor. He defined the terms of the covenants and the rewards and punishments tied to them. By his power he enforced the terms of the covenant (Robertson 1996).

2 As in all the surrounding countries, Israel had a cadre of health practitioners who practiced healing crafts outside terms of the covenant. Minor injuries and illnesses as well as the timely death of the elderly were not considered divine punishment. A cadre of practitioners treated wounds and injuries, usually through anointing with oil and binding wounds. These also appear as metaphors for God's healing work (Brown 1995).

3 Most North American or European readers will think of "family" in terms of a husband, wife, and their children and have presented that as a biblical ideal. I am not using "family" to refer only to the nuclear family but to the extended family, which I believe more closely expresses God's blessing of shalom. I am also not suggesting that God's blessing means having as many children as possible.

Chapter 2

The Shadow "Covenant":
Health, God, and the Spirits in African Belief

We'll take a second look at Daudi, not now as the King of Israel in the covenant of *shalom* but as a rich and successful businessman in Cameroon, and see how his story would be different. (The context for this interpretation is taken from Eric De Rosny's *Healers in the Night* [1985]).

♦ ♦ ♦

Daudi came into the clinic. I immediately saw that he had not improved since his previous visit. As a younger man Daudi had been full of boundless energy and as he aged, he had retained his vigor and love of life. The last-born son, he had been a herdsboy for his father's cattle. But he was extraordinarily gifted. He had achieved fame in competition with others in business and now was the richest man in the region with numerous wives and children.

But today he was listless. When I asked him a question, he paused for several seconds before answering as though he hadn't heard me. When he did answer, he spoke softly and without energy or passion. Normally he stood straight but now he stooped over like a very old man. He complained of severe back pain. He could not sleep because of the pain and at times his heart would begin racing even when there had been no exertion. He had two or three infected abrasions that I had treated earlier but that were not healing properly. Previous diagnostic tests had been equivocal. I had discovered no injury or disease to account for his back pain.

I was uncertain how to proceed. He was slowly dying before my eyes and I could not discover why.

I continued to probe. Although Daudi had been generous, he had nevertheless been aggressive in his business. Business owners of his own clan, who were not as capable or aggressive, had lost their businesses because they were unable to compete. One of his uncles, who had mortgaged his family's farm to secure funds to remain in business, but who was now on the verge of losing both his business and his land, went to the nganga *(diviner) to discover why this misfortune had befallen him. The nganga said that Daudi practiced* ekong *(sorcery). The nganga reminded the businessman of three young men and women who had died prematurely in the surrounding community in the past few years. He said that Daudi had purchased them and that after he had caused their deaths, they were trapped into helping him as his slaves in the unseen world. These unseen slaves worked against his competitors, bringing misfortune to their lives and driving customers from their shops.*

The embattled businessman was thankful to understand why this had happened to him and soon spread the word within the community. Many who resented Daudi's success were anxious to believe the nganga's divination. Together they sought protection and approached one of the most powerful witches in the region to protect them from Daudi's power, to counter it with a curse against him, and to purchase a poison to use against him. Though I could find no trace of toxic substances in Daudi's system, he was nevertheless convinced that the power of the witch was now working against him.

I felt out of my depth. Was Daudi mentally ill? It didn't seem so. He spoke rationally about the actions of his enemies and did not demonstrate paranoia as I understood it clinically. Was it the power of his belief that was causing him to be sick or was he under true spiritual attack? Had he actually ingested something toxic in his food or drink that we had not been able to discover with the tests we had available?

Those questions were beyond my ability to answer so I gave him the help that I could. I had run cultures on his lingering infections and discovered resistant bacteria that were not addressed by the antibiotic I had originally prescribed. I explained why his sores had not yet healed and gave him a new prescription for an antibiotic that should effectively address the infection. I also gave him some mild medicines to take at night to help him relax and sleep.

◆ ◆ ◆

In Africa, neither good nor bad things happen by chance. The task of traditional healers involves discovering what has upset the balance of powers within the complex network of relationships that bind African people into unwritten "covenants" with God, the spirits, and one another. There is no written authority for African belief. Belief is not creedal but experiential and relational. Additionally, each ethnic group has its own mythology and belief system, handed down from one generation to the next.

In this chapter, I will examine themes of health and healing that emerge from African thought. Because there is not just one set of beliefs but rather thousands throughout Africa, these themes appear in varied customs, and, in some instances, may not be present at all. A Christian health and healing ministry, therefore, must reflect not only the themes but also the specific variations in those themes that characterize the people to whom they minister.

The task of an author who presumes to write about African belief is not unlike the job of the traditional healer. To discern underlying principles of health and healing from the myriad and distinctive sets of beliefs that fill Africa is no less complex a task than discovering the imbalance in relationship that has caused an illness. I approach this task with humility and gratitude. As an outsider, I am keenly aware that I am writing about things that I have not experienced in my own culture. I am thankful to the authors, both Africans and non-Africans, who have helped me to understand the forest through which I walk in the pages I have written about Africa. I am also thankful for the Holy Spirit who helps me discern how the truth of the Bible illumines the path I tread.

When I began to examine African beliefs and practices regarding health, I expected to find parallels to the holism of God's covenants and to the power of healing in God's kingdom. The parallels are there as surely as men and women bear the image of God. But God's image in us has been distorted by sin; apart from Christ it cannot be restored. Likewise, the "covenant" of health in African belief bears the image of God's revelation. But it too has become distorted by sin and, apart from Christ, it cannot be restored. I recognized what many Africans know through their experience – that traditional beliefs and practices surrounding health and disease are shadowed by fear.

HEALTH AND DISEASE

The edges of the years have met,
I take sheep and new yams
And give you that you may eat.
Life to me.
Life to this my Ashanti people.
Women who cultivate the farms,
When they do so,
Grant that the food comes up in abundance.
Do not allow any illness to come.
                              Ashanti prayer
                              (Mbiti 1975, 44)

God! give us health.
God! give us raided cattle.
God! give us the offspring
Of men and cattle.
                    Nandi prayer
                    (Mbiti 1975, 71)

Mulungu, here is your food.
We wish for rain, for wives,
For cattle and for goats to raise;
And we pray, God, that our people
Do not die from sickness.
                    Ila prayer
                    (Mbiti 1975, 112)

Like the Hebrews, the African perspective on health is experiential and holistic. In some African languages, the word that is most commonly used to translate health shares some of the same richness as shalom. Even when there is not any single word with the same wholeness of meaning as shalom, health is intimately linked to all of God's blessings; prosperity, freedom from illness, fertility, and victory. For many peoples, health also entails a sense of inner peace.

> *Yaada gabbatu male, nyaata hingabbatan.*
> Only when one is at peace in his/her thoughts does s/he become fat; eating alone does not fatten. (Oromo proverb)

Health depends upon maintaining a balance of power within the network of relationships that affect the welfare of the individual or community

(Jansen 1973; Dube 1989). Appiah-Kube, a Ghanaian church leader, described health in terms of balance. "Most Africans think that health is symptomatic of a correct relationship between people and their environment, which includes their fellow beings and the natural as well as the supernatural world. Health is associated with good, with blessing, with beauty; all that is positively valued in life" (Atkins 1990). In contrast, disease, injury, "unnatural" events in the cycle of life, environmental catastrophes, financial setbacks, in fact any bad thing that an ancient Israelite would interpret as God's punishment, results from an imbalance in the powers that determine the fate of men, women, and communities (Atkins 1990; Dube 1989).

Some African peoples think of health in terms of a life force that is either diminished or strengthened through the network of relationships and events (Jansen 1973). A life force may be depleted by others but may also be given, often through the services of a diviner.

Traditional African beliefs about the nature of health, goodness, and blessing and about disease, evil, and cursing are as holistic as that of the Hebrews. Like the Old Testament, most African traditions teach that these blessings and curses emerge from the quality of relationships to God and spiritual beings, to family and community, and to the environment. Each of these relationships involves a characteristic blending of light and shadow, of hope and fear, and of wisdom and distortion.

THE DISTANT BUT IMMANENT GOD

In Psalm 38, the Hebrew King David personally addressed Yahweh in his anguish; the African businessman Daudi does not look first to God to find the cause or the solution to his problem. The Creator God of most African peoples is paradoxical. He[1] is removed and unknowable, yet often on the lips of men and women who seek gifts from him; he is impersonal, yet his actions, particularly his punishments for injustice, affect the lives of men, women, and communities; his specific identity and name varies from one people to the next, yet many of his characteristics are the same from one myth to the next (Mbiti 1992; Taylor 1963).

The Distant God

In most African traditions, a single high God created the universe and all that it contains. More importantly, this initial creation had all that was required for the welfare of men and women also created by God. God gave them land and livestock and made them fertile (Mbiti 1992; Shenk 1983). In some myths, God also lived with the men and women he had created. Then, because of carelessness, accident, or misdeed, God moved away, making his residence in the heavens.

In some myths, God moved away because of carelessness. God moved away from the Ashanti people because a woman pounding out *fufu* kept hitting him in the face with her pestle. God moved away from the Mende people because they kept asking for things and gave him no rest. In other traditions, God moved into the heavens to prevent smoke from getting into his eyes or because an arrow was carelessly shot through the clouds at him (Mbiti 1992; Kirwen 1978).

Other myths more closely parallel the story of Eden. God moved away because men and women failed a moral test given to them by God (Mbiti 1992). Finally, for some peoples, it was simply an accident. Some groups said that the rope that once linked the heavens and earth was cut accidentally by a hyena or trickster (Mbiti 1992; Shenk 1983).

All the myths share two characteristics in common. The separation of God from men and women was disastrous and also irreparable. Death is the most frequently mentioned consequence of the separation (Shenk 1983), though there were others.

> However the separation occurred, it brought disadvantageous and tragic consequences to men: man was the main loser. These consequences disrupted the original state of man. According to the Bambuti, God left men alone, death came, and man lost happiness, peace, and the free supply of food. The Banyarwanda tell that when a woman decided to hide death, contrary to God's law not to do so, he decided to let men keep death, and so death has ever since remained with men. The Bushmen tell that man lost the gift of resurrection, and death came among men. According to the Chagga, when disease and old age came to men, they lost the gift of rejuvenation, and death came as well (Mbiti 1992, 98).

Once the relationship was severed, there was no remedy. Because God and his creatures were so unlike one another, living together in relationship was unthinkable (Shenk 1983; Kirwen 1978). Mbiti laments: "Behind these fleeting glimpses of the original state and bliss of man, whether they are rich or shadowy, there lies the tantalizing and unattained gift of the resurrection, the loss of human immortality, and the monster of death. Here African religions and philosophy must admit a defeat: they have supplied no solution. This remains the most serious cul-de-sac in the otherwise rich thought and sensitive religious feeling of our peoples" (1992, 99).

The daily relationship of the African to God, then, does not focus upon reconciliation but upon how to avoid punishment and preserve God's blessings.

The Immanent God

God as Judge

> *Waaqayo utu madeessu, deebise fayyisa.*
> God brings both wounding and healing.
> > (Oromo proverb)

> *Bulani nafse Waaqa gargara.*
> God helps the one who lives well.
> > (Oromo proverb)

> Thou, O Jouk, who hast created all men:
> Let my family be forever happy,
> I have not offended against my father and my mother,
> I have not sinned with my neighbor's wife,
> There is no sin in me, I am innocent:
> I have stolen nothing;
> I have killed no one without cause.
> Great contentment to everyone of my house.
> > Guir prayer (Mbiti 1975, 32)

For most African peoples, God is present in everyday life because he is just and he punishes sin. The more devastating the communal or individual calamity, the more likely it is that people will attribute it to God rather than to spirits or evil forces.

As the supreme judge, God accepts only the serious cases or those that have moved through the lower spiritual courts without resolution. In most African thought God, like a judge, is not accomplishing a grand plan. "God's active part in human history is seen in terms of his supplying them with rain, good harvest, health, cattle, and children; in healing, delivering, and helping them; and in terms of making his presence felt through natural phenomena and objects" (Mbiti 1992, 47).

And, like a judge, the African God is not vulnerable or affected by the crimes of those who come before him for judgement. Unlike the God of the Bible, the African God is not personally offended or saddened by sin because he is separate from it and it cannot touch him (Taylor 1963).

Traditionally, most Africans regard an action as sinful because of its consequences to others and not because it is a personal offense against God. Also, because God is removed from men and women, sin brings no eternal consequences for misdeeds. In traditional religious belief, the offender is concerned only about proximate consequences in this life (Mbiti 1992).

Because God punishes sin, African traditions suggest a kind of covenant between God and humanity. The biblical parallels to the covenant between Israel and Yahweh, however, are shallow (Shenk 1983). Yahweh was close to the Israelites, not far away. He was personally angered and personally offended by their transgressions and blessed by their obedience. Finally, like a judge who holds the power of reward or punishment, God is addressed by those who stand before him. God is distant in African belief because he is unknowable and is separated from his human creatures by a gap that cannot be bridged. He is near because his human creatures can and do "approach the bench," sometimes directly but often through their intermediaries. The high God of traditional Africa is too remote to enter into covenant with his human creatures. He is near enough, however, to intervene in their lives.

The First Leg of the Stool of Fatalism: God's Immutable Will

> *Ky'aleeta: tokizzaayo*
> You cannot send back what God sends you.
> (Lugandan proverb)

> If you say that she will die,
> She is yours, this child of yours.
> It is your affair;
> As for us, we long that your child may recover.
> ...
> If she dies, this child of yours,
> We can only speak your names;
> We cry to you for help.
> Ngoni prayer (Mbiti 1975, 49)

I don't know for what Imana is punishing me: if I could meet with him I would kill him. Imana, why are you punishing me? Why have you not

made me like other people? Couldn't you even give me one little child,
Yo-o-o! I am dying in anguish! If only I could meet you and pay you out!
Come on, let me kill you! Let me run you through with a knife! O Imana,
you have deserted me! Yo-o-o!

Banyarwanda prayer (Mbiti 1975, 86–87)

Fe-aa Rabbii finqilli himbuusa.
The burden of the Lord: one turns it over
and over but does not put it down.

(Oromo proverb)

Like the ceremonial stool of an elder, the stool of fatalism in Africa rests
on three legs that are bound together in common belief. Their paradoxical
relationship to God is the first of the three factors that contribute to a
fatalistic approach to life.

Dr. Dan Fountain (1996) wrote that transformation in Africa cannot
take place until the fatalistic worldview of Africans is challenged and
changed. As a physician, Dr. Fountain faced the daily frustration of trying to motivate change in health behaviors among local people who felt
that their actions would have little or no effect upon the "will of God."
Instead of taking action to prevent disease and lessen its effects, they
responded either passively (the Ngoni prayer) or with anger and anguish
(the Banyarwandan prayer) but not with positively directed action.

Because God is immanent in his actions but distant and unknowable in
his person, all men and women can do is passively accept his will. In the
Bagre initiation rites of the LoDagaa in northern Ghana, the elders
lament that the ways of God are unknowable.

The matters of old
who can know them?
Alas, alas,
it is God
who created us
and who punishes us.
Our forefathers' matters,
who can know them,
sit and know them?

(Goody 1996, 7)

The elders conclude that though men and women may perform, the
knowledge of God and his actions are beyond human knowing (Goody

1996). A person has little or no influence on the actions of those with whom there is no relationship. Without knowledge of or relationship to God, Africans traditionally have little power to change or even anticipate his intervention in their lives.

The African God and the God of the Bible

The parallel between the God of the Bible and the God of African tradition is only a partial one. God in both worldviews created the universe and established the laws that govern it. In both views, God is now separated from his creation, bringing death into the world. The separation in African tradition, however, is attributed to distance (Taylor 1963) while the separation in Christian thought is attributed to the personal offense of sin. Petitioning the God of African tradition might affect his actions but there is, in fact, little that will change the exercise of his will. The God of the Bible is immanent and near. Reconciliation and a restored relationship to him are possible through Jesus as the mediator. The God of African tradition is immanent in his actions but far away. The gap can only be bridged; the relationship cannot be restored.

This gap is not empty, however, but crowded with spirits. This "world in between" (Milingo 1984) is a lively one that blends with the activities and relationships of everyday life. The following prayer of the Luguru weaves together all the worlds in a plea for healing.

> You, Father God,
> Who are in the heavens and below;
> Creator of everything and omniscient;
> Of the earth and the heavens;
> We are but little children
> Unknowing anything but evil;
> If this sickness has been brought by man
> We beseech you, help us through these roots.
> In case it was inflicted by you, the Conserver,
> Likewise do we entreat your mercy on your child;
> also you, our grandparents, who sleep in the place of the shades,
> We entreat all of you who sleep on one side.
> All ancestors, males and females, great and small,
> Help us in this trouble, have compassion on us;
> So that we can also sleep peacefully.
> And thus do spit out this mouthful of water!

Pu-pu! Pu-pu!
Please listen to our earnest request.
(Mbiti 1975, 45)

THE WORLD IN BETWEEN

And though this world with devils filled should threaten to undo us...
Martin Luther

The world of traditional Africa is filled with spirits. Some are evil; some are not. Daudi, the businessman, sought the protection of some even while being threatened by others. The spirits are the mediators between God and persons but may also act on their own. They are not all knowing. Spirits can be bent to the will of men and women by those who know how to relate to them.

As a Westerner, I was surprised not by the belief in spirits but in how "matter of fact" it was to some people. I once interviewed a Ugandan priest who told me of a naming ceremony (a ceremony in which family members decide which name, from among the ancestors, should be given to the child). The conversation went like this.

"The child was colicky, crying, restless, and not eating well. We wondered if we had given the child the wrong name so the elders of the clan met together to consider it. After a long discussion, the child's grandfather finally said that the child should be named after him, and the others agreed. Once we named the child after the grandfather, he became well again."

I asked, "The child's grandfather, was he still living?"

"Oh no, he is dead."

A council in which ancestral spirits and living relatives consider important matters together was, for this highly educated priest, not in the least unusual. E. Milingo, formally the Catholic Archbishop in Zambia until he became involved in an active spirit-healing ministry, appealed to his own experience in refuting the strong rationalism of his European colleagues. Their arguments denying the existence of the spirit world did not convince him because he conversed regularly with the dead (Milingo 1984).

Many missionaries and Christian health workers do not deny the existence of the spirit world, but they often ignore it in their practice. The only niche in scientific medicine for belief in spirits as the cause of poor health is a mental disorder. Christians in health care in Africa must know how to respond to the role and place of spirits in the lives of their patients.

A Spiritual Taxonomy

Any attempt at a firm classification of spirits in Africa is doomed to failure from the beginning because of the great variation between peoples. In day-to-day practice, even within a single oral tradition, different thoughts exist as to the types of spirits and their work. Nevertheless, some distinctions are important.

- *Divinities* are manifestations of God. These spirits serve "as the hands of God" (Moreau 1990, 103) in doing his bidding. Moreau distinguishes three classifications of these spirits. Created spirits serve as the agents of the high God. Other divinities are associated with natural objects such as the sun and moon, a mountain, rain or thunder. Among some groups, the name of the high God and the divinity for the sun or rain is the same (Mbiti 1992) even though the divine spirit of the sun or rain is not God. Finally many peoples recognize those who belonged to the royal line, who were champions or heroes, as divinities apart from the ancestors (Gehman 1989; Bediako 1990). These spirits have passed from the personal memories of succeeding generations into the collective memory of the people and thus have been deified.

- *Ancestral spirits* continue to be a part of the everyday life of their families and clans so long as they remain in living memory. They retain their names and are invited to participate in important family events as well as in the daily life of their clan. Pobee suggests that among the Akan not all the dead become ancestors but that they must earn it by a good life. Other peoples believe that spirits of the dead cannot enter a restful state as ancestral spirits if their death was brought about through witchcraft (De Rosny 1985), or without a respectful funeral.

- Many *spirits* are neither divinities nor ancestral spirits. The composition of this vast spirit horde varies considerably from one tradition to the next. These spirits may include ancestral spirits that have passed out of living memory (Kirwen 1978) or who belong to a different clan (Hammond-Tooke 1989); spirits commanding important aspects of life such as the hunt, black-smithing, or initiations (Christensen 1990; Moreau 1990); the spirits of natural objects such as a tree, stream, mountain, or animal (Christensen 1990; Gehman 1989; Shorter

1985); natural events such as a storm or lightening or natural resources such as iron (Moreau 1990); territorial spirits (Christensen 1990); a spirit double or guardian (Moreau 1990); and spirits of destruction, evil, or witchcraft[2] (Christensen 1990; Milingo 1984; Daneel 1990; Shaw 1996; Taylor 1963; Moreau 1990).

- *Satan and demons* are not a part of the spirit world in traditional African thought[3] but are now important spiritual beings because of the influence of Christianity and Islam. In many African languages a transliteration of the Hebrew is used (*shetani* in Kiswahili). Without a traditional referent for Satan, some Africans come to regard this spirit as the evil side of the High God, a divine manifestation, or even as his firstborn son (Bosch 1987).

Archbishop Milingo told of a conversation that he had with a spirit through the person the spirit had possessed. The spirit bragged that it was only one of millions, far too many to count. The world of the spirits is confusing in its ambiguity and complexity but remains a part of the everyday life of many Africans. What does this mean? What are spirits like? What do they do? Are all of them "devils who threaten to undo us"?

The Work, Character, and Control of the Spirits

According to LoDagaa tradition, Bagre is the offspring of the High God, one of the spirits that would be classified as divinities. In the initiation rite, Bagre is rebuked as "the thieving god, the lying god, the troubling god." When Bagre objects to being addressed in this way, the elder praises him as "the god of fertility, the god of farming...., the god with a good heart" (Goody 1996, 8–9).

Bagre is accused of lying and theft because he does not deliver what he has promised; yet he requires offerings and sacrifices. In the next breath he is described as good. Africans traditionally feel ambivalent about the spirits, and consider many as neither good nor bad. The ambivalence extends even to ancestral spirits who have the most intimate ties to their descendants.

Ancestral Spirits

The ancestral spirits continue to play a vital role in the lives of their descendants, often acting with benevolence, protecting and guiding those in whom they continue to live, and mediating their requests to God or to

more powerful spirits. The people, in prayer, appeal to this continued
relationship.

> MOTHER: O spirits of the past, this little one I hold is my child: she is
>   your child also, therefore be gracious to her.
>
> WOMEN, *chanting*: She has come into a world of trouble: sickness is in the
>   world, and cold and pain: the sickness with which you were familiar.
>
> MOTHER: Let her sleep in peace, for there is healing in sleep: let none
>   among you be angry with me or my child.
>
> WOMEN: Let her grow: let her become strong: let her become full grown:
>   then will she offer such a sacrifice to you that will delight your hearts.
>
>   (Mbiti 1975)

The favor of the ancestors is not certain, however, but must be earned and
maintained through respect, sacrifice, thanksgiving, and the maintenance
of relational taboos. The ancestral spirits demonstrate all the diversity in
personality and emotions that they did when they were alive. The complex
web of mutual obligations and responsibilities of family must be continued after death.

Among the Zulu, for instance, if a man's sister dies without children of
her own, he is obligated to perpetuate her name through the names of his
daughters. His sister earned this right because the bride-price that was
paid for her helped her brother, in turn, to pay the bride-price for his wife.
She therefore becomes the *vamwene* or owner or possessor of her
brother's wife. If the brother fails in his duty, his dead sister may come as
an apparition and "grab hold of the womb" of his wife and prevent con-
ception or complicate the birth. He must meet his obligation to her in
order for his wife to regain her fertility (Daneel 1970).

But why would a sister who might have been loving in life turn against
her brother? The relationship between the living and the living-dead is a
reciprocal one. Without a living person to bear her name, the spirit of the
sister could soon pass out of living memory. The ancestral spirits require
continued sacrifice and recognition. The living must carry on the work
and preserve the teachings and traditions of the ancestors.

The living, therefore, are not without power over their ancestors, as
this Zulu prayer indicates.

> When have we ever forgotten to make sacrifices to you and to enumerate
> your honourable names? Why are you so miserly? If you do not improve,
> we will let all your honourable names fall into oblivion. What will your fate
> be then! You will have to go and feed on locusts. Improve: else we will

forget you. For whose food is it that we make sacrifices and celebrate the praises? You bring us neither harvests nor abundant herds. You show no gratitude whatever for all the trouble we take. However, we do not wish to estrange ourselves completely from you and we will say to other men that we do not completely possess the spirits of our forebears. You will suffer from it. We are angry with you.

(Mbiti 1975, 106)

The ancestral spirits give special attention to vital events in the cycles of life – birth, initiation, marriage, death, the naming of children – and continue while in living memory to participate in these events. Fulfilling the expectations of both the living and the dead in a complex web of relationships is an impossible task. As with living relatives, the ancestors are impossible to please all of the time, but unlike living relatives, the ancestors have greater power to cause harm or good. Mazrui even suggests that the problems of modern Africa represent a collective curse of the ancestors upon African leaders who have ignored the lessons of cultural continuity.

You will multiply in numbers but not always have the food to feed your hungry children. Your economic institutions will atrophy. Your warriors will ignore honour; your leaders will betray you; your trains will rust; your roads decay and your factories grind to a standstill. Behold chaos replace order! Behold hunger replace harvest! (Mazrui 1986, 11).

If the ancestral spirits, who have familial intimacy with their descendants, are ambivalent in their relationships, the other categories of spirits, even those who are not regarded as inherently evil, are even more volatile.

Spirit Possession

The activities of the legions of spirits who inhabit "the world between" intersect everyday life. They animate objects, cause social problems, and bring sickness and calamity (Moreau 1990). The spirits may act on their own accord, perhaps punishing a person for tearing the web of relationship by breaking a taboo, or they may be summoned and sent to do harm by a living enemy.

Health problems are often attributed to the work of spirits, usually in the service of a declared or undeclared enemy. Diviners and sorcerers manipulate the spirits either by discovering what they demand or by countering their strategy or power to reestablish a balance in the world of the sufferer. In preparation for a closer examination of the work of diviners, healers, and exorcists in the final chapters of Section 1, I will briefly address spirit possession here.

In many African traditions, spirits are able to possess any created thing in the physical world; animals, objects, and people (Moreau 1990). Daneel (1990) distinguishes between four kinds of possession. First, diviners and medicine men are often possessed by spirits in order to carry out their diagnostic and healing work. The possessing spirit is an intermediary to other spirits. The spirit comes upon invitation and leaves when the healing work is complete. Enemies seeking revenge for a wrong done to them, their family, or ancestors may also negotiate with a spirit to possess or harm the offender.

Amafufunyana possession in South Africa is only one example of virtually countless variations that can be found throughout Africa. The possessed person hears disembodied voices, is ill, and becomes extremely agitated. An enemy, perhaps motivated by envy, causes the possession by mixing the blood of a person who has been violently killed, or ants from a new grave, and giving it to the victim in food (Edwards 1989).

Secondly, neglected ancestral spirits, who desire attention or who wish to preserve tradition, may also possess someone. Shorter reports an incident in which a spirit possessed a girl because she had refused to marry the young man that her father selected for her. The spirits in the girl said that they were only going to "trouble her for a while" (Shorter 1985, 184).

Thirdly, a person may be possessed by a witchcraft spirit. Unlike a morally neutral spirit that possesses a diviner, a witchcraft spirit is always evil.

Finally, Christian and Islamic teaching has become intricately interwoven with traditional beliefs about possession in much of Africa. People are also believed to be possessed by demonic spirits or *majini*.

"And though this world with devils filled..." We return to the question that began this section. Just what or who are the spirits in African belief? Are some of them beneficial, or are they devils?

A Biblical Perspective

Dr. Scott Moreau has exhaustively examined the biblical references to created, non-human spirits. Angels are the only category of created non-human spirits specified in the Bible. The good angels worship and praise God, minister to his saints, and are the mediators of God's power that they exercise in both judgement and blessing. In the prophetic books they appeared in a number of fantastic forms but in their appearances to people, they took on human form, sometimes with their glory veiled, as in their meal with Abraham at Mamre when they announced that Sarah would give birth to his son (Gen. 18:1–19:26). But normally their glory was revealed.

In the visions of heaven, though angels such as the cherubim (Ezek. 1:4–28) are described by similes, they would never be mistaken for an animal or natural object. Good angels do not act independently but only to fulfill the will of God. They refuse worship of themselves. They act as mediators in only one direction – from God to people, and never from people back to God. Angels sometimes exercise God's judgement, bringing death and illness, but they are never involved in healing ministry. They sometimes prevent harm from coming to God's people.

Though the Bible is silent on the origin of demons, they are most often regarded as angels that followed Satan in rebellion against God. Though they are under the command of Satan, Satan did not create them since he is himself a created angel. There are no instances in the Bible of possession by a good angel, but in his healing ministry, Jesus cast out demonic spirits who had possessed people. In addition to self-destructive acts that often accompany possession, demons cause some sicknesses (Lk. 13:11,16) and engage Christians in spiritual warfare. The Bible implies that demons may be able to use their powers to bring about disasters such as droughts and floods (Job 1:16,19).

Human spirits live on after death, and there are at least two instances of their appearance in the Bible aside from the post-resurrection appearances of Jesus. Samuel apparently returned to speak to Saul when he sought him through the medium at Endor (1 Sam. 28:3–20). Moses and Elijah appeared with Jesus on the Mount of Transfiguration (Matt. 17:1–13).

When God rescued Peter from jail, Rhoda, the servant girl, thought that it was his angel or spirit that came to the house where they had been meeting (Acts 12:15). Several passages imply that the saints who have died may be aware of events on earth. The writer of Hebrews encourages Christians to persevere in the race of their faith because they are surrounded by a cloud of witnesses (Heb. 12:1), probably other saints, now dead, who had demonstrated faithfulness in their own lives (Heb. 11). In Jesus' account of Lazarus and the rich man (Lk. 16:19–31), the rich man, suffering torment after his death, pleaded unsuccessfully that Lazarus, the beggar, be permitted to go to his living brothers and warn them of the fate that awaited them.

Several very clear principles emerge from the Bible.

1. *There is a very real spirit world that affects the lives of men and women.* Both angels and demons intervene in the lives of men and women. Even though socio-psychiatric arguments may be used to explain some instances of spirit possession, some spirit possessions are genuine.

2. *There are both evil and good spirits at war with one another.* Angels and demons engage in a spiritual warfare but it is unclear that humans, by their actions, can alter the course of that warfare in spiritual realms. There seems to be a level of conflict that happens independently of human intervention.

3. *Spirits can cause illness, bad events, and death.* Evil spirits can bring about illness and death through self-destructive and aggressive acts by those who are possessed, through spiritual attack on the body, and through the effects of fear and hopelessness mediated by bodily responses to these negative feelings. Angels may sometimes be involved in punishment of wrongdoing as God's messengers.

4. *Good spirits are not involved in healing.* In their protective roles, good angels may prevent harm from coming to a person. Milingo stated that good spirits gave him comfort in the midst of his ministry though he did not specifically identify them as angels. There is no biblical evidence, however, that angels serve as mediators from men and women to God or as healers. Good angels apparently receive their directions from God and are not manipulated or controlled by human will or technique. God reserves those roles for himself through the work of Jesus and the Holy Spirit.

5. *Men and women are instructed very clearly to avoid diviners and mediums in the search for healing, though we should not be surprised if they are effective in some instances.* God forbade the involvement of his people in any demonic practice (Deut. 18:9–14). Because evil spirits possess power, they may bring about changes that appear positive, including apparent healing, but serve only to draw people further from God. Additionally, as we will discover in following chapters, diviners and other traditional practitioners have learned to employ God's gift of dominion and the power of healing that he has built into his creation to bring about healing.

6. *Only God is to be worshiped.* Though evil spirits may play a mediating

role in bringing people into Satan's kingdom, good spirits never mediate between people and God. Rather we are instructed to approach God only through the mediation of Jesus and the Holy Spirit. Good spirits refuse worship directed toward themselves.

7. *Ancestral (human) spirits may exist but do not act as intermediaries to God.* On the basis of the biblical record, we cannot firmly deny the presence and influence of ancestral spirits, but we are forbidden from calling them up or seeking their assistance.

What are the spirits in Africa?

Some non-African missionaries and scholars, and many fewer Africans, deny that spirits really exist at all. They argue that manifestations such as possession happen more frequently when cultures are in transition or when an individual, troubled by guilt or fear, externalizes those emotions in order to cope. Many who believe in the reality of the spirits also recognize that their influence is amplified by the culture of fear and suspicion that they create.

> I do not for a moment deny that there are spiritual forces outside man which seem sometimes to function within human history and human society. But the belief in the mystical power is greater than the ways in which that power might actually function within the human society. African communities in the villages are deeply affected and permeated by the psychological atmosphere which creates both real and imaginary powers or forces of evil that give rise to more tensions, jealousies, suspicions, slander, accusations, and scapegoats. It is a vicious cycle (Mbiti 1992, 209).

Christians who believe in the reality of the spirit world, but who reject the traditional idea that some spirits are morally neutral, gravitate toward one of two positions. Some regard the non-human spirits as demonic without similarly condemning the ancestral spirits. Archbishop Milingo appeared to have embraced this view. He regarded the spirits who possess diviners or victims as demonic spirits who must be cast out.

Milingo, however, was not ready to call ancestral spirits demonic because they are too bound up with African identity. "These (marriage ceremonies, funeral rites, naming rituals, etc.) are the areas where the Africans have still remained themselves and thanks be to God that this has happened or otherwise we should have no identity" (Milingo 1984, 76). One young seminary student argued that it would not be a sin for Africans to ask their dead relatives to mediate their requests directly to

Christ. He wrote: "To deny people the right to identify themselves with their own culture is not only to challenge and despise their ancestors (the founders of such cultures), but is to create a society of those who have been torn away from their ethnic roots; and who, feeling insecure and belonging nowhere, are open to all kinds of unstable behavior" (Rakotsoane 1996–97, 21).

Many African Independent Churches that recognize diviners and possessing spirits as demonic are also more tolerant of ancestral spirits. An ancestral spirit that out of jealousy or anger brings a member of the church under attack is exorcised while one who simply participates in the important ceremonies of community life is tolerated.

Moreau concludes that whether ancestral spirits are truly human spirits or demons posing as ancestors, they are willing or unwilling allies of the demonic. Gehman concludes that all human and non-human spirits involved in African tradition are demons. In this he reflects the perspective of the rapidly growing Christian movement in Africa that has been termed Pentecostal evangelicalism (Kailing 1994). Pentecostal evangelicals are characterized by a Christocentric and near-literal approach to the Bible. They retain their African identity by accepting the reality and power of the traditional spirit world, but also reckon it as under the dominion of Satan and his forces.

"Behind all spiritual reality which is not directly connected with the Holy Spirit is the power of a real and personal Satan who, with a host of demonic spirits at his command, seeks to fulfill the biblical description of his role in the world: 'to kill, steal, and destroy' " (Kailing 1994, 496). With the power of Christ and the Holy Spirit, Christians must therefore oppose the world of the spirits. I believe that this position, though in practice it may give the spirit world a visibility that amplifies its influence, is close to a biblical one.

Do the spirits threaten to undo us? Milingo (quoted by Shorter) reports the following conversation between himself and a spirit that had possessed a client who had come for healing.

> "Why do you deceive people claiming that you can heal them
>   when you know that you cause the diseases?"
> "If they follow our instructions some are healed."
> "But why do you cause diseases and then heal again?"
> "So you will know that we are clever."
>
> (Shorter 1985, 189)

An academic discussion concerning spirits discounts the influence they have in Africa, both directly and through the fear that belief in them engenders. Even Africans who regard some spirits as morally ambivalent avoid encounters with them and fear those among the living who befriend them. Because ancestral spirits are so unpredictable, Africans who believe in them often are ambivalent – wanting their favor but wishing that they would simply go away (Mbiti 1992). In Gehman's survey of Akamba church leaders in Kenya, the vast majority felt that the missionaries were right in opposing ancestral spirits and that these spirits would invariably draw those who consorted with them away from Christ and into fear.

A Covenant of Shadow

The covenant of the Hebrews with their God involved fear of punishment, but also a sense of longing after Yahweh as the source of life and healing. Their fear of Yahweh was based on their knowledge of him, his character, and his expectations. In the New Testament, the covenant became one of healing grace and salvation. With the punishment paid, the Christian could be free from fear. God jealously guarded his relationship to his creation and invited men and women to relate directly to him.

The covenant between Africans and the spirit world is one of fear. The spirits themselves are of uncertain character and may punish or reward without warning. Even the Old Covenant is a new covenant for Africa. Healing is performed in a climate of fear. Ancestral spirits and living humans are each obligated to the other. The requirements of the shadow covenant are uncertain and the paths to forgiveness and restoration often ill defined and ambiguous.

Notes

1   Because of the limitations of the English language, I will follow biblical convention and use the masculine pronoun to refer to God. In many African languages, a personal but gender neutral pronoun is used to refer to God who is a spirit and without gender. Among African peoples, both masculine and feminine imagery is used in reference to God (Milingo 1984).

2   I will discuss witches and the African concept of evil in the section on community relationships later in this chapter.

3   In an exception to this, Pobee and Bediako report that the Akan people believe in a spiritual prince of evil forces named *sasabonsam*. This red-eyed spirit leads

the *mmoatia*, tiny creatures with superhuman strength that wait suspended from trees in the darkness of the forest to prey upon hunters. The Akan use this name to refer to Satan (Bediako 1995b).

Chapter 3

God's Environmental Order
in the Covenant of Shalom:
Dominion, Creativity, Wealth

◆ ◆ ◆

In 1996, Bishop Desmond Tutu visited Nairobi. During one of his addresses, he told of the debilitating effects of apartheid on the sense of dominion among his people. Early in his ministry, Bishop Tutu was invited to address a conference in Nigeria. As he boarded the Nigerian airliner in Johannesburg, he immediately noticed that the entire flight crew were black Africans. The contrast to South African airlines at that period of time was striking; the flight crews on South African airlines were all white. He boarded the airplane with a sense of pride and belonging. Shortly into the flight, however, the airplane ran into turbulent weather. As the airliner bounced through the sky, Bishop Tutu said an unbidden thought came to his mind. "We are really in trouble now – in the middle of a storm and not even one white person in the cockpit."

◆ ◆ ◆

In the above story, Bishop Tutu recognized that his unbidden fear was rooted in the oft-repeated message of South African society. Apartheid not only barred black South Africans from professions requiring a high level of technical skills and critical decision-making but also promoted the belief that they were racially inferior to whites in these areas. By strengthening the perception among black and white South Africans that black South Africans were fit only for subjection rather than mastery, the system of apartheid denied the gift and responsibility of dominion. Pastor Oscar Muriu of Nairobi Chapel maintained, "Absolute powerlessness corrupts absolutely." Men and women who are denied all opportunities to exercise dominion cannot be whole or healthy. God's image is corrupted as much by a chronic sense of helplessness as it is by a presumption of total control.

The exercise of dominion is central to the covenants of shalom in the Old Testament. The responsible exercise of dominion is rooted in the relationship between people and the natural world. Adam and Eve, and later Noah, were made responsible to work the land and subdue it. Eden was a good place, but it was not a tame place. Adam and Eve reflected God's image as through creative, productive work, they exercised dominion over his creation. The work of Adam and Eve in naming the animals symbolically demonstrated their exalted position. Naming something demonstrates the power and responsibility of the name-giver.

But how is dominion to be exercised within the covenants of *shalom*? What is the relationship between our fullness of health and the natural order?

- We must exercise dominion as stewards rather than owners.
- We must understand the characteristics of the natural order, both good and bad, in order to maintain harmony in our relationship to it.
- We must manage the wealth of the natural order wisely.

STEWARDSHIP AND DOMINION

Our dominion over the natural order is delegated to us by God (Genesis 1:28–30) and we are therefore accountable to him. Because we are under God's authority, we do not exercise unrestrained rights over his natural creation.

We cannot wantonly destroy God's natural creation for our own apparent benefit. Owners may scrap or discard possessions if they feel it is to their benefit. Stewards do not have that right. If we fail to protect the natural assets given into our charge, we fail as stewards. The destruction of the natural environment carries many consequences. First, just as the deliberate destruction of a painting or sculpture shows contempt for its creator, so our deliberate or careless destruction of the natural environment shows contempt for its Creator. Our relationship to God is affected by our attitude and actions toward the gifts he has given into our charge. Secondly, poor stewardship of the natural world directly affects our health through the release of environmental toxins and indirectly through the destruction of resources that may contribute toward our health and welfare. The careless destruction of species of plants and animals not only demonstrates contempt for their Creator but also affects the balance of nature in sometimes unpredictable ways and may deny us healing resources of great but as yet unrealized value.

We are sometimes called upon to limit our exercise of dominion. Our ultimate accountability is to the Creator and not the creation. First, our relationship to God is of primary importance in our management of his creation gifts. The Old Testament frequently contrasts the eternity of God with the temporality of our interaction with the created world. The teachings of the New Testament not only continue this theme but also reveal that the natural environment itself will be destroyed and God will make a new heaven and earth. Our accumulation of wealth[1] and possessions, therefore, is ultimately futile. If we truly are able to hold lightly to possessions, we will not only suffer less from stress but can freely enjoy them and expend them in building a community of mutual concern and care for one another in sickness and in health.

> But godliness with contentment is great gain. For we brought nothing into the world, and we can take nothing out of it. But if we have food and clothing, we will be content with that. People who want to get rich fall into temptation and a trap and into many foolish and harmful desires that plunge men into ruin and destruction. For the love of money is a root of all kinds of evil. Some people, eager for money, have wandered from the faith and pierced themselves with many griefs.
>
> Command those who are rich in the present world not to be arrogant nor to put their hope in wealth, which is so uncertain, but to put their hope in God, who richly provides us with everything for our enjoyment. Command them to do good, to be rich in good deeds, and to be generous and willing to share. In this way they will lay up treasure for themselves as a firm foundation for the coming age, so that they may take hold of the life that is truly life (1 Timothy 6:6–10, 17–19).

Secondly, environmental and scientific ethics must be rooted in the teachings of the Creator. Dominion, whether expressed in the power of wealth or the power of knowledge, may be used for good or evil. Every successful exercise of dominion carries the seeds of our eventual defeat. Nations, businesses, and individuals use the power of the wealth they control to master and dominate others. Increased energy use produces thermal, chemical, and nuclear pollution. Our mastery of disease processes not only permits us to combat illness but also to use sickness as a weapon against our enemies. Our increased ability to understand and intervene with the genetic code threatens to extend our dominion beyond our ethical wisdom.

As God's image bearers, we are commanded to exercise dominion. Our dominion over the natural world is a function of our unique position as God's image bearer. In the created order, we are a little lower than the angels but rulers over God's creatures (Psalm 8:5–8). We are of greater value than the plants and animals. As creatures of greater value, we are free to use God's creation for our benefit as we bring it into subjection. Our ethical treatment of animals and the physical environment, therefore, is based not on a sense of equality but one of sovereign responsibility. Finally, we cannot be whole people without the exercise of dominion in some areas of our life. In the fear that he experienced in flying in an airplane with a black African flight crew, Bishop Tutu recognized that the most debilitating result of apartheid was the deeply rooted conviction that one race somehow belonged by divine right in a position of domination above another. A fatalistic response in the face of a hostile environment is no less debilitating and dangerous. If we believe that we have no power or authority to challenge the constraints of our environment, we cannot maintain our health or take steps to fight disease. Passive acceptance of our "fate" denies our humanity and shortens our lives.

UNDERSTANDING AND MAINTAINING HARMONY WITH THE NATURAL WORLD

Coping with the Curse

> For the creation was subjected to frustration, not by its own choice, but by the will of the one who subjected it, in hope that the creation itself will be liberated from its bondage to decay and brought into the glorious freedom of the children of God. We know that the whole creation has been groaning as in the pains of childbirth right up to the present time (Romans 8:20–22).

The entire creation is under the curse of God (Genesis 3:14–19), who "subjected it to frustration." The goodness of God's creation is marred by pestilence, tragedy, and decay. The natural forces designed by God to express the goodness of his creation are the same ones that work toward its destruction.

Creation is the source of wealth and beauty but it is also a terrible enemy. The natural powers of creative adaptation have become weapons used against us. Bacilli and viruses mutate and then mutate again. The struggle with a hostile environment continues. The land still begrudges us its produce, and men and women are still killed by others of God's creatures. The battle has also become more complex as it shifts from dangers of the plains and jungles to the lethal pollutants and daily stresses of the urban environment and to the micro-organisms emerging from the rain forests – but it is no less deadly.

Men and women are alienated from the natural world. As part of the curse, work as creative stewardship has been compromised and become, in part, a battle for survival. In God's judgement of sin, the wildness of creation was transformed to hostility. Creation mounts defenses against its domination by human industry. Plants not only protect themselves individually by sprouting thorns and thistles but collectively they conspire to throttle agriculture. The same forces that nourish the growth of food also nourish the even greater productivity of weeds and pests.

Moses warned the Israelites that disobedience to God's law would result in creation itself turning against them. They would plant and cultivate but through political or natural disaster would not enjoy the produce. Their herds would become infertile. The climate would conspire against them – the earth would become as hard as iron resisting the plow while heat and drought overtook them. Mildew and blight would attack their possessions. Their bodies would finally decay and return to the elemental substances of which they were formed.

But God subjected the creation to frustration "in hope." In the Romans passage, Paul refers to the hope of redemption. The redemption of men and women from the power of sin is the promise of the eventual redemption of the entire creation that will culminate in the creation of new heavens and earth free from God's curse.

A second, more immediate hope lies in the redeemed relationship of the people of God to their environment. God has gifted all men and women with the power to understand and cope with the environment.

Despite the effects of the curse, men and women throughout the world cultivate the land, tend their flocks, and harness the latent energy of the creation to survive and often to prosper. Medical science is itself an exploration in dominion. The work of development agencies in countering the effects of God's curse in enabling men and women to exercise creative dominion over the environment is part of the redemptive work of God, even though its impact is temporary.

There is another common finding, however, that has been repeated throughout the world as people embrace the gift of life in the Lord Jesus. Poor men and women who become Christians often, in time, become healthier and more prosperous than they were before. Why? First, God still enjoys giving good gifts to his children. The Israelites certainly expected national prosperity as one of the fruits of obedience to the terms of God's covenant. Secondly, the new believer joins the helping community of God's church. Finally, poor Christians often enjoy a better quality of life because of a transformed relationship toward God's creation. God redeems the fatalism of poverty into a more hopeful and active exercise of dominion. One key to this redemption is found in a changed perception of time and contingency.

Time, Contingencies, and the Cycles of Nature

> Let there be lights in the expanse of the sky to separate the day from the night, and let them serve as signs to mark seasons and days and years (Genesis 1:14).

> As long as the earth endures, seedtime and harvest, cold and heat, summer and winter, day and night will never cease (Genesis 8:22).

Time is marked by the rhythmic dance of God's creation. The rhythms of creation weave in upon themselves in the seasons of the year and of our lives. Without this grace of the ordinary, God's creatures could not survive. Shalom is rooted in the rhythms and cycles of the creation. Health and well-being depend upon the repeated cycles of day and night, and upon the cycles of work and rest captured in God's covenant gift of the Sabbath.

The welfare of all of God's creation depends upon the cycles of the seasons. Without the certainty that one season invariably follows another, survival would be threatened. The fertility of the land depends upon the cycles of depletion and renewal. The laws of the Sabbath addressed these cycles and reinforced them by requiring that fields remain fallow every seventh year. Survival of plants and animals depends upon the cycles of the days and seasons. Bees could not find flowers if it were not for the predictable rise and fall of the sun nor would plants flower without the cycles of the seasons. Animals could not migrate, hibernate, or in many cases, reproduce.

The cycles of worship, fasts, and celebrations defined community for the Israelites and was intimately tied to a just society. The laws of social justice were based upon the Sabbath cycles of years. The requirements of the Covenant reflected the relationships between environmental domin-ion, renewal, and social justice. Without the marking of time there would be no cycle of ceremony and celebration, and the cohesiveness of commu-nity would begin to disappear. Without the cycled movement of the heav-ens, there could be no marking of time.

Unlike many pastoralist people, the cycles of life for the Hebrews hap-pened in the context of a linear flow of history controlled by their God; more as repeated rhythms than eternal circles (Boman 1960). Their rela-tionship to Yahweh was marked by his interventions in their past and in their future. Linear time was measured by these events, their relative position to one another in history, and their significance to the present (Wolff 1981; Boman 1960). History was not a matter of days and years but of "times" of blessing and trial, of obedience and disobedience.

For the Israelites, God's assurance that the rhythms of life would con-tinue framed a secure and predictable environment, while their linear view of history gave them personal significance. What they did today had consequences for the "times" of the future. Their actions made a differ-ence not only to them today but to their descendants in times to come. They could change their future because what Yahweh would do was con-tingent upon their daily responses to his instruction.

The New Testament reinforces a linear sense of history. The creation itself had a beginning and will have an end. The coming of Jesus and growth of the church marked the beginning of the people of God in the New Covenant, and its final union to Christ as his bride will mark its ful-fillment. Individuals too have a linear and not cyclical history. We are con-ceived and we die. Our fate after death is contingent upon our actions in the intervening period of years.

Why is a linear perspective that transcends the cycles of the natural world important? People who perceive the events of the world only as a series of cycles unaffected by their actions develop a fatalistic attitude toward life. Poverty strengthens this perception because the poor cannot control many of the forces that affect them. When we believe that what we do now has no impact upon what happens to us in the future, we learn to be helpless. "What is the use?" The entire concept of preventing disease and promoting health demands a sense of contingency – that what we do now will make a difference to us in the future. A sense of contingency, in turn, demands a perception of time that retains some linearity, and a perception of the created world that affirms our ability to shape its events. When the poor embrace a worldview transformed by Christianity, they often become more prosperous. Christianity enables them to address and change their environment with hope for the future.

NATURAL RESOURCES, JUSTICE, AND PROSPERITY

Ultimately, God's natural creation is the only source of personal and national wealth. In pastoralist and agrarian cultures, this relationship operates more directly than in multi-layered economies, but the ability to acquire and control God's gifts of creation remains the basis of wealth even in the developed world. In the Mosaic covenant, therefore, God established complex safeguards that were designed to prevent the long-term division of God's people into the rich and poor.

In many developing countries, the primary cause of poverty is the inequitable distribution of land and its decreased productivity as its nutrients are depleted. The Law of Moses, however, provided for the periodic redistribution and renewal of the land.

- Every seventh year the Israelites were not to sow or harvest, allowing the fallow land to replenish itself as it produced its fruit naturally.
- Every fiftieth year (Year of Jubilee), the land that had been leased (for none of it was to be sold since it was the Lord's) would be returned to its original owner, providing for the redistribution of the wealth of the nation (Leviticus 24:1–25). Because the lease would be based upon the productive capacity of the land itself rather than ownership, the value of rural land would remain linked to its productive capacity, helping to control speculation.
- Those who were forced to lease their fields could redeem them at any time before the Year of Jubilee by paying a fair price for the remaining productive capacity of the lease (Leviticus 25:31).

- Property in walled cities could be redeemed within the first year after sale but otherwise was sold permanently (Leviticus 25:29–30). This provision recognized that the value of land and buildings in urban areas was based not on its agricultural productivity but other market factors, and it allowed for the growth of commerce.

Cycles of Injustice

How do rich people increase their control of resources and cyclically increase the gap between themselves and the poor? Marginal farmers are highly vulnerable. The failure of even a single crop often pushes them to the edge of survival. Other emergencies or cultural obligations, such as the provision of a dowry, consume what little reserves they might have, even in a productive year. They borrow money from the rich at high rates of interest with their land or animals as security, and eventually lose all. They are reduced to tenant farmers or day laborers, becoming virtual slaves of their oppressors. "A poor man's field may produce abundant food but injustice sweeps it away" (Proverbs 13:23). Just as the Mosaic laws provided for the periodic redistribution of national wealth, they also protected the poor from this form of oppression.

- Israelites could charge no interest on loans nor take items essential to the well-being or livelihood of the borrower as security for the loan (Exodus 22:25–27; Leviticus 24:6, 10–13). All debts were to be canceled every seventh year and the Lord promised to bless the Israelite who loaned money shortly before the sabbath year (Deuteronomy 15:1–11).
- Hired laborers were to be paid their fair wage daily to permit them to purchase the essentials of life (Deuteronomy 24:14–15). "Company stores" that charged unfair prices to poor laborers were forbidden. Lenders could not sell food at a profit to poor debtors (Leviticus 25:37).
- If a Hebrew became poor and sold his labor to another Hebrew as a slave, he and his family were to be freed after six years and provided with the essential resources to permit them to reestablish a viable livelihood. During the period of his service, he was to be treated not as a slave but as a hired worker (Exodus 21:2–4; Leviticus 25:39–43; Deuteronomy 15:12–18). Slaves who successfully escaped were not to be returned to their masters but were permitted to live in any town in

Israel (Deuteronomy 23:15).

The principles underlying these specific provisions – the equitable distribution of wealth, protection from economic exploitation, and the security of the resources required to maintain a living – retained the vitality of commerce while halting the cycles of oppression that result in ever increasing gaps between the rich and the poor. Violation of these principles in any economic system results in the ascendancy of the rich persons, institutions, or nations at the expense of the poor. Ill health is an intimate partner of poverty.

Our relationship to nature becomes exploitative when we fail to recognize that God is the Creator and we are his stewards, accountable to him for our management. Our hope for the redemptive transformation of the created order lies in God's power; his acceptance of us as his children is the harbinger of emancipation of the entire creation from the frustration of the curse.

Notes

1   Money represents the ability to acquire and control resources that are a part of the natural creation. The power of money is therefore derived from the natural environment.

Chapter 4

The Environmental Covenant in Africa:
Maintaining a Precarious Balance

◆ ◆ ◆

Miyunga was renowned in all the villages of the Kimbu people. He snared more birds than anyone else within memory and almost never failed. One day, however, all of his snares were empty until he reached the one furthest from the village. The two birds trapped in that snare were like none he had ever seen before – beautiful beyond measure. Instead of killing them, he bound them to bring them back to the village. On the way the birds began to sing in Miyunga's own language. They sang of Miyunga's skill in snaring birds but rather than a song of praise, it was a song of accusation, that he had killed too many. Frightened, Miyunga released the birds but it was too late. Birds flew from the forest around him, including birds he had killed and eaten, and pecked him to death.

◆ ◆ ◆

This myth of the Kimbu (Shorter 1985, 25–26) warns of the danger of upsetting the balance between people and the environment where humans must live in interdependent partnership with other creatures (Taylor 1963). The African "loves the environment, he fears it, and he senses something mysterious about it. The elements, plants and animals, the land and all that is within and on it – these play a vital role in the African's apprehension of reality" (Bediako 1995b, 14). The land, in particular, is the root of the African existence. "To remove Africans from their land is an act of such great injustice that no foreigner can fathom it" (Mbiti 1992, 27).

In traditional belief, there is no firm distinction between the natural order and the spiritual world. Everything has a significance beyond what is seen, and all is interconnected. The sun and sky are images of God, the earth and the rains and streams that water it represent life and fertility, the gifts of God. The owls and hyenas are the familiars of the witches, carrying out their evil tasks cloaked in darkness (Shorter 1985). Satan may take on the form of a wolf or lion in order to destroy life (Bediako 1995b). Totemic animals link the natural world with the world of the ancestors and the history of the people. An animal that, in myth, helped the founder of a clan in a time of great distress may be revered. Age mates, linked symbolically by rites of puberty, or clan members, linked by a common ancestry, may identify themselves by a totemic animal (Goody 1996). Hunters who kill for food must follow proper ritual to prevent vengeance from the spirit of the animal (Morris 1995), a lesson that Miyunga might have forgotten.

> *Eyeemanyi amalwalira: tatega nnaali.*
> One who wants to guard against illness does not kill the crested crane.
> (Lugandan proverb)

Those who upset the balance of the spiritual ecology must restore it again. Friends among urban Zulu in South Africa asked a researcher how he had been affected by his move to their area. In asking this question, they were interested in more than how he had coped with the disruption that accompanies any change of residence.

> They would explain that every person, due to his particular make-up, was in balance and harmony with the powers in the area where he was living. When a person changed his residence, and particularly when this involved ecological changes, he was susceptible to natural forces over which he had not control (du Toit 1981b, 91).

These friends were expressing concern that the balance of forces governing this person's life might have to be restored through the intervention of a diviner. Healing among many Africans has two goals: to cure the ailment and to restore the balance of the patient with his or her environment. The distinctions that are drawn in English between the natural and supernatural have no parallel in Bantu languages (du Toit 1981b, 151–179).

The sacramental approach to nature is a basic reason why Africans seek integrated healing (Shorter 1985). Their traditional medicines come from the products of the earth that are themselves the symbols of the spirits that lie behind them. Illness is an imbalance or a draining of the life force that must be restored, and there is no reason to draw a distinction between the work of the diviner and the work of the herbalist or physician. All are working with tools imbued with spiritual power to restore the life force (Jansen 1973; Nyansako-ni-Nku 1981; Shorter 1985).

Almost paradoxically, while Africans traditionally share a kind of kinship with the environment, they also use it without sentimentality just as each creature acts out its own nature in the cycles of life. "Behind the visible substance of things lie essences or powers which constitute their true nature. Nature has power which may be revered as well as harnessed to man's benefit" (Pobee 1979, 48).

THE ENVIRONMENT AND ANTHROPOCENTRISM

We were attending a staff retreat at Lake Baringo in Kenya, an area known for the many varieties of birds. The lodge where we were staying employed a resident ornithologist who conducted tours. I asked one of my African colleagues if he thought we should go. He said that I should do what I wanted but he would not accompany us. He then went on to say that Africans are often not welcome on bird-watching tours with white expatriates. I asked why that was so. "Because we are always asking, 'But how do they taste?'"

Along with respect for nature, Africans traditionally have a very practical approach. Morris tells of one woman who had captured a young forest deer and kept it as a pet. She cared for it affectionately. She also eventually put it into the cooking pot. A counselor once expressed to my wife how hard it was for him, despite his extensive training, to counsel Europeans and North Americans. He said he really got into trouble when one of his white clients came into his office weeping and said that her cat had died. His response communicated, "Yes, so what? Now tell me what has made you upset." Respect for nature and for maintaining the balance of powers that it represents concerns many Africans, but sentimentality is not part of their response.

In the creation myths of many African peoples, plants and animals that are used for food come into being at the same time as men and women because they are part of God's gift. The Maasai believe that all cattle were created by God as their possession and have often "liberated" the stock of surrounding tribes to enjoy their God-given destiny. The Akamba say that livestock were lowered from the sky along with men and women; the Zulu say that cattle sprang up from the same spot as men and women (Mbiti 1992). From the beginning, then, the natural resources that assure the well-being of men and women were the gifts of God.

The belief that God creates resources at the same time as he creates human life continues to be expressed in attitudes toward family planning. The argument that the number of children should be limited because of limited resources often fails. There are many reasons why Africans value large families. Identity, particularly for women, is bound up with the bearing of children. Children provide a safety net for old age. The number of children increases the strength of the family and clan and also of the tribe in relationship to other tribes. In traditional belief, many children increase the likelihood that the memory of the mother and father will live on through more generations. Children are a gift of God not to be denied, and God would not give children as a gift unless he also was going to give the resources to provide for them.

The expectation of God's provision for children, however, demonstrates more than faith in the good gifts of the giver of life. It also hints at an attitude of dependence that characterizes a traditional African approach toward the environment. Maintaining a balance with the environment and expecting that God will provide is not the same as exercising dominion. Men and women may be at the center of the natural order but not exercise dominion over it.

THE SECOND LEG OF THE STOOL OF FATALISM: THE ENVIRONMENT AND DOMINION

Among the Malawian peoples, a strong conceptual distinction is drawn between the control over nature in the village (*mudzi*) and the struggle for control over opposing powers of nature in the woodlands (*thengo*). The village (controlled by men and women) is the place of living; but the source of life is in the woodlands, where men (for women rarely go to the woodlands) struggle to exercise an uncertain dominion. The spirits live in the woodlands, including the spirits of the rain that exercise control over life and death, prosperity and want in the cultivated fields of the village.

Ancestral spirits hover around their burial sites in the woodlands, and the wild animals live there. The medicines that restore life and health are primarily composed of the plants and animals of the woodlands (Morris 1995). The environment represented by the woodlands is one where human creatures do not exercise dominion but must maintain balance. The belief that the natural environment is unpredictable and largely uncontrollable constitutes the second leg of the stool of fatalism.

Most Africans are more vulnerable to the effects of drought or other natural disasters than those of us who live in Europe and North America. While Europeans and North Americans exercise no more control over nature than Africans, they have access to more resources that buffer the effects of natural catastrophes. Americans and Europeans recognize cognitively that drought, earthquakes, floods, and hurricanes are outside their ability to control, but they also trust, perhaps with a sense of presumption, in their ability to control their effects either through taking precautions or through resources that are mobilized for relief and rehabilitation. Except for those who live daily with the vulnerability that attends poverty or minority status, Europeans and Americans tend to project that sense of control or dominion into other areas of their lives. They assume that we can either change those things that threaten them, protect themselves from them, or counter their negative effects.

When our sense of control is violated, we often feel violated as people. In setting ourselves apart from, and in many senses above, nature, we are better able to maintain a sense of control and reconstruct meaning when we become victims of forces beyond our control. Our attribution of a natural evil that befalls us to a chance happening or even to God's permissive will provides greater comfort and motivates a more active response in addressing its immediate effects than an attribution of a natural evil to the actions of an enemy, witch, spirit, or the active punishment of God.

Most Africans recognize that nature is unpredictable. The primary force buffering the effects of natural evil is the network of relationships and mutual support, particularly within family networks (Twesigye 1987). Assistance from other sources is less sure and is even less likely to be available at the time it is most needed.

Traditionally, however, Africans carry a greater burden than Europeans and North Americans because, while natural evil may be unpredictable, it is not entirely uncontrollable. Natural evil has a cause that must be addressed, or it will repeat itself in another form. Efforts to prevent natural evil are less likely therefore to be addressed toward proximate causes such as the maintenance of vehicles or roadways, the uncontrolled grazing of livestock, or the control of infection. These precautions may delay the evil happening or cause it to come in another form but will not prevent it. If it is fated to happen, and the ecological roots of the problem are not addressed, it will happen. Passivity toward proximate causes of evil happenings prevents the exercise of dominion in the very areas where exercising it is most likely to be efficacious.

The sense of dominion is also compromised by the assumption that each living thing is helpless to act in ways that are contrary to its essential nature. To do so would be to upset the ecological balance. Lions will always be carnivores. To be anything but a meateater would mean being something other than a lion.

> *Jaalala adurref hantuutaa / utu taphattu wal nyaatt.*
> The love of the cat and the mouse; they eat each other while playing.
>   (Oromo proverb)

Even if a cat and mouse have every intention of playing together, the cat will eventually make a meal of the mouse. Both the cat and the mouse are trapped by essential natures that they cannot control through intentions. Even survival is not a strong enough motivation for living things to act contrary to their natures. One folk tale tells of a young wildebeest trapped on an island with a snake. The water is rising and will soon flood the island and the snake pleads with the wildebeest to be carried across the river to safety. The wildebeest hesitates but finally agrees when the snake convinces him that he will not bite him because that would bring death to them both. Halfway across the swollen river, the wildebeest feels the fangs sink into his neck. As both are about to sink beneath the water, the wildebeest asks the snake why he caused their deaths. "A snake is a snake," the snake replies.

A Sukuma proverb expresses the same idea. *Mpija wa shima? Buka twishiganilwe* (The healer of a wound? Get up, let's compete). Because it is part of his essential nature, the man whom a healer has helped rises up to compete with the very person who healed him.

Survey interviewers asked Nigerian men and women, "Is one woman sufficient for a man?" Half of the men and a third of the women answered that men could not be confined to one sexual partner. When the interviewers asked why that was so, almost all, both men and women, answered that it was simply a part of the fundamental nature of men to need multiple partners (Orubuloye et al. 1997).

In contrast, the creation gift of dominion in the new covenant of the kingdom is empowered by God so that followers of Christ may extend his power over the basic desires of their nature. This has important implications for health-related behavior. In the study cited above, the authors credit Christian belief, specifically the ideology of self-control, as a factor that lowers risk of sexually transmitted diseases.

> Although traditional society is still a reality in the input it makes to shaping contemporary society, the Christianization of much of southern Nigeria is not superficial. The Christians are deeply Christian in a way that is now a memory in much of the West. People mean it when they talk about a Christian way of life. Throughout this project, a way of life subject to less risk of sexually transmitted disease was consistently described as Christian behaviour. Furthermore, the two imported religions (of Islam and Christianity), especially Christianity, are the only ideologies with much capacity to erode older beliefs in the near-unrestrainability of male sexual desires (Orubuloye et al. 1997, 1205).

The first leg of the stool of fatalism is based in traditional concepts of God as practically immanent in his irresistible actions but distant, unapproachable, and unknowable in his person. The relationship between God and humanity is forever broken. The second leg is based in the compromised sense of dominion. Natural evil fated to happen cannot be prevented by attention to proximate causes. The natural and ultimate sources of well-being and life are beyond the control of humans who, along with other living beings in the creation, are fated to live according to their essential natures even when life is at stake. The Yoruba believe that fate is determined by the person's selection of his or her "head" (basic character) prior to birth and the irresistible interventions of God and the spirits (Hallgren 1991). The last leg of the stool, bound together with the rest, also lies in traditional beliefs about the nature of the environment, particularly in concepts concerning time.

THE THIRD LEG OF THE STOOL OF FATALISM: THE TIMES AND CYCLES OF LIFE

> In traditional African thought, there is no concept of history moving 'forward' towards a future climax, or towards the end of the world. Since the future does not exist beyond a few months, the future cannot be expected

to usher in a golden age, or even a radically different state of affairs from what is in the Sasa and the Zamani. The notion of a messianic hope ... has no place in the traditional concept of history. So African peoples have no 'belief in progress,' the idea that development of human activities and achievements move from a low to a higher degree. The people neither plan for the future nor build 'castles in the air' (Mbiti 1992, 23).

Mbiti maintains that the African concept of time is a key to understanding other aspects of their worldview. Like the Hebrews, Africans conceive less of *time* than of *times*. The movement of time, therefore, is tied to experience or events. Some of these events, such as eating, work, and rest happen in daily cycles. Others, such as cultivation or the coming of the rains, happen in seasonal or annual cycles. Some of the pastoralists such as the Gabra in Kenya also count cycles of droughts and plenty (Robinson 1994–1996). These cyclical events are captured in the measurement of time. For some peoples, the lunar months, for instance, are named after the work or predominant weather pattern that characterizes that time in the seasonal cycle (Mbiti 1992).

Mbiti suggests that Africans see time in two dimensions. One is what he calls the *Sasa* (Kiswahili for now) or the "time region in which people are conscious of their existence, and within which they project themselves both into the short future and mainly into the past" (Mbiti 1992, 22). The length of the *Sasa* would vary according to a person's experience. An elder's *Sasa* would be longer than that of a young person; a community's *Sasa* would be even longer because the past time that is relevant to their present experience is longer.

The second region of time is the *Zamani*. This could be called the time beyond immediate experience or perhaps the time beyond counting. The *Zamani* is best described as a region rather than a time. It is where "everything finds its resting place" (Mbiti 1992, 23). Ancestors who have passed beyond memory as well as unborn children of the future both occupy the region of the *Zamani*.

Mbiti analyzes the verb tenses among the Kikuyu and Akamba, two Bantu tribes of Kenya. Like many Bantu languages, the grammar has no mechanism for describing actions in the future beyond about six months. The past tenses of the languages group anything before the recent past into broad categories. Mbiti's analysis of African time was basically supported by Gehman (1985) in his independent study of the Akamba.

Those who do not conceptualize the future cannot fully appreciate that their actions of today may either build or destroy their own well-being in the future. A construct of contingency lives only in the future.

> *Owu nkum oyarefo, okum onipa a ne wu adu so.*
> Death does not kill the sick person, it kills the
> one whose time of death is due.
>
> (Akan proverb)

This proverb involves no call to action. It may be applied only retrospectively. The sickness that kills cannot be determined ahead of time, only by looking into the past. Because death cannot be prevented, the sickness that kills also has no prevention. If the future beyond a period of a few months is not contingent upon the present, many preventative strategies make no sense. Successfully preventing AIDS as well as many other diseases and injuries demands a sense of contingency that extends beyond a few months.

The African concept of time is anthropocentric. The cycles of African time correspond closely to the rhythms of Hebrew time that were also centered on human activity. The Hebrews, however, also embraced a linear view of time that was theocentric and corresponded to the activities of God. African time has no equivalent to this linear perspective because the activities of the High God have no goal or end. Without a linear concept of time and history, the cycles reign forever unchallenged. There is no power that can rescue men and women from the cycle.

> *Ennaku zisembera nga kikande.*
> Misery creeps in upon you like uncultivated land.
>
> (Lugandan proverb)

The end of every man and woman begins with the diminution of the life force of their youth. Death brings escape from the limitation of the body but also commences the process of a new dying as the spirit must face the inevitable end of passing from human community to a nameless existence in the *Zamani*.

After death, a person remains in the *Sasa* as long as there are living people who remember and can greet him or her by name. After the person has passed from living memory, even if the name is remembered in a genealogy, he or she is truly dead. The now nameless spirits pass into the region of the *Zamani* where they join the company of other spirit beings that no longer have an identity. These unknown spirits become a source of fear and dread when they intervene in the lives of the living.

A distant and purposeless God, an uncontrollable environment, and a cyclical perspective on time that provides a very limited perspective of the future are the three legs of the stool of fatalism. In contrast, biblical belief imbues humanity with the significance latent in contingency but also hope. In the kingdom of God, identity is never lost; men and women are forever members of his family and are known to him by name.

Finally, even the security and meaning that emerged from the cycles of life is itself being destroyed. Africans must now deal with a world culture of commerce rooted not in the present but the future. The cultural transition to the idea of an extended future contingent upon the actions of today is one that many Africans have made, but not without cost. The poor of Africa pay those costs most heavily in the loss of their well-being.

THE ENVIRONMENT, POVERTY, AND SOCIAL JUSTICE

The poverty of Africa has many causes. Dr. George Kinoti identifies nine factors that contribute to the poverty of African peoples: bad governance, inequitable competition within the world economic order, negative aspects of African culture, poor management, moral failure, low standards of formal education and lack of access even to these poor services, over-population, low standards of science and technology, and misuse of environmental resources (Kinoti 1994).

The colonial legacy and the economic and political dominance of European countries certainly contribute to these problems but, like many other Africans, Dr. Kinoti feels that the blame for Africa's problems can no longer be fully attributed to the North.

Kinoti specifies the African attitude toward time as a contributor to the continent's inability to compete in a world economy based upon efficiency and timeliness. At a deeper level, however, the lack of regard for the future also contributes to poor management and governance since each of these disciplines demands an orientation to future events.

The undeveloped concept of dominion not only contributes to fatalism (Kinoti lists this as another cultural factor that causes poverty), but also to the slow growth of science and technology. Kinoti laments that "hard and honest work" and "pride in work well done are largely alien concepts in Africa" (1994, 29). Without a sense of dominion, work is characterized either by unremitting toil or by the extrinsic rewards of wealth.

Finally, in regard to the use of natural resources, the utilitarian ethic is no longer in balance with the ethic of respect for the land. In company with multinational organizations from Europe and North America, Africans have exploited their mineral, land, and forest resources. Traditional practices of cultivation have given way to the monocropping of export crops for Northern markets. "In some countries unjust land tenure, bad land-use policies, and corruption give fertile lands to a few wealthy or powerful Africans. The poor majority, the peasants, who are thus deprived of ownership of good land, become tenants of rich land-owners and have no incentive to care for the land, while others are driven into ecologically fragile, marginal lands. The result is extensive erosion of soil and water resources" (Kinoti 1994, 32).

Chapter 5

Community Health:
Rediscovering Shalom and Healing
in Biblical Communities

♦ ♦ ♦

During the months that I wrote this book, my mom was dying after a prolonged struggle with cancer. One Saturday morning in May her heart, weakened by chemotherapy, hypertension, and diabetes, finally gave up as my father was driving her to the hospital. My father's lover, friend, and dearest companion of 55 years slumped against him as he waited for a light to change, and was gone.

My dad immediately called his children but none of us could get to his home that day. My father, a pastor and a man of faith who had comforted many in times of loss, immediately reached out to others in the shock and sorrow of Mom's death. His pastor came immediately. When the pastor learned that none of the family would be able to reach my father that day, he spent the night with him. During the course of that day, my dad broke away from calling friends and extended family to call a younger pastor who had specialized in the problems of aging and the grieving process. My father talked to this pastor at length to discover what he could expect to happen over the next few weeks and months as he grieved over Mom's death.

The following day, a Sunday, my father realized that he would soon have a house full of family and guests. Though my mother had been a meticulous housekeeper, she had been too weak to maintain the cleanliness of the house to her usual standards over the previous weeks. My father called the people at the mission agency where he and my mom worked. Within a couple of hours, they had mobilized a cleaning crew of ten people who not only cleaned and ordered the house but polished it. The president of the mission, my dad's boss, spent an hour scrubbing every inch of the bathroom. Throughout the next week, people from the church and mission not only provided food and emotional and spiritual support but also participated in honoring my mom and dad.

What is most staggering about the support my father received from the healing community of the church is that it is not unusual. Throughout the world, many times a day, the church community closes around its members to support them in sickness, misfortune, death, loss of a job, and all of the tragedies that come with living in a broken world.

◆ ◆ ◆

THE HELPING COMMUNITY OF SHALOM

"It is not good for man to be alone."

The account of God's creation in Genesis is punctuated by his repeated observation that what he had made was good. Suddenly that sequence is broken. God declares that it is *not good* for Adam to be alone. His declaration was even more surprising because Adam shared a relationship with God that had not yet been marred by disobedience. Apparently, not even God met Adam's needs for companionship. Though Adam was created in God's image, he remained one of God's creatures and needed the company of a fellow creature who perfectly complemented him. In his creation of Eve, God established not only the family but also the human community. When my father suddenly found himself without his companion and helpmeet of more than half a century, he reached out to the community[1] of shalom embodied in the church.

Ministry within the Community of Shalom

As my father reflected on the days immediately following my mother's death, he marveled at how well he did. He concluded that he coped not through a false show of spirituality or protective detachment but through the power and presence of God in his life, enabling him to remain simultaneously vulnerable and strong. The church was for him an incarnate expression of God's presence. The help he received was not motivated by the duties of kinship or the fear of God's punishment. Rather, the root of kindness was love (1 John 4:16–18; 1 Peter 1:22).

The community of shalom ministered practically to his needs. They assisted in bringing food, cleaning the house, providing hospitality to overnight guests, organizing the details of the funeral and memorial service, assisting with the costs of the funeral, and in many other ways. They became an extended family with resources for service that far exceeded those of the actual kin.

Helping Ministries of Law and Grace

The practical helping ministries of God's people extend beyond assistance to individuals who have suffered a sudden loss. In the Law of Moses, God codified the relationships of community members to one another in an extensive, integrated body of law that defined moral, civil, and criminal behavior. In the Law, God explicitly specified the rights, responsibilities, and obligations of the individual community members to one another as well as to the entire community.

Individual and corporate health within the community of shalom depends upon the practical assistance of God's people. Because ill health is a companion of poverty, provision of helping services for the poor is a critical component within a community of shalom. Diseases cluster among the poor – the result of lack of access to health care, poor nutrition, lack of personal and public hygiene, crowded living situations, poor educational standards, and many other reasons.

The Law of Moses contained specific provisions addressing the basic needs of the poor. Most poverty among the Hebrews was addressed through the assistance of the extended family or the community but when that safety net failed, the Law assured that the poor would be provided with their basic survival needs while preserving their dignity.

- To meet immediate needs, any Hebrew was permitted to enter fields, vineyards, and orchards to eat freely from the produce, though not to harvest it (Deuteronomy 23:24–25).
- Additionally, anything that remained on trees or in vineyards and fields after a single harvesting, as well as any sheaves that were forgotten in the field, were to be left for the poor to harvest and take to their homes (Deuteronomy 24:19–22).

- Every third year, a tenth of the produce from the entire land was to be given to the Levites and the poor (Deuteronomy 26:12). During each seventh year, when the land was left fallow, the poor were permitted to take and eat whatever grew there (Exodus 23:10–11).

The laws of social justice and charity grew out of Israel's oppression in Egypt. The Hebrews were urged by God to remember their heritage as slaves. Because Yahweh was the protector of the vulnerable men and women in Hebrew society, he commanded his people to side with the orphans, widows, aliens, and poor (Leviticus 19:33–34). To oppress the poor was to show contempt for Yahweh, who created them (Proverbs 14:31).

In the new covenant, giving is uprooted from the soil of fairness and mercy and replanted in the very character of Jesus Christ. Paul wrote to the Corinthians encouraging them to participate in meeting the needs of their sister church. "I am not commanding you, but I want to test the sincerity of your love by comparing it with the earnestness of others. For you know the grace of our Lord Jesus Christ, that though he was rich, yet for your sakes he became poor, so that you through his poverty might become rich" (2 Corinthians 8:8–9). The grace of giving encompassed not only individual acts of kindness, such as those that assist the sick, injured, or grieving but also institutional acts of sacrificial giving to alleviate poverty and disease.

Yet Paul did not call the Corinthian church to fully emulate Jesus. He did not expect them to become poor so that their sister church could become rich. Rather, he called them to equality.

"Our desire is not that others might be relieved while you are hard pressed, but that there might be equality. At the present time your plenty will supply what they need, so that in turn their plenty will supply what you need" (2 Corinthians 8:13–14a).

HELPING MINISTRIES IN EMOTIONAL
AND SPIRITUAL HEALING

Jaal-lalti goggoduun lafe nama dhukkubsiti.
Love that is dry makes the bones sick.
(Oromo proverb)

My father recognized that the community of the church helped by providing a climate for spiritual and emotional healing. In order to heal, my father required more than the resources of food, money, and labor. "Dry love" can mobilize a gift of food, but it cannot heal the spirit.

Dorothee Soelle distinguishes between three stages of human suffering (Wind 1995). The first, "mute suffering," happens immediately after a loss or catastrophic illness or injury. The community is comprised of those who support the suffering person during that time of relative helplessness. Those who meet pressing demands include not only friends who are immediately available to satisfy practical needs but also health professionals who provide emergency care, or even caring strangers. Those who brought food to my father and some of those who worked hard to clean the home participated in the first stage but not necessarily the next stages of his journey.

The next stage is "lamenting suffering," when the person begins to speak and cry out his or her hurt. The lament may involve anger and protest as well as cries of pain. The suffering person names and begins to accept the injury or loss. During this time suffering persons require a listening community, people who can compassionately reflect their pain and sorrow.

The last stage of "changing suffering" happens when the sufferer "begins to experience trustworthy relationships with others, and, together with them, finds a way to reorganize life" (Wind 1995, 155). "Changing suffering" requires an interactive community that shares the same perspectives as the sufferer about life and living. It requires a common "language" of belief and understanding that permits reflection and builds solidarity.

As my father reflected on his experience, he recognized that he depended upon the church as a helping community in the deeper levels of need. His Christian friends and colleagues in the church and mission shared his suffering and helped him to reconstruct meaning and direction in his life by interacting in the same "language," reflecting common values and beliefs.

Like instrumental assistance, this second level of the church's role as a helping community is also rooted in the example of Jesus Christ. Paul opens his second letter to the Corinthians by praising the God of comfort.

> Praise be to the God and Father of our Lord Jesus Christ, the Father of compassion and the God of all comfort, who comforts us in all our troubles, so that we can comfort those in any trouble with the comfort we ourselves have received from God. For just as the sufferings of Christ flow

over into our lives, so also through Christ our comfort overflows. If we are distressed, it is for your comfort and salvation; if we are comforted, it is for your comfort, which produces in you patient endurance of the same sufferings we suffer (2 Corinthians 1:3–6).

This passage and the rich system of shared belief that lies beneath it not only empowers compassion but also provides a shared basis for interaction so that suffering moves beyond lament to change and the reconstruction of personal meaning.

My father identified prayer as the final way in which the helping community of the church contributed to his ability to cope with mother's death and begin to reconstruct his life. On the morning of my mother's death, my wife, in the middle of her devotions, sensed a strong direction to pray more intensely for my mother and father than she had in the past. As my mother was dying a thousand miles away, my wife was praying that God would be a refuge and strength for both my mother and father, delivering them from fear and making his presence real in their lives. The power of prayer in the extended community of God began even as my mother was dying, and my father was facing the initial shock of her loss.

As word of Mom's death spread through the churches my dad had pastored and the missionaries throughout the world to whom he and Mom had ministered, many people began to pray, write, and E-mail. Because the missionaries were scattered throughout the world, his family of faith literally prayed for him 24 hours a day.

He was also strengthened by praying with many other people. Prayer represented a common language bringing strength, comfort, and new direction in the midst of shock, lament, and change. The act of praying together with others, particularly when hugging or touching each other, became a sacrament of healing; the intimacy of shared prayer was itself a channel of God's grace.

THE GRACEFUL COMMUNITY OF SHALOM

◆ ◆ ◆

The Gabra and Janjamtu, two pastoralist peoples of northern Kenya and southern Ethiopia, lived close to each other; sometimes competing for, sometimes sharing, water and range lands. At one time the camps of both peoples were side by side, and their two elder sages enjoyed each other's companionship and counsel. Then a terrible thing happened; the son of the Gabra sage accidentally killed the son of the Janjamtu sage. Though neither man wanted more blood to be shed, they and the elders agreed that the customary law of both peoples demanded the death of the Gabra young man. After prolonged discussion, the two sages and their elders agreed on a compromise. The Janjamtu sage would choose whose blood would be spilled to avenge the killing.

Seeking to mollify the warriors and yet preserve his friendship with the Gabra sage, he chose the priest's daughter. By this time, the hour was late and the deed could not be done until the following morning. The Janjamtu warriors, fearing that the girl would escape during the night, demanded that she be brought to a neutral ground under the elders' tree between the two camps, to spend the night in a thorn enclosure.

At first light, the two sages, accompanied by elders and others, left their camps, walked toward the ritual tree, and found the warriors sleeping. Inside the thorn enclosure, the girl slept peacefully on her mat on the ground. As the sages approached the tree, they noticed that the girl cradled something in her arms. It was a lamb, a lamb that they described as without deformity or fault.

Very much disturbed, the sages and elders consulted one another as to what the meaning of this could be. No one had approached the tree during the night. None of the livestock of either camp were missing. Where had this lamb come from, and for what purpose?

In the end, both the Janjamtu and Gabra elders could reach only one conclusion. God must have sent the lamb to be slaughtered in the place of the girl, to make restitution for the Janjamtu young man. They anointed the lamb and slaughtered it. No more blood was spilled (Robinson).

◆ ◆ ◆

This story from the oral tradition of the Gabra people demonstrates the conflict of grace with law. The Law of Moses, as well as the Gabra and Janjamtu, recognized that transgressions were not only individual but collective. In breaking their joint relationship of intimacy with God, Adam and Eve broke the intimacy of their relationship to each other. They suddenly had to protect themselves from each other. They each blamed another for their sin. Eve blamed the serpent, Adam blamed Eve, and together they blamed God as their Creator. Where they had once been one flesh, they became competitors.

Their self-protective competition became codified in the "life for life, death for death" law of Noah that justified retribution in kind. On the one hand it strengthened the role of community in enforcing justice, but, on the other, it fractured the solidarity of community by building a culture of retribution.

The selection of the priest's *daughter* as the sacrifice in place of the young *man* reflected another consequence of breaking the covenant with God. When Adam and Eve sinned, the balance of power changed. God told Eve, "I will greatly increase your pains in childbearing; with pain you will give birth to children. Your desire will be for your husband, and he will rule over you" (Genesis 3:16). Of physically greater strength than Eve, Adam was able to dominate her. Eve, in turn, became dependent upon Adam for her place in society. Women became valued as bearers of children and not as companions. Though the daughter of the Gabra priest accepted her fate gracefully, even able to sleep through the night, she had no choice but to obey the decree of the elders.

The parallels between this story and the covenants of God's law and grace are remarkable. The sacrifice of God's lamb not only made possible the reconciliation of men and women to God but also to one another in community. Linking the old and new covenants by an explicit reference to God's "chosen people," Paul urges the Colossian church to embody their calling to shalom in a graceful community that models the forgiveness of Christ.

> Therefore, as God's chosen people, holy and dearly loved, clothe your-selves with compassion, kindness, humility, gentleness and patience. Bear with each other and forgive whatever grievances you may have against one another. Forgive as the Lord forgave you. And over all these virtues put on love, which binds them all together in perfect unity. Let the peace of Christ rule in your hearts, since as members of one body you were called to peace. And be thankful (Colossians 3:12–15).

The community of God confesses sin to one another. Within the new cove-nant, men and women are to confess their sins not only to God but also to one another. James links healing to corporate prayer and to the confession of sins. "Therefore confess your sins to each other and pray for each other so that you may be healed" (James 5:16). In his personal reflection on the East African revival and how it affected his own home, Dr. Dan Kesege maintained that the power of the revival was rooted in confession of per-sonal sins rather than attributing blame to others (Granberg-Michaelson 1995).

The verbal confession of sins is essential to the experience of shalom within community. First, the person who confesses may be cleansed, forgiven, and restored. Secondly, verbal confession is an active rather than passive response to the presence of evil. The person who never confesses to sin never progresses beyond a culture of victimization. Without confession, "guilt becomes a menacing fetish" (Taylor 1963,177). In the African story, if the son of the Gabra sage had denied his offense, every questioning look or word from another member of the community would have become, for him, a curse. The one who sins becomes the victim of the community that he or she wronged.

The community of God forgives and cleanses one another. Why is forgiveness given a central role in the healing community of grace? First, forgiveness permits the one who is forgiven to be cleansed of guilt. As a high priest, Jesus Christ does not merely cleanse bodies of ceremonial uncleanness, but sprinkles our hearts "to cleanse us from a guilty conscience" (Hebrews 10:22). Just as unclean diseases separated ancient Israelites from temple worship and from the community, those with guilty hearts are alienated from God and from one another. In guilt and disease, symbol and reality are intimately linked. Disease was for the Israelites a sign of guilt. Unresolved guilt is the root cause of many diseases and interpersonal conflicts.

The person who experiences the grace of God in forgiveness is able to forgive; the one who forgives is able to be forgiven. Our own forgiveness, as well as our ability to forgive, springs from our experience of Jesus' forgiveness. Without forgiveness, we "miss the grace of God" (Hebrews 12:15) and permit the growth of a "bitter root" that defiles the entire community. Bitterness is the natural consequence of being either unforgiven or unforgiving. Unforgiven people become bitter in their continued isolation from community; unforgiving people become bitter as they horde offenses in the treasury of their hearts, counting them in secret and recounting them openly. In the Old Testament those who touched an unclean person themselves became unclean and had to be cleansed before returning to a fullness of relationship within the community of Israel. Bitter people defile those whom they touch and destroy community.

The community of God confronts and restores those who alienate themselves from it. In both the Old and New Testaments, those of God's people who cut themselves off from one another could be restored to the community. In the Old Testament, shalom was linguistically linked with the compensation that had to be paid to a person who had been wronged. There the verbal form of the root word for *shalom* (*shlm*) is most often used in the context of legal agreements and is frequently translated as "repay" or "compensate." The commands in Exodus 21:33–22:14 specify the compensation that offenders are to pay to aggrieved parties in numerous instances of the intentional or unintentional destruction or loss of property. These civil penalties consistently use the verbal form. "If a man steals an ox or a sheep and slaughters it or sells it, he must pay back (*shlm*) five head of cattle for the ox and four sheep for the sheep" (Exodus 22:1).

The purity and unity of the community were preserved through exclusion of the sinful, sick, and unclean. The way back into the community for the sinful, unclean, or diseased required that they follow the steps indicated in the Law of Moses.[2]

Grace was certainly not absent in the Old Covenant. Repeated sacrifices performed in faith and sincerity atoned for sin against Yahweh in the Old Testament. Yahweh promised healing and restoration to those who were contrite and lowly in spirit. "I have seen his ways, but I will heal him; I will guide him and restore (*shlm*) comfort to him" (Isaiah 57:18). Nevertheless, the person who caused loss to another was required to bear the burden of that loss. Obedience often sprang from fear of punishment and loss, a fear that drained inner peace and strength and prevented fullness of life in community (1 John 4:18).

In contrast, in the new covenant, the purity and unity of the community are preserved through confrontation and restoration of those who are sinful, sick, and unclean. Virtually nothing is written in the New Testament concerning compensation of the victims of injustice. The community of God in Christ is preserved by grace, not by justice.

> Brothers, if someone is caught in a sin, you who are spiritual should restore him gently. But watch yourself, or you also may be tempted. Carry each other's burdens and in this way you will fulfill the law of Christ (Galatians 6:1–2).

In the new covenant, Jesus instructs offenders to be reconciled with those who hold something against them, making right the losses they might have suffered (Matthew 5:23–26). If the offenders fail to take action, however, God lays the burden of reconciliation upon those who are offended, not only calling upon them to forgive the offender but also to bear the burdens and consequences of their sin so that they may be restored (Galatians 6:1–2). Consequently, in his letter to the disputatious Corinthians, Paul writes that if the church cannot adjudicate a dispute between its members, it is better to be defrauded than to divide and shame the body through appeal to the civil courts (1 Corinthians 6). In the same way, God calls the members of his community to "cover" the unintentional and unconfessed sins committed against them with love and graceful forgiveness (1 Peter 4:8).

When the elders of the Gabra told the story of the lamb to my friend, they also said that it was a topic of continuing debate. Though it had taken place many years ago, some elders maintained that the law of the tribe should have been honored. To them the story was one of moral failure – first in the substitution of the priest's daughter and later in the substitution of a lamb. They concluded that the elders at that time had taken a great risk. By their decision, they might have not only divided the two peoples but perhaps even catalyzed open warfare.

Other elders argued that their forefathers had taken the right decision. By accepting the lamb as a gift from God intended for sacrifice, they were able to preserve the unity of two peoples without human bloodshed. The sacrifice of the lamb permitted the son of the Gabra elder once more to enter the Gabra community with his sin fully covered, and further violence was averted.

The Old Covenant would affirm the arguments of the first set of Gabra elders; the New Covenant would affirm the argument of the second set. The pathway to communities of shalom in the Old Testament was hedged in by fairness and justice. The final goal was the preservation of community through the application of the Law of Moses. The pathway to communities of shalom in the New Testament involves confrontation, forgiveness, and restoration. The final goal is the restoration of community through grace.

True community cannot exist for long apart from grace. In the new covenant, the model for the restoration of community was not the law but the nature of Jesus' relationship to his people. He forgave those who offended him even though they did not repent, and he bore the burdens of all sinners. In transforming the basis of community reconciliation, Jesus established the church as a graceful, forgiving, healing community.

THE HEALING COMMUNITY OF SHALOM

◆ ◆ ◆

The missionary father was riding his motorcycle back home to his house in western Tanzania when he lost control and crashed. His leg was broken in several places. He endured a long trip to a large church hospital but the injury was beyond the skills, or perhaps the technologies, of the doctors. His leg continued to swell and soon circulation of blood to the leg began to shut down. He was rushed to a better equipped hospital in Nairobi, a short distance from Nairobi Chapel, his home church. Members of the Chapel, as well as his own mission, came to visit him many times a day, praying for him and encouraging him and his wife in his sickness. His condition stabilized but soon the leg began to deteriorate once more. The doctors felt that he was too ill to be evacuated and began to prepare to amputate the leg. He and his wife called for the elders of the Chapel to come and pray for him and anoint him with oil. I joined the elders in the hospital room. One of the elders traced the sign of the cross on his forehead with oil, and we all prayed. Circulation in the leg improved and the crisis passed. Members of the church and the mission had also begun to identify orthopedic specialists in the United States. Eighteen months following the accident, after treatment and rehabilitation in the United States, he and his wife credited their healing to the power of God that began to operate in a new way at the time of his anointing.

◆ ◆ ◆

After his anointing, this seriously ill man did not jump out of bed and run through the hospital leaping and praising God. His expression of thanks to us after our prayer was hushed and weak. His healing and recuperation continued over a number of months. He and his family drew heavily upon the resources of scientific medicine as well as the healing prayers of God's community. In fact, the members of God's community provided access to a quality of scientific medicine that he might not have otherwise obtained. Yet he and his wife attribute his healing to this time of community prayer. The passages on the community's role in healing in James and 1 Corinthians do not address the issue of whether or not a healing was miraculous.

Healing within Community

James gave his instruction on healing in the context of teaching on prayer.

Is any one of you in trouble? He should pray. Is anyone happy? Let him sing songs of praise. Is any one of you sick? He should call the elders of the church to pray over him and anoint him in the name of the Lord. And the prayer offered in faith will make the sick person well; the Lord will raise him up. If he has sinned, he will be forgiven. Therefore confess your sins to each other and pray for each other so that you may be healed. The prayer of a righteous man is powerful and effective (James 5:13–16).

This instruction on healing reveals several important lessons about the community of healing in the church.

1. *It is a community response.* James clearly specifies that the sick person should call upon the community of the church represented by the elders. In healing, the community becomes the agent of God's blessing and the recipient of his grace. As agents of God's healing, they anoint and pray for the person who is sick. As recipients of God's grace, they confess their sins and are themselves forgiven and restored.

2. *The act of healing mobilizes the other healing resources of the church.* The elders who minister to the sick person also mobilize church members to gather around the one who is sick, as a graceful and helping community.

3. *The healing involves more than recovery from sickness.* When James wrote about the sick person being made well after anointing and prayer by the elders, he spoke of a person being "saved" [*sozo*] (Brown 1995). Later in the same chapter, he used the same word to emphasize that turning "a sinner away from his error will *save* him from death." In both of these passages, James referred to community interventions that result in the healing or salvation of an individual. In the same passage, James also referred to the healing of the community, effected through the group confession of sins and prayer. In this passage, he used the word *iaomai* that implies not only physical healing but restoration as well. In the same passage therefore, James embraced a fullness of healing that transcended physical recovery – salvation for individuals and restoration of the community.

4. *This is a symbolic intervention.* The anointing with oil "in the name of the Lord" indicates that the oil carried a symbolic rather than medicinal significance.[3] The oil represented God's blessing and the power of his presence. There is no indication in the passage that this is a ceremony reserved only for dire circumstances.

5. *The act of healing is not magic.* There are no magic words or rites prescribed by James in this prayer for healing. The instruction is simple and general. It prescribes no specific procedure for anointing with oil or any ritual to sanctify or otherwise empower the oil for healing. It involves no diagnostic procedures either of the physical or of the unseen worlds. The healing is not mediated by angels or other spirits.

6. *It does not require healers or prophets with special power or knowledge.* Later in the chapter, in fact, James emphasized that these prayers could be made by people of faith who are "just like us" (James 5:17). The ministry of healing established in this passage is one of the church, not of healers.

7. *It is an effective intervention.* God says that he will honor the prayers made in faith for the sick person by healing (saving) him or her. Why are prayers sometimes not met with physical healing? This passage gives no answer. Two possible answers may be derived from reflection rather than exegesis: a) Because the word for healing refers to salvation and is associated with the forgiveness of sins, the prayer offered in faith effects salvation even if the person dies, or b) After the knowledge of the new covenant, prayers offered in faith may remove the fear of dying and of death by renewing the assurance that they will be "raised up." To argue that the person's continued sickness or death demonstrates that the prayers were made with insufficient faith is not justified. Only a short while before in the same letter, James had emphasized the brevity of life and God's sovereign control (James 4:13–17).

THE GIFTS OF HEALING

In his first letter to the Corinthians, Paul wrote that the Holy Spirit gives gifts of healing to members of the church. In other biblical passages regarding the spiritual gifts, the gift of healing is not mentioned. The Old Testament has no parallel either to Christian healing ministry or the ministry of spiritually gifted healers.

Priests in the Old Testament combined the roles of health (shalom) educator, public health officer (Avalos 1995)), and spiritual mediator. In teaching the Law of Moses to the people of Israel, the priests also showed them the way to shalom. As public health officers, the priests had limited powers of quarantine. They diagnosed some infectious diseases according to the Law of Moses and isolated those who suffered from them. They also supervised the destruction of objects and possessions that might have been infected. Finally, the priests examined those who said they had been cured and restored them to the community. Most importantly, as spiritual mediators, the priests enabled repentance and restoration of the people of God's covenant through the rhythmic system of sacrifices and rites. Sacrifices addressed both individual and collective sins, both intentional and unintentional sins.

Because God was the only healer for Israel, their priests were not given a ministry involving physical healing. They did not conduct rites or ceremonies of healing. There were very few instances of physical healing in the Old Testament and only four that involved the mediation of a healer. Elijah and Elisha accounted for three of these and Isaiah the fourth. It is therefore not surprising that Jesus' contemporaries identified him as Elijah or another of the prophets (Matthew 16:13–14). There is not a single instance in the Old Testament where the blind, lame, deaf, or dumb were healed (Brown 1995). It almost seems that God reserved these miracles to announce his kingdom.

In evaluating the many healing practices of the church, it is important to make some observations about healing as a spiritual gift.[4] The gifts of healing may encompass a variety of interventions and practices. Paul used the word *iaomai* to express the gift of healing. Spiritually gifted healers include not only those who serve God by bringing miraculous recovery from sickness and injury but also those who restore others to wholeness, individually and in community. Spiritually gifted healers include the peacemakers. These healers are men and women who are able in love to confront sinful and alienated members of the body so that they repent, seek forgiveness, and are restored. These healers include those who are able to confront embittered people who need to forgive others and enable them to discover and express God's grace in their lives. Finally, some members of the Body of Christ have a special ability to transcend denominational and ethnic boundaries to bring others together in fellowship. These may also have the gift of healing.

The goal of the healing gifts is the common good of the church, not individual healing. The spiritual gifts are meant for the common good of the church. The Holy Spirit gives the gifts to "prepare God's people for works of service, so that the body of Christ may be built up until we all reach unity in the faith and in the knowledge of the Son of God and become mature, attaining to the whole measure of the fullness of Christ" (Ephesians 4:12–14). The Holy Spirit does not intend to establish a branch of alternative medicine. True unity of the church and the maturity of its members require healers who are peacemakers and reconcilers. Spiritually gifted healers recognize that biomedical approaches to healing, though essential, often fail to address the root causes of illnesses caused by stress, alienation, broken relationships, hopelessness, or excess.

The gifts of healing are meant for use in the context of all of the gifts. Paul makes clear that the gifts of the Spirit are interdependent, just as one part of the body depends upon another. The gifts of helps, encouragement, teaching, and administration are close partners of the gift of healing. When one gift dominates the others or is used as the single criterion of spirituality, the church is unbalanced. Ignoring the gifts of healing within the church increases susceptibility to division, bitterness, and discouragement. A church or movement that takes its sole identity from healing ministry heightens its susceptibility to unbiblical excess, pride, and pretense. Finally, the exercise of the gifts must mesh with the overall ministries of the church. The healing ministry of the elders described in James, for instance, is more intimately bound to the community of the church than to the exercise of individual spiritual gifts.

The healing ministry of Jesus is not necessarily a model for the exercise of the spiritual gift of healing. The healing ministry of Jesus was an expression of his compassion for those who were sick and afflicted. The exercise of the spiritual gift of healing must share that aspect of his ministry. His healing ministry also served as a proclamation of the kingdom of God, a proof of his divinity, and a visible demonstration of his teaching. While the exercise of spiritual gifts of healing may accomplish some of these same purposes, its goal is to strengthen the church. Likewise, there is no instruction in this passage that the exercise of the spiritual gifts of healing emulates the actual practices of Jesus in healing.

Unlike tongues and prophecy, the gifts of healing are not referred to by Paul as "sign" gifts. The gifts of healing are often grouped together with the "sign" gifts of tongues, prophecy, and sometimes miraculous works. There is no biblically justifiable reason for doing so. Paul makes no reference to gifts of healing in his further teaching on the gift of tongues as a "sign" gift (1 Corinthians 14:22). To mistakenly associate the gifts of healing with only charismatic expression or the working of miracles often, in practice, violates its core value and work of restoration at the level of the church community. The gifts of healing may find expression in all Christian traditions and, in fact, should bring Christian traditions together, not divide them.

Like the other gifts, the gifts of healing must be expressed as a reflection of God's love. Paul places his great passage on love between his general teaching on the spiritual gifts and his instruction concerning the practice of two of the gifts that, today as well as in first-century Corinth, are most likely to become unbalanced and divisive. When the ability of healers to discern and express the power of God in physical healing becomes the central focus of their ministry, they are in grave danger. They are tempted to build their identities, and sometimes livelihoods, as powerful healers rather than compassionate servants. All the gifts involving a public display of power carry the danger of pride, self-seeking, and boastfulness.

The people of God suffer in spite of the gifts of healing. When Jesus chose the path of compassion and grace above the path of immediate power, he chose it not only for himself but also for his followers. Men like Peter had certainly not missed one of the implications of Jesus' healing ministries. A commander with the power to co-opt nature as an ally, and, even across great distances, to heal those injured in battle and raise dead soldiers to life, would be a formidable commander indeed. Neither Joshua nor Jesus' ancestor David, the two greatest conquerors in the history of Israel, wielded such power.

However, Jesus chose a different path. In the last recorded miracle of healing before his death, Jesus, for the first and only time in his life, healed the battle wound of an armed man; not for his ally but for one of his enemies (John 18:10–11). In choosing this path for himself, Jesus consigned his followers to suffering even as he bought their salvation. The spiritual gift of healing was not given to deliver all those in the church from suffering. Healing, in fact, presumes suffering. The spiritual gift of healing within the body does mean that none of its members should suffer alone. "If one part suffers, every part suffers with it…" (1 Corinthians 12:26).

God intends his church to become a place of healing for its members. The missionary family received a gift of healing from the church. It came through the elders as they prayed for the father and anointed him. It came through those with a gift of healing as they ministered grace to the family, turning them toward God and away from bitterness that threatened to take root in their suffering. It came through those who were skilled in healing interventions. But their healing did not mean an escape from suffering.

THE COMPASSIONATE COMMUNITY OF SHALOM

♦ ♦ ♦

On one of our trips back from Bangladesh, we stopped in Germany to enjoy the hospitality of Christofel Blindenmision, one of the organizations that supported our program. A young American couple had also stopped there on their way back home from Afghanistan. As we sat together, the couple began to tell us of their experiences. Once they began their story, we sensed their urgency in completing it. A Finnish couple who had been their colleagues had been killed by one of the armed factions. They had been shot and stabbed in their beds. Their young children, disturbed by the noise, had gone into their parents' room after the intruders fled. They remained by the bodies of their parents until well into the morning when they had been discovered. The couple who told us the story had taken care of the slain couple's children until arrangements could be made to return them to their relatives in Finland.

The pastor of the murdered missionaries had come to Afghanistan to conduct the memorial service and accompany the children home. In his meditation, he said, "Where was Jesus when this was happening? He was right there beside them as they suffered and remained beside the children throughout the night."

♦ ♦ ♦

As this young couple related their experience, I realized that something was happening to me that I had not experienced before. Sitting in a comfortable German home, the reality of suffering broke through to me in a way that it had not done on the streets and villages of Bangladesh where I had encountered it daily over many months. I was more deeply affected by the account of this tragedy than our ministry to thousands of people in Bangladesh over the previous two years.

In later years, I have come to realize why that was so. I was ministering in Bangladesh with dedication, energy, and humility but with a limited capacity for compassion. I was not able to adequately bridge the cultural gap to enter into the suffering of a poor rural farmer in Bangladesh.

Those affected by the deaths in Afghanistan were more like me. I was a young father. I could imagine our two young children trying to understand why their mommy and daddy would not wake up. I was a leader and could identify with the young couple sitting across from us, and the struggle they had in taking care of the recently orphaned children even while they searched for meaning. I shared in their now shattered sense of invulnerability – the belief that God simply would not let these bad things happen to young people who served him overseas. I could identify with the pastor, struggling to comfort the slain couple's children and the frightened, stricken colleagues, even as he struggled with God to make sense of what had happened and to find words of comfort and hope. I experienced helplessness in this comfortable room that I did not face in Bangladesh. I couldn't fix anything. I could not mobilize human and material resources. I could not draw up plans or solicit donors. But I could enter into the suffering of another and know compassion.

Compassion is the immune response of the body of Christ. The church is a suffering community, first of all, because it is a human community. What sets it apart is not that its members suffer, but that the whole body responds to that suffering by sharing it.

The immune system responds to protect the body from destruction. The immune system responds to threats against the integrity of the body. The discovery of an infectious organism or destructive substance activates an immune response as the resources of the body are mobilized to disempower the intruder. If the immune system fails to respond either because it is weakened or the invader somehow disguises itself, the invader's destructive power is increased. In the same way, a compassionate response is triggered within the body of Christ when a member of that body is threatened or suffers loss. If the compassionate response fails, the infection may gain power within the body to harm not only the member of the body that is immediately threatened but eventually the life of the entire body.

The immune response is intimately identified with the nature of the problem. Compassion includes suffering with another person. Compassion, therefore, involves more than activism in meeting needs. It requires identification with the person affected by suffering. My relationship to rural Bengali farmers was one of mercy and help, but because I could not deeply identify with their suffering, it was not one of compassion. The immune system produces antibodies that are specifically identified with the substance or organism that threatens the integrity of the body. The effectiveness of the immune response depends upon its specificity – it must "know" the threatening agent through previous exposures or "learn" it by genetic and biochemical sensitivity to its distinctive characteristics.

Within the church, then, no one member can be equally compassionate in all circumstances. An older man in the church may be better able to suffer with another older man whose wife of many years passed away than with a young woman who just suffered a miscarriage. While compassion in the body may certainly transcend differences of age, culture, and gender, these differences are nevertheless real. Christians have greater confidence to approach God as a loving Father than did ancient Israelites, not because God's character changed but because Jesus identified with the suffering and temptation of men and women (Hebrews 4:14–5:10). "The mystery of God's love is not that he takes our pains away, but that he first wants to share them with us" (Nouwen et al 1982, 18). Just as the immune system requires a variety of white blood cells that are sensitive to the specific threats to the body, the church requires diversity in order to embody compassion.

The immune response is systemic. The immune response is at the same time localized and systemic. The response immediately surrounding the threatening organism or substance is most visible, but all of the systems of the body contribute to its effectiveness. The circulatory system increases the flow of blood to the infected area. The bone marrow is signaled to produce additional white blood cells to fight the infectious agent. The entire body often becomes feverish as its resources are rapidly mobilized. In the same way the entire body of Christ suffers together with the threatened member. While the suffering is not equivalent throughout the entire body, the spiritual, social, emotional, and physical resources are diverted to the person most at risk. The threatened member is most aware of those who surround him or her and visibly share in suffering, but in a broader sense the entire body is moved by the suffering of the one member and shares in it.

The immune response is strengthened by defending against attacks of disease. Compassion is deepened and made more effective by suffering. This miracle takes place in two ways. First, personal suffering increases the member's capacity for identification. Had I grown up in the home of a poor rural farmer, I would have been better able to respond compassionately to rural farmers in Bangladesh because I could better understand their fears and sufferings. Compassion is also strengthened as members of the Body experience God's grace expressed in the comfort they receive in their time of need (2 Corinthians 1:3–7). Those members who, in their suffering, cut themselves off from grace and the comfort of other members sow bitterness, not compassion. The effectiveness of an immune response is increased as the antibodies become more diverse through exposure to disease. One reason that adults are less vulnerable to sickness than children is that they have a heritage of successful fights against disease archived in the diversity of specialized antibodies.

The immune response is often itself painful. Anyone who has experienced a boil recognizes that the immune response itself may be very painful. The accumulation of sacrificed white blood cells around the isolated core of the battle causes swelling and tightness. The heat of the battle produces inflammation and fever. The nerve endings become highly sensitized to pressure so that the person gives the boil the attention it requires and protects it from further injury that could spread the infection. Compassion hurts. It requires vulnerability. A person cannot be compassionate and self-protective. Shared suffering is genuine suffering.

The immune response may be compromised or turned against itself. Finally, in some conditions such as rheumatoid arthritis, the immune system turns against the body it was designed to protect. The immune system mistakenly identifies another part of the body as an external threat. The power to heal becomes the power of self-destruction. The immune system may also be compromised or overwhelmed by repeated or highly virulent infections, continual stress, and diseases such as AIDS.

The body of Christ sometimes fails in compassion as well. Like an auto-immune disease one member of the body may passionately attack another whom he or she identifies as a threat. There is a failure to identify with the struggles and sufferings of a brother or sister. The compassionate response may also be exhausted. Ideally, healers have all of God's grace as a resource; practically, a healer may find that compassion is compromised when the fifty-third patient of the day walks through the door.

Finally, compassion may atrophy through isolation or through a hardening process that destroys all passion. Those members of Christ's body who never leave their own comfort zone geographically, culturally, or socio-economically never learn to identify with anyone's sufferings but their own. Without outside referents, they may come to regard even their moderate discomfort as great suffering. Displacement is required for compassion to develop. The Greek word for church, *ekklesia*, means the people who are called out.

> Through voluntary displacement (from our areas of comfort and control), we counteract the tendency to become settled in a false comfort and to forget the fundamentally unsettled position that we share with all people. Voluntary displacement leads us to the existential recognition of our inner brokenness and thus brings us to a deeper solidarity with the brokenness of our fellow human beings. Community, as the place of compassion, therefore always requires displacement (Nouwen et al 1982, 64).

Christians may also fail to be compassionate because they build walls of protection against all passion or suffering. They refuse to be touched by the weakness or sufferings of another, just as they refuse to share in their joys. But in cutting themselves off from the passions of the body, they also slowly cut themselves off from its very life.

THE TRANSCENDENT COMMUNITY OF SHALOM

In the Old Covenant, the people of God were defined by race, shared ancestry, culture, and the provisions of the covenants. In calling out Abraham to establish the people of God, God also defined an ethnic community.

- He called Abraham out from others. One essential aspect of community is that it has boundaries – a way to identify members from non-members.
- He gave them a Patriarch. Descent from a common ancestor defined the community ethnically and gave them a unique story. To be a community, members must have a shared story that holds them together. The Semitic languages eventually grew from this heritage.
- He promised them a homeland. Communities are defined by their real or mythical attachment to a homeland, particularly in agrarian and pastoralist cultures.
- His promises became exclusive for the first time, shared only by the members of the community. Just as the shared ancestry of Abraham defined a common heritage for his descendants, the shared promise of a homeland defined their common destiny.
- He gave Abraham the symbol of circumcision – a ritual scarring that signified membership in the community.

In fulfilling God's command, Abraham did not start his journey with only a staff and bundle of food. Though he left his father's household, he left with his family, servants, and relatives. God's individual blessing to Abraham involved the establishment of a lasting community. The Law made no provision for a person to become a beneficiary of the blessings of shalom without also being grafted into the nation of Israel.

But the church is a community open to all who come to Christ in faith. Paul wrote many of his epistles in part to counter the arguments that members of the Body of Christ culturally had to embrace the life and customs of a Jew. The earliest of the church councils successfully addressed this problem when the conflict over the cultural expression of Christianity threatened to split the early church (Acts 15). In the new covenant, the community of shalom retained its identity but membership became open to all.

- God still calls people into the community of shalom. Identity with the healing community of the church is now a choice to accept the Lordship of Christ in response to God's call rather than the artifact of birth as a descendant of Abraham and Isaac.
- Men and women now choose to be born into the church community as descendants of God and heirs of the covenant promises given to his son Jesus, displacing Abraham or another genetic ancestor as one who gives them identity.
- The members of the community receive a heavenly kingdom as a homeland but all of the present creation as a gift to be enjoyed and cared for.
- The blessings of the new covenant extend to all those who respond to God's invitation to join. The shared headship of Jesus Christ defines a common heritage to graceful, compassionate service, and the shared promise of a kingdom defines a common destiny.
- Membership in the healing community of the church is signified by participation in its ordinances/sacraments.

◆ ◆ ◆

My father and mother had accepted the Lordship of Christ and had served him with compassion. Therefore, at the time of my mom's homegoing, my father had all the resources needed for his healing inside his biblical community. He was able to rediscover shalom.

Notes

1   *Community* may mean many things. I use the word in several contexts throughout this book. First, as I have done here, I use it qualitatively to signify a sense of mutual obligation and support between people who identify with one another. Elsewhere, I will use it to refer to the *community* of God's people that, in reference to the Old Testament will signify the people of God's covenants, and in reference to the New Testament, the church. When I later refer to the church as a *healing community*, I integrate the qualitative and biblical meanings. Finally, I use it to refer to geographic *communities*. The phrase *community participation* or *community health* refers to participation and health of people living together in geographically distinct communities. In instances where the meaning of the word *community* is not obvious from its context, I will provide some additional explanation.

2   The cleansing ceremonies also protected the Israelite community from the spread of infectious diseases. The priests diagnosed infectious skin diseases that required isolation of the infected person from the rest of the Israelites. Likewise, when people were cured of the disease, the priest would be called to examine them. If the disease was cured the priest would accept their sacrifice and ceremonially cleanse them with water mixed with the blood of the sacrifice and oil to return them to the community (Leviticus 13–14).

Similarly, Israelites who were made unclean by a bodily discharge, contact with a carcass, or childbirth were required to wash themselves and either wash or destroy objects that had been soiled. In most cases, secondary contact with these unclean emissions also required washing and temporary isolation. People who were made unclean carried the responsibility for washing themselves and objects that had also been made unclean. Additionally, if persons or objects had been made unclean by contact with the dead body of a person, they had to be ceremonially cleansed. In these circumstances, everyone and everything that had become unclean had to be sprinkled with water mixed with the ashes of a red heifer that had been sacrificed and placed in an accessible location outside the camp (Numbers 19). In most cases, the unclean Israelites who had washed and, if necessary, been ceremonially cleansed, presented themselves to the priest with the prescribed sacrificial offering. By accepting the offering the priest restored those who had been unclean to community (Leviticus 11:24–12:8, 15:1–33).

3   Some have suggested that the oil used for anointing in this passage was medicinal and without symbolic significance. Because oil was used medicinally to cleanse wounds, they conclude that the procedure described in this passage should be followed only when all recourse to scientific medicine has failed. This interpretation cannot be justified from the passage itself. The anointing was done "in the name of the Lord," taking the form of a blessing rather than the administration of a medicine (Brown 1995).

4   I am not going to enter into the theological debates surrounding the spiritual gifts. I believe that the Holy Spirit still gives gifts of healing to members of the church today, but I also believe that they may be expressed outside of "charismatic" churches.

Chapter 6

The Ambivalent Covenant of African Community

◆ ◆ ◆

The sense of mutual obligation in an African family runs deeper than a list of traditional obligations. I recently met a Kenyan colleague at a conference near Washington, DC. During the days before the conference, she had stayed with relatives in the area — distant relatives by American standards. I asked why she was moving into the hotel. "Because he will insist on driving me in every morning at rush hour even though the conference is on the opposite side of town from his work. When I've come before, he has taken me to my morning appointments regardless of where they are. I object and point out that the Metro (rapid transit) will take me there. However, he just says, 'But you're family.' "

◆ ◆ ◆

COMMUNITY AND IDENTITY

Whatever happens to the individual happens to the whole group, and whatever happens to the whole group happens to the individual. The individual can only say, "I am because we are; and since we are, I am" (Mbiti 1992, 109).

Like the ancient Hebrews, most Africans cannot maintain their individual identity apart from their identification as a people. The Akan people identify three components to individual identity that link the person to his or her community and heritage. Traditional rites and customs progressively link the person and the extended community. The individual man or woman bears the name of an ancestor, a link to the communal heritage. Rites of passage are rites of incorporation and seasonal celebrations also affirm group identity (Taylor 1963). Shaking the hand of every person in a room acknowledges that each person belongs to the group and affirms his or her identity. Knowing the right form of greeting for those who are older or younger, or this relation or that, is not only good manners but essential symbols of belonging in relationship to one another (Shenk 1983).

A 55-year-old man, testifying to why he had joined the Zionist movement in Zimbabwe, equated exclusion with loss of identity. "The Dutch Reformed Church does not accord the African recognition as a human being. The missionaries even close the door when they eat. The Zionists differ from them in this respect, because we regard each other as truly God-created Africans" (Daneel 1970, 19).

> To think that life is a gift given to an individual as his or her own personal possession fails to comprehend the nature of human procreation. The helpless baby at birth is totally dependent on the care and concern of the family. It cannot talk, walk, or help itself. It only knows how to feed by sucking. The life force of the baby grows and increases only with the care of the family. It is clear to all that the nurturing of this one new life is a nurturing of life itself – the great gift of Kiteme (life) given to the family to be shared. Human growth and life are inconceivable without the family community. The family community is the greatest asset of humankind. There is no identity outside the community (Kirwen 1978, 71–72).

If there is no identity outside of community, alienation from one another is not just unfortunate but depletes the life force of isolated men and women. As with the Hebrew community, belonging to an African community carries its own set of mutual obligations and responsibilities.

Covenant, Community, and Health

> In (the African's) case as well as in the Jew's, significance and ultimate survival are the boons of a covenant of mutual responsibility and obligation (Taylor 1963, 119).

For the Hebrew, shalom was rooted in community. The mutual

obligations of one person to another defined by the Law as well as their corporate identification with Yahweh brought individual and community wholeness in every sphere of life.

The promise of well-being to an African is also rooted in community. Identity, security, health, resources for living, the bearing and rearing of children, and even the hope of continued life after death are interwoven in belonging. "The future is unpredictable, consequently requiring collective solidarity and mutual support in case of any eventualities such as misfortune, accidents, hard times, and most of all, death. Humanity and harmonious, reliable, supportive human relationships are considered to be the highest value in the community ..." (Twesigye 1987, 102). Relationships must be maintained and guarded. Health, too, is rooted in community. The African community contributes to the promotion of health in three basic ways beyond providing a sense of individual identity and belonging. First, basic needs are met within community. Secondly, the community provides accountability. Thirdly, the community is a base for health action.

The Community Meets Basic Needs

Africans have traditionally said, "There are no orphans in Africa." Where community remains intact, this statement is basically true. The network of mutual obligations in community provides for the basic needs of its members. While there are many variations throughout Africa, tradition defines specific obligations for the care of the elderly and of widows and orphans, as well as others who would otherwise be marginalized, such as children born out of wedlock or wives deserted by their husbands. As the structure of the African family is weakened by urbanization, the acquisition of wealth based upon individual accomplishment rather than group effort, and the ascendency of the nuclear family as a functional unit, the safety net is also weakened. The African family remains strong, however, in spite of the forces arrayed against it.

The Community Provides Accountability

Mary (not her real name), a young, single woman, worked for us in Nairobi. Mary was orphaned[1] by the death of her father. Her mother worked as a domestic helper in a nearby town. Mary came from Kakamega, where she was a member of an independent Luhya church. When Mary announced that she was coming to Nairobi, the church leaders gave her a letter of reference to give to the local assembly of that church in the city. Once they received the letter, the elders of the Nairobi congregation not only welcomed Mary to the Luhya fellowship but also instructed her in urban survival skills and assigned an older man to be her "guardian." This man provided parental guidance, served as a mediator to other, often ethnic-based helping networks, and held Mary accountable to the teachings of the church.

In this case the ethnic and religious communities paralleled one another, providing assistance and identity in the midst of transition, as well as accountability designed to maintain a healthy lifestyle in a large, otherwise bewildering multi-ethnic city.

In a study of male sexuality in Nigeria, the researchers made a surprising discovery. The women in the rural areas were more likely to confront their husbands concerning their sexual behavior.

> In the villages husbands and wives are part of larger groups of relatives. There are incessant complaints – not merely about sexual behavior – but, in a situation where husbands and wives are rarely alone together, such nagging is unlikely to disrupt marital relations. Furthermore, in rural life such disruptions are not just the business of husband and wife but of all the relatives surrounding them ... It is very different for those who live in town. Marriages can easily break up when the sole disputants are the wife and husband. An angered husband can seek immediate solace in commercial sex. Divorced wives are well aware of the risk of breaking up an economically advantageous marriage and having to return to the village (Orubuloye et al. 1997, 1200).

Threats to health and well-being such as risky sexual behavior, alcohol abuse, and child or spousal abuse or neglect is less likely to occur and, when it does, will be more quickly addressed within the context of an extended family or church community than in the isolation of unconnected nuclear family units. Employers in South Africa often favor the members of the Zion Christian Churches (ZCC) because the accountability that they have to their church community for honesty and abstinence from alcohol makes them better employees. The community strengthens the influence of those who alone have little power.

The Community is a Base for Health Related Action

The community health program at the Tenwek Christian Hospital achieved a high level of community participation. Community members responded to the health interventions by adopting many of the innovations that they promoted. Additionally, community health committees assisted in managing and running mobile clinics. Well over one hundred voluntary community health workers delivered simple curative and preventative care and promoted behavioral change for good health. Just under half of the community health workers reported that community members had helped them in their chores at home or, less frequently, given them a gift or money (W. Long 1992).

Not only at Tenwek but throughout the continent of Africa, health and development workers mobilize community participation in community based interventions. The roots of community assistance, however, are embedded deeply in traditional life.

> Helpfulness to blood relations, to relations by marriage, and neighbors in the *kokwet*[2] is a fundamental rule of Kipsigis social life. Women help one another in all forms of domestic work: cleaning the house, grinding corn, making beer, sewing clothes and ornaments, picking vegetables, carrying water and wood, especially if there is a sickness or rush of work. Groups of families band together as a routine to perform these duties, and lend children to herd goats or look after the younger children. There is no obligation to perform these duties except for relations. It is, however, the custom and there is no special word for working without remuneration (Orchardson 1961, 40).

> The kokwet are those people with whom you are living. Maybe you are living in a place where you do not have any relatives. You do not need to worry because you know that your neighbor is going to help you (Marie, an elderly Kipsigis woman cited in Thomas 1989, 20–21).

Not all African communities have traditions of community service as strong as those of the Kipsigis. Throughout Africa, however, communities unite to challenge problems of community and individual health and well-being.

The community in Africa is a powerful force but it may also turn against the promotion of shalom. The covenant of community may also become a covenant of shadow.

The Shadow Covenant: Sin and Community

> *Banja ndi gombe, hinanensa kugomoka taiu.*
> *The family is like a steep river bank, it crumbles quickly.*
> *(Sena proverb)*

The African community is fragile. The river bank offers protection from the waters that would sweep all things away but is itself vulnerable.

> Within this tightly knit corporate society where personal relationships are so intense and so wide, one finds perhaps the most paradoxical areas of African life. This corporate type of life makes every member of the community dangerously naked in the sight of the other members. It is paradoxically the centre of love and hatred, of friendship and enmity, of trust and suspicion, of joy and sorrow, of generous tenderness and bitter jealousies. It is paradoxically the heart of security and insecurity, of building and destroying the individual and the community. Everybody knows everybody else; a person cannot be individualistic, but only corporate (Mbiti 1992, 209).

In the covenant between Israel and Yahweh, sin destroyed community; in Africa that which destroys community is sin. The turbulent waters of jealousy, hatred, bitterness, and mistrust that the banks of community are to hold in check are the very waters that erode the banks. The covenants that were meant to maintain peace are defeated by evil (Shenk 1983). Returning to the story that opened chapter two, though Daudi had been generous to his clan, fulfilling many of the obligations of kinship, he had also been aggressive and ambitious. The fragile bank had crumbled and those who should have stood with him to protect him had, out of jealousy, made themselves his enemies.

Bediako (1990, 17) states, "The essence of sin is in its being an antisocial act. This makes sin basically injury to the interests of another person and the collective life of the group." A sense of personal sin, therefore, is not inherent to the state of the heart or even the act itself, but rather to its effects upon relationships. The degree of goodness or badness of an act is in its effects upon others (Taylor 1963). Sin in Africa, therefore, tends to relate to others within the community and not to God, who is distant and suffers no consequences because of personal sin (Mbiti 1992; Kirwen 1978; Bosch 1987).

Because moral sin is measured more by its consequences than by the nature of the act itself, a behavior that is indulged in with discretion is ethically different from the same behavior indulged in with careless disregard of relationship. In many cultural settings, for instance, because marriage was consummated by the birth of a child rather than in sexual union, wide latitude is given to sexual behavior.

Two-thirds of the married men in a large survey in Nigeria indicated that they had sexual relationships outside their marriage (Orubuloye et al 1997, 1204). Traditionally, these kinds of behavior were tolerated by societies as long as the people involved were discreet. "Traditional religion did not condemn non-marital male sexuality. Nor did it extol it, but simply ignored it. The society was not macho, although it did respect virility. It just assumed that male sexuality was biologically uncontrollable and hence inevitable, although it usually demanded that it be reasonably discreet."

Rather than commandments that establish moral principles, therefore, African thought protects relationships through taboos that prescribe and proscribe specific kinds of behavior between persons dependent upon their relative status. "As a rule, a person of lower rank, status, or age commits an offense against another person or being of a higher rank or age. One may also offend against a person of the same status. Never or rarely does a person or being of a higher status do what constitutes an offense against a person of a lower status" (Mbiti 1992, 209). Personal sin is social, not spiritual.

Moral evil, then, is rooted in what one person does to another. The "law" for moral evil is comprised of those traditions and customs that define how one person is to act toward another. These customs differ according to the relative status of the people involved. Either individuals or communities may sin, but the consequences of the sin are never suffered alone but in community.

Moral evil begets physical (Shenk 1983) or natural evil – "those experiences in human life which involve suffering, misfortunes, diseases, calamity, accidents, and various forms of pain" (Mbiti 1992, 214). For the African, physical evil lies at the heart of their experience of the world, for everything bad that happens springs from evil. Because evil is rooted in relationship, nothing happens by chance but is caused by a person or being external to the one who is suffering.

> Every form of pain, misfortune, sorrow, or suffering; every illness and sickness; every death whether of an old man or of the infant child; every failure of the crop in the fields, or hunting in the wilderness or of fishing in the waters; every bad omen or dream; these and all other manifestations of evil that man experiences are blamed on somebody in the corporate society. Natural explanations may indeed be found, but mystical explanations must also be given (Mbiti 1992, 209).

The truth of this statement is reflected in the vocabulary of illness. As one example, the terms used to describe sexually transmitted infections (STIs) among the Goba fall into three major categories (Bond and Ndubani). Generic terms are rooted in history, patterns of life, and shame. Some of the elderly people in this people group in Zambia refer to STIs as *Kenya* or *Kariba* referring to the belief that they were introduced by young men conscripted to fight in Kenya during the Second World War, or the growth in fishing commerce (and movement of people engaged in that trade) introduced by a dam named *Kariba*. Some generic terms are borrowed from the languages of other peoples who migrated into the area. Finally, some generic terms carry the idea of shame; a prefix is attached to the common word for disease to indicate that it came about through failure to maintain self-control, an offense against social relationships.

Symptomatological terms refer to the physical symptoms of the diseases. Folk terms refer to the causes of the diseases. The folk terms that refer to STIs carry either the idea of having violated a taboo, such as having intercourse with a woman who had suffered a recent abortion or miscarriage or who was menstruating, or of having been victimized by witchcraft. People say that a woman who becomes infertile after contracting an STI had "her veins cut" by the intervention of a witch.

None of the terms parallels scientific understandings of STI symptoms and causality. Bond and Ndubani (1997, 1215) understate the vast gulf that is fixed between traditional and scientific understandings of disease. "These (traditional) causal concepts are not easily understood by using modern scientific analysis and/or the germ theory. They are socially and culturally constructed and perceived. They do not succumb credulously to any scientific explanation and yet they exist from the community viewpoint."

> Natt hindhufin / sitt nan dhuffa jette busaan.
> "Don't come to me, I will come to you," said the malaria.
> (Oromo proverb)

The buffeting of physical evil upon African life falls as blows from external agents and is as pervasive as the curses and punishments specified in the Hebraic covenants. But who are these external agents who cause evil things to happen? By what powers is physical evil introduced?

The Mediators of the Shadow Covenant

First, evil events may be catalyzed by the living. One person may pronounce a curse upon a person who has offended them (Gehman 1989). Other living people who have been wronged, or who are motivated by envy or hatred, may consult with diviners or witches to employ the spirit world as allies in an attack on their enemy, through illness, misfortune, or possession (Daneel 1970). Finally, some evil may be caused unintentionally by those who have the power of an evil tongue (Gehman 1989).

Secondly, the spirit world may act independently. God and divinities may punish evil, particularly if it is collective. Spirits may bring disaster to the lives of those who have broken taboos or otherwise harmed relationships within community. Ancestral spirits may also take retribution if they have been personally offended by a lack of respect (Daneel 1970; Jansen 1973).

Finally, a person may be the victim of witchcraft or sorcery (Jansen 1973; Gehman 1989; Mbiti 1992). Witches are evil incarnate, capturing in their behavior the very essence of sin (Taylor 1963). They may be employed by an enemy to cause harm to another, but they may also act independently because they hate goodness and community. Witches and the evil spirits who are their consorts do evil because it is their nature to do evil (Shaw 1996).

Evil from the Living: The Destructive Power of Words

Exasperated with a mother who repeatedly refused to give a desperately needed antibiotic to her very sick baby because "he doesn't want it," I told her exactly what would happen to that child if he did not get the medicine. He would die. A dear African friend who overheard the conversation took me aside and gently told me that I must never say such a thing, because, by saying it, I would cause it to happen. She said that what I had said was true, and we both knew it, but the mother of the child did not understand that. She told me I had better pray hard that the child would survive; if I did not, I would be viewed as the one who took away its life! Happily, the child lived, and I learned to make my point in a less direct manner (Brodeen 1995, 22).

The ancient Hebrew would better understand the power of a curse than the modern clinician. Words in Africa bring about the events for which they are symbols. The Gbaya proverb, *Fara wen ne fara fio* (The place of words is the place of death), warns against the exchange of harsh words in a quarrel or fight (Christensen 1990, 100). Among the Kamba as well as other groups, an expression of admiration may destroy the object of praise, especially if the admiration hides an envious spirit. If a person makes a remark that might be misunderstood, he or she would spit to demonstrate that there was no evil intent (Gehman 1989).

Curses are intentional, and usually pronounced by one who is older, or higher in status, on one who is younger. The young woman who worked in our home had to purchase expensive gifts for her extended family when she went "up-country." Though a Christian, she feared the tongue of her aunties who might criticize or even curse her if she failed to respect them by bringing them a gift. The power of a curse is increased by the status of the one who pronounces it in reference to the accursed. A curse from one's father or mother is particularly powerful. If a father is unable to command respect and obedience from his son, a curse becomes a force that cannot be resisted. The Oromo proverb, *Ilmi abbomi abbaa dide / abaarsa hindidu* (The son who refused the orders of his father will not refuse his curse), warns children of the consequences of disobedience.

In a similar way, a curse may be the final appeal to God or to the spirits for justice. The Anyuak people who feel they have been wronged by another may repeat a curse against the offender over a number of months or even years. The curse is not fulfilled until after the death of the one who pronounces it, whose spirit may remain restless until justice is done. These curses are regarded as a common cause of death among these people (Brodeen 1995).

Some curses and oaths are conditional. The curse affects only the one who is guilty and is harmless to the one who has done nothing (Mbiti 1992). These curses and oaths may be accompanied by a ritual, trial, or the drinking of a 'poison.'

Once spoken, a curse may destroy all that is associated with well-being; disease, infertility, economic disaster, and even death may follow a curse. A curse may persist for several generations. Because a curse can normally be withdrawn only by the one who makes it, a deathbed curse is particularly powerful and dreadful. Many peoples have proverbs and stories that warn against the danger of a deathbed curse. After the death of one who curses another, a relative or ritual specialist may stand in his or her stead in withdrawing the curse but it leaves a stronger legacy of fear (Gehman 1989).

Evil from the Living: Vengeance, Jealousy, and Anger

> *Moetsuoa ha a lebale, moetsi oa lebala.*
> The victim does not forget though the victimizer might.
> (Sotho proverb)

In the story that opened Chapter 2, Daudi's enemies, moved by envy toward him, sought the assistance of a diviner in placing a curse upon him. Envy and anger are strong motivators of evil; people overcome by these emotions may easily believe that they are victims of another person who is more successful than they without apparent cause. They then feel that they have adequate reason to seek redress through magic or sorcery. My brother, who is a missionary in Botswana, reports that some of the young people to whom he ministers either rein in their individual initiative or disguise their success to prevent themselves from becoming too different from those around them and thus the object of envy and anger.

> *Embi erumire ennungi okugitta.*
> A mangy dog bites a healthy one to kill it.
> (Lugandan proverb)

In many other cases, people are truly victims of others. While they cannot oppose a powerful oppressor openly, they are able to seek the assistance of the spirit world in secret. The Oromo capture this approach to the world in another proverb, *Yo argatte ebbisi / yo dhabde abaari* (If you get, bless! If you lack, curse!). If all evil things have an outside cause, poverty is the mark of a victim, and cursing the person or being who is the cause of the poverty becomes an appropriate response. How this attack is mounted varies greatly throughout Africa. It may involve the use of body parts, such as hair or fingernails of the person targeted by the diviner. It often involves mixing 'poisons' in the food or drink of the targeted person, or the placement of charms or other symbols such as severed animal parts in his or her home or compound.

Evil from the World in between: The Work of the Spirits

When I asked how much the belief in spirits affects life in Africa today, especially among educated urbanites, the pastor of my church answered with this account of one of his Christian friends. When a relative of this man's family died, the other family members debated the customs that should be followed in his burial. Because many of the people in the family were well educated and prosperous, they finally decided that the dead man should be buried in the suit and tie that characterized his profession and were symbols of his success in life. In the weeks and months that followed the burial the family suffered the sudden deaths of other kin who had not been expected to die. Though the deaths had proximate causes, the family members began to suspect a mystical cause as well.

After consultation with a diviner, in which the Christian man did not participate and which he tried to discourage, the family members concluded that they had made a mistake in dressing the body for burial, and that the man who had died was expressing his discomfort by causing the death of other kin. At a significant expense, they exhumed the body, opened the coffin, loosened the tie and unbuttoned the top collar button. They then closed the coffin and laid it back in the grave. The ancestral spirit, apparently comforted by his less constrictive apparel, stopped his assault upon the family. The Christian, though he did not believe the family deaths were associated with this ancestral spirit, nevertheless expressed his frustration to the pastor. He, the Christian, was the one who had seemed foolish. It appeared senseless for him to argue that the diviner's solution had been incorrect when, in the belief of his extended family, it had obviously worked.

Natural evil may also have its origin in the world of the spirits without human manipulation. Ancestral spirits may act independently either to punish or to express their dissatisfaction. Spirits who cause accident, disease, or misfortune for some identifiable cause may be appeased, and, given proper respect, may choose to bring good rather than evil. They are feared but they may be manipulated. The greatest fear, however, surrounds the work and person of witches and sorcerers who, in company with evil spirits, bring about physical evil simply for its own sake and seek to destroy individual and community well-being.

Witches and Sorcerers: The Incarnation of Evil
Witches are the enemies of life.

> The Xhosa have a word, *umona*, which, in conflict with all grammatical rules of the Xhosa language, is a noun belonging to the human class. *Umona* means malice, avarice, envy, selfishness, individualism, exclusiveness, vindictiveness. In Xhosa culture *umona* signifies the quintessence of witchcraft, the personification of evil. The person who has umona has turned his or her back on the community and is seeking gain at another's expense, acting in vile self-interest and refusing to share with others what

he or she possesses. For the witch, "hell is other people"; the witch is the utter egoist whose behavior subverts the social order (Bosch 1987, 46).

Witches or sorcerers, driven by a power to harm and kill, seek through their secret ways to tear apart community. Witches and the powers that drive them are the African expression of the devil. The Kamba term these inexplicable evil powers *uoi* and the person who wields them is *muoi* or a witch (Gehman 1989).

The Gbayan proverb, "A trickle of water that goes alone goes crooked," describes the character of the witch (Christensen 1990). He or she is the outsider who hides malice behind smiles and does evil work in secret, in the dark of night, by charm or by spell, by transformation into a creature of the night, or through familiars that wait upon him or her to destroy (Taylor 1963; Hammond-Tooke 1989).

Witches and sorcerers and the spirits that attend them are often cited as the causes of physical evil – the disasters that fall upon men and women for no apparent reason. Two-thirds of women living in urban Ile Ife, Nigeria, cited witchcraft as a cause for infertility (Renne 1997).

◆ ◆ ◆

Among the servant community in our set of flats, one older woman gained a repu-tation for evil and was feared by the other workers. Mary (not her real name), the young, unmarried woman who worked for us earned more than this older woman, and dared to express disagreement with her. Mary became the focus of her evil intent. She threatened Mary with death. On one occasion, she told Mary that she had hired two men to kill her on her way from the bus stand (not an impossible thing to believe) but that Mary had been saved because she walked home that evening with an elder from her church. Finally, Mary came to Kendra, my wife, very frightened by the threats that had been made against her.

Kendra sought the advice of friends who urged her to bring the threats out into the open. Kendra called together all of the servant community as well as others from within the compound who were available. She set the woman in front of them and said that she was an evil woman who had threatened Mary. Kendra told them that if anything were to happen to Mary, they would all know who was responsible. Kendra told me later that she found some severed chicken parts thrown into our back garden shortly after this meeting, but that the meeting had its desired effect of tempering the woman's attacks against Mary. Whatever evil this woman intended toward us had no effects that we are able to identify. Shortly after this incident, the woman lost her job and was forced to move from the quarters shared by the servants.

◆ ◆ ◆

Three lessons from that experience illustrate aspects of the effects of this evil within society. First, it was not until we arrived back in the United States that Kendra told me about our being targeted in retaliation for her actions in exposing the evil. We never told our children. Kendra was worried about the effects that fear might have. As we discussed this story I remembered at least two occasions when I was targeted with a curse in Bangladesh that I never mentioned to the family either. The power of evil is amplified by fear. In regard to ill health, fear has the power to multiply many times whatever power of evil may reside in the spirit or evil person.

Second, like most people, we could, in retrospect, identify instances of physical evil in our lives that followed these events. If we had chosen to attribute these events to the power of evil, we would have increased the power of evil over our lives. As the father of lies, Satan wants to perpetuate lies concerning his power. I believe Satan revels in any lie that exaggerates his power and brings fear.

Third, by bringing these matters into the open and identifying these threats with a particular person, we solved one problem but precluded other possible solutions. By externalizing the problem and naming this lady as the victimizer, we precluded possible reconciliation between Mary and this woman and blinded ourselves to areas of Mary's character and relationship that might have contributed to the destruction of this relationship. We also ran the risk of scapegoating a person who might not have been as evil as she had been described. In a rural village, our public accusations, though we did not call her a witch, might have endangered her life.

While after reflection we feel that we did do the right thing in this particular incident, the sense of mutual suspicion that characterizes the fear of witches has its own destructive effect on community. The effect of this suspicion upon community life is captured in proverbs (Nussbaum 1996).

"He is doing an impossible thing: like one who quarrels with a nursing mother." It is unwise to argue with a nursing mother because, if her child dies, the person who quarreled will be accused of having caused the death.

"The kind neighbor is accused of witchcraft." This Sukuma proverb warns against being too kind to a neighbor, particularly in providing food. If a neighbor is kind to another person beyond the bounds of social obligations, he or she might be accused of witchcraft or poisoning if the person subsequently becomes ill.

The Jabo proverb, "One never knows when a witch is present" and the Kaonde proverb, "An owl (witch) awaits those who go to the grave" both warn against witches who appear harmless but work in secret with evil power. Suspicion of others destroys a sense of community.[3]

African Community and Biblical Shalom

The most vivid picture that Moses gave in his warning to Israel concerning the consequences of God's punishment was the dainty mother, secreted in an inner room away from her family eating her newly born child (Deuteronomy 28:56-57). This horrific depiction is an apt metaphor for the African concept of evil. It is a power, disguised by smiles in everyday life, that consumes the very life force of the community. This evil, if permitted to continue, destroys the life which nourishes it, just as the Hebrew mother, in order to survive, destroyed her own future by eating the offspring who would carry her own life into future generations. In consuming her child, she consumed herself.

For Israel, however, the destruction of community was a consequence of their sin against Yahweh. For the African, that which destroys community is itself sin. The ancient Hebrew, the Christian, and the African all recognize that life is found in community and death in its destruction. There are two additional relationships that are essential to our understanding of African perspectives of health, healing and disease; self-identity and relationship to the environment.

IDENTITY, BELONGING, AND ALIENATION BEYOND THE COMMUNITY

Community and identity are inseparable for African peoples. Identification with one's family community is the defining factor of life and living and continues after death.

- While the constituent elements of personhood vary from one tradition to another, they provide a link to kinship. The constituent elements of body, soul, and spirit for the Akan link the person to the lineage of both father and mother (Pobee 1979). The individual Akamba is comprised of body *(mwii)* and spirit *(veva)* or breath that comes from God but both together constitute a person *(mundu)* who is "a physical representation of the dead, the living, and the yet unborn" (Gehman 1989, 56). At the naming ceremony, a Dogon child receives eight souls drawn from among his or her ancestors and other members of the community (Brodeen 1995).

- In the naming ceremony a child receives the name of an ancestor, linking that child to the extended family community of the living dead (Taylor 1963).

- At circumcision (or the equivalent rite of puberty) the shedding of blood in many traditions symbolically links the person to the life of the ancestors and the land of the people.

- During life, men and women live on through their children. As for the Hebrews, fertility is an essential part of a woman's identity. Infertility is a curse because it alienates that woman from the life force of the family.

- Roles in life are defined primarily by relationship to others within the family community and provide an identity as well as constraining expressions of individuality.

- After death, the disembodied person continues as a member of the family community. When the person is no longer remembered by the living, their fate is unclear in many traditions but they lose essential aspects of personhood.

Identity, Alienation, and Transcendence

Identity, health, and physical welfare are bound up with the community of the extended family, clan, and tribe. Inclusion within this community may be threatened, however. Alienation from the family community often brings death or illness, both because of the loss of the physical assistance and also because of the loss of meaning and identity. Membership within the community may be threatened in several ways.

A person may be excluded from the family community by failing to fulfill the obligations to others that his or her role entails. Among urban Nigerian women, for instance, only 30 percent dared to confront their husbands with questions concerning their extramarital sexual relationships, even though many of the women knew that their husband's behavior put them at risk for AIDS and other diseases. Half of the rural women, who were less isolated from the buffering effect of extended family and therefore less vulnerable to unilateral decisions of their husbands, complained. Some wives refused to complain because of fear of their husband's rejection that would deprive them of present and future children as well as their place in the family community (Orubuloye et al.1997).

Widows in western Kenya who refuse to be sexually cleansed (have sexual intercourse with a relative of their deceased husband) and "inherited" may be rejected from the family community. When they lose their place within the family, they also lose their livelihood. The fear of losing one's place within the community continues after death. The living may exclude an ancestral spirit who fails to provide blessing or protection to the family. People accused of witchcraft or sorcery not only run the risk of losing their places in the community but also their lives.

Changing circumstances in the family's composition and welfare may also threaten an individual's well-being. Children within a polygynous family whose natural mother dies may lose their rightful share of the family's wealth for school fees or even in the sharing of food and medical attention, particularly if their father's co-wives had been jealous of the natural mother. The increasing number of deaths from AIDS has also placed tremendous pressure on the family safety net. Numerous AIDS patients within the same family community impoverish the family through the search for care as well as the income lost as family members become unable to work because of the sickness.

The urbanization of Africa and the struggle of the new generations with the pluralism and individuality of modernity is slowly eroding the family community. Extended families can rarely live together in urban areas. Formerly, in rural Africa, much of a person's behavior was determined by their roles in the different stages of life. The number of individual decisions that faced a person throughout life was limited, and there were many advisors. The young person growing up in the city is faced with many choices about schooling, life style, and profession. Formerly, the number of relationships that a person had to maintain fell within the boundaries of family and village. People living in the city have many different layers of relationships outside the family. High expectations for the maintenance of relationships remain part of the society but can no longer be fulfilled in the expanded relational network. This slow disintegration of life and relationship produces stress and threatens loss of a firm identity.

> Social deprivation is not only a cause of emotional distress and of physical disorders, it can also be said to *be* a sickness in itself ... In the urban situation, the inability to achieve, the frustrations of endless and unsuccessful job-seeking, of failing to set up one's own survival network, being an outcast or a member of the unwanted 'surplus' population of the shanty-towns, having a disability which renders employment impossible – all these factors are causes of social deprivation in which people need to restore or renew their social personality...anxieties about getting employment and the shame they feel in forced idleness give them headaches and cause them sleeplessness (Shorter 1985, 59).

The reconstruction of a social identity aside from family has proved elusive. There are few, if any, transcendent elements to African concepts of community. National identity often falls apart along ethnic lines. The former Prime Minister of Ghana, who was removed from office by a military coup, reflected on this problem. "Whereas the bond of union of the tribal community has been that of kinship, a modern state consists of many different tribes. How is one to achieve an extension of the African family spirit to the nation as a whole? How can one shift the emphasis from kinship groups to the state?" (Bediako 1995a, 239). No African state has satisfactorily discovered the answer to that question.

There is also no tradition of an African identity. Europeans gave Africans their identity as Africans (Mazrui 1986). While many Africans strive to build a sense of African identity free from the negativism of the colonial heritage, very few, while still living in Africa, find their identity in being African. Nobody in Africa expects people to help with the costs of a funeral or wedding because they share identity as *Africans*. The African identity fails the test of practicality.

Community and Kingdom; Identity and Shalom

The Hebrew and the African share much in common in regard to identity and community. Like the Hebrews, Africans have no firm sense of identity outside of belonging to a family community. The sense of identity was strengthened by the exercise and enjoyment of the mutual obligations and privileges that attended the fulfillment of the role specified by age, law, and tradition. To be separated as an individual from one's community is for the African, as it was for the Hebrew, to be separated from the source of life. Like the Hebrews, Africans highly value fertility and the bearing of children as the perpetuation of community life.

The theocentrism of the Hebrews, however, gave them a transcendence in community and a security of identity that is not a part of the anthropocentric theology of African tradition. The person in community is at the center of the African worldview. God is relevant only so far as he relates to "this life, this existence, and its concerns and cares" (Bediako 1995a, 100).

> Bantu primal religion assembles its fundamental beliefs around two vital centres: God and man. The high place that God occupies is however seen as the basic presupposition which underlies the purpose of the Creator, who has oriented everything towards the perpetuation of the summit of his work: humankind (Bediako 1995a, 100).

For the Hebrew, however, God alone occupied the center of the worldview. The Israelite communities as well as the individual Israelite were expressions of his creative power and transcendent grace. The traditional African, after death, fears being forgotten by the living and therefore losing identity as a living person. The Israelite expected to be forgotten. His or her eternal identity lay not in the community of the living or even in his or her descendants, but rather in relationship to Yahweh.

In the New Covenant, identity was still rooted in community, but the community itself became transcendent. God's family community not only defines identity in relationship to the creator himself, but, through the Church, meets the test of practicality for "this life, this existence, and its concerns, its cares, and its joys."

The inability to define a sense of community that effectively transcends ethnic identity also contributes to the maintenance of corruption in government, business, and industry. This becomes an everyday and debilitating part of African experience. Justice is a personal and not legalistic concept (Shenk 1983). While this relational conceptualization of justice contributes toward personal reconciliation when a wrong has been committed, it also redefines what is just and moral behavior in the public and private sectors. What is "just behavior" toward a friend or relative is different from "just behavior" toward a stranger.

Kudadjie and Aboagye-Mensah likened the period of intense and widespread corruption in Ghana (*kalabule*) to the state of Israel during the judges when, because there was no king (rule of law), everyone did what was right in their own eyes (relationally defined justice). The result in Ghana was general demoralization of the society.

As honest, hardworking people could not meet their obligations to family, etc., and they were humiliated for not being clever, many began to feel that the pursuit of righteousness and excellence was foolish. Life was becoming purposelessness. The national moral fibre completely broke down and sank to the lowest levels that anyone could remember (Kudadjie and Aboagye-Mensah 1992, 23).

Ironically, the appeal to solidarity becomes a weapon to squash protest against injustice. Those who publicly criticize a ruling government or sitting ruler are breaking relationship with the nation and acting as traitors. Legitimacy in protest requires the effective rule of a transcendent law.

Our greatest strengths are often the root of our greatest weaknesses. A great love may conceive possessiveness, jealousy, and hatred. Great wisdom may give birth to hopelessness and despair. African community is no different. It is the greatest strength of African peoples. Health and healing ministries must build upon these strengths. But it is also a powerful source of evil – of suspicion, vengeance, division, and hatred. Sickness and natural evil as well as health and healing draw the sources of their power from the strength of community. We will explore healing themes more deeply in the next four chapters.

Notes

1   In most of Africa, a person is considered an orphan if one of the parents has died.

2   Local Kipsigis community.

3   Shorter attributes the belief in witches to the need of Africans to explain evil, particularly at a time when they are struggling with conflicts between tradition and modernity and community and individuality. Witchcraft, in this view, springs from unresolved stresses in society and fades away when stability is restored as it did in Europe and North America. Jansen and Taylor also suggest psychological explanations. "Witchcraft is the active embodiment of the brooding anger which in Africa is the essence of sin" (Taylor 1963, 190). Witchcraft permits guilt to be projected through a scapegoat and provides a safety valve for aggression (Jansen 1972). Kirwen, who denies the reality of witches, believes that the strength of those identified as witches lies in the intensity and expression of their evil feelings of jealousy, envy, hatred, and anger that "once set loose, seek out and wreak havoc on the victims" (1978, 22). Bosch (though he disagrees with these interpretations) sums them up

well. "Belief in witchcraft, in fact, fulfills an important social function in traditional Africa. It provides a channel through which people can deal with hatred, hostility, frustration, jealousy, and guilt" (1987, 43). Africa needs witchcraft then as a buffer for change and a mythology to reconstruct meaning when evil befalls a person.

I believe that there is a spiritual reality underlying the practice of sorcery and witchcraft, but that the destructive work of evil utilizes the sociological and psychological forces that multiply its power and influence. Satan is good at contextualization. He will fit his attack to different cultural and historical frameworks in order to increase its destructive potential.

Chapter 7

Restoration and Power in
the Kingdom of Healing

◆ ◆ ◆

*Millions of Africans have eagerly embraced Jesus. Nevertheless, many recognize
that their churches and ministries incarnate an image that reflects not Jesus' face
but the face of Western culture. They recognize that true health and healing happen only in community. Some are seeking to conform the face of Christ and his
church to their own culture. Others struggle to define an authentic incarnation of
Jesus' kingdom in transforming their own cultural traditions – not a distorted
reflection of the West but a redeemed expression of themselves.*

◆ ◆ ◆

"… Rabbi, who sinned, this man or his parents, that he was born blind?"
(John 9:2).

Jesus' disciples, like us, wondered why. Why is this man blind? But
they gave Jesus only two options – either the blind man or his parents had
sinned. No other possibility occurred to them. The man, blind from
birth, was for them a stumbling, groping object lesson of God's judgement. Jesus, too, saw the blind man as God's object lesson, but the lesson
he wished to teach was a very different one than the disciples expected.

Both the disciples and the Pharisees agreed that the blind man in John
9 must be suffering God's punishment for sin. Even after reluctantly

admitting that the formerly blind man could now see, the Pharisees still ejected him from the synagogue. On what basis? Because he was "steeped in sin at birth" (John 9:34). They could explain his blindness. God had punished him terribly for some terrible generational sin. What they could not explain was his restoration.

Though they tried to deny his restoration, even calling his parents as witnesses, the facts were plain. The blind man had been restored.[1] But they also knew that Yahweh jealously guarded his place as Israel's *rope* or healer.[2] If God was the only *rope*, the healer, the restorer and mender of Israel, and Jesus, *for the first time in the history of Israel's relationship to their God*, restored sight to the blind, then Jesus must be…

The Pharisees gagged on the words. The very thought was blasphemous. One group of Pharisees argued, "This man healed on the Sabbath. He is the one who deserves God's judgment. He must be a sinner." Another group replied, "If he were a sinner, how could he heal? Healing comes only from God." The now restored blind man taunted them with the absurdity of their position. "Now that is remarkable! You don't know where he (Jesus) comes from, yet he opened my eyes. We know that God does not listen to sinners. He listens to the godly man who does his will. Nobody has ever heard of opening the eyes of a man born blind. If this man were not from God, he could do nothing" (John 9:30–33).

The formerly blind man, though, completed the sentence the Pharisees refused to end. He acknowledged that Jesus was the Christ. He did not simply thank Jesus but worshiped him (John 9:36–38). Jesus then declared that he came into the world so that "the blind will see, and those who see will become blind." The Pharisees took offense, replying, "Are we blind too?" Turning common wisdom on its head, Jesus replied, "If you were blind, you would not be guilty of sin; but now that you claim you can see, your guilt remains" (9:41).

The Pharisees' perspective on God and healing was too narrow. Jesus had brought a new revelation of God's healing power that did not operate according to the rules of the Pharisees' legalistic formulas. They thought that the blind man must be "steeped in sin" because he was blind. They saw only part of the truth. The blind man was sinful. He did need restoration. But they were blind to their own sin. Because the Pharisees had no sickness or disability, they assumed that God was pleased with them. Both the blind man and the Pharisees were blinded; but only the blind man acknowledged his blindness and sought healing and restoration. Because the Pharisees claimed to see, their guilt remained untouched and unforgiven.

In their pride the Pharisees failed to see what the blind man both saw and embraced; that the kingdom of God had come upon them. God had permitted the man to be born blind; but not because of his sinfulness. He was blind "so that the work of God might be displayed" (John 9:3).

JESUS' HEALING MINISTRY AND THE KINGDOM OF GOD

When Jesus sent out his seventy-two followers, he commanded them, "When you enter a town and are welcomed, eat what is set before you. Heal the sick who are there and tell them, 'The kingdom of God is near you.' " (Luke 10:8–9). Jesus' compassionate healing ministry proclaimed his sovereign authority over a powerful kingdom.

The Kingdom of Healing Power

Jesus' ministry of healing and deliverance opened the eyes of the blind to the light of God's kingdom. With the light, however, the shadow of Satan's rule and power became sharp-edged and deep. Before Jesus' advent, the Hebrews attributed sickness and injury, health and disability to Yahweh. Satan is rarely mentioned in the Old Testament and not in reference to sickness or possession. In the New Testament, many maladies, particularly demon possession, are attributed to the work and power of Satan. Even in the Old Testament, the presence and power of evil was most sharply defined in God's presence. Even though Job was not guilty of the sin laid to his charge by his friends, he repented in the presence of God. Isaiah became keenly aware of his own and his people's sins when confronted with a vision of God (Isaiah 6:5).

When Jesus began to heal, the brightness of God's kingdom burst upon the people. Satan could no longer hide in the twilight preceding the dawn. Again and again Satan and his demonic spirits confronted Jesus only to recoil in defeat. Jesus did not attribute all sickness to Satan's work. He usually discriminated clearly between the casting out of demons and the healing of sickness. In statements that summarize Jesus' healing ministry, however, the healing of sickness and deliverance from evil spirits are almost always paired (Brown 1995).

Jesus' power to heal was sometimes almost palpable. Luke writes that

"... those troubled by evil spirits were cured, and the people all tried to touch him, because power was coming from him and healing them all" (Luke 6:18–19). On at least one occasion, when the hemorrhaging woman reached out and touched his robe in the crush of a great crowd, Jesus sensed that power had gone out from him. When confronted with her act the frightened but healed woman confessed to her deed, an act that would have made Jesus ceremonially unclean. Rather than rebuking her, however, Jesus commended her faith and sent her away with his blessing of shalom (Luke 8:42–48).

In the Old Testament, restoration and healing was premised upon a response of obedience to God's commands. Healing in the New Testament often rested in an act of faith in response to Jesus' authority. Jesus said that the Pharisees would remain in their figurative blindness because they failed to respond in faith to his authoritative claim to be the Son of Man (John 9:35–41). Many people in Jesus' hometown remained lame and blind because they refused to recognize Jesus as more than the son of the local carpenter. Because they did not respond in faith to Jesus' teaching about himself, Jesus did not do many miracles there (Matthew 13:53–58). People who came to Jesus were not healed because of a strong inner conviction that they would be healed but because they came to *Jesus*. Healing faith was rarely an expression of certainty in the outcome but a believing response to Jesus' authority.

The relationship between faith and healing, then, is not a direct one; there is no "dose response." Individuals do not experience more or less healing in proportion to the level of their faith. Jesus delivered the demon-possessed son of the father who approached him in doubt (Mark 9:14–29) as surely as those who approached him with certainty. Healing is about relationship because it is mediated by a person, Jesus Christ. Because healing is relational rather than linear, we are not able to discern any "standing orders" for miraculous healing in the Bible. Jesus chose to test the faith of the Canaanite woman by first refusing to answer her and then by questioning her request (Matthew 15:21–28). In contrast, he healed a paralytic not because of the ill man's faith but because of the faith of his friends (Matthew 9:1–8). Jesus' healing encounters cannot be properly understood out of the context of the relationships surrounding them. Faith does not bring healing; faith brings people to Jesus who heals.

The importance of this intermediary relationship becomes evident in the differences between the two gospel accounts of the disciples' failure to cast out a demon. In Matthew's account (17:14–20) Jesus ties the disciples' failure to their lack of faith. In Mark's account (9:14–20) Jesus also links their failure to a lack of faith but adds that "This kind can come out only by prayer" (29). These two themes make sense only if healing faith is faith in the power of a mediator and not faith in the certainty of healing or command over healing power. Turning to prayer in uncertainty reflects weak faith in an assured outcome but strong faith in the mediating power of God. Faith in God is not misplaced because the kingdom of power is also a kingdom of compassion.

The Kingdom of Compassionate Service

> He forgives all my sin and heals all my diseases; he redeems my life from the pit and crowns me with love and compassion.
>
> The Lord is compassionate and gracious, slow to anger, abounding in love. He will not always accuse, nor will he harbor his anger forever; he does not treat us as our sins deserve or repay us according to our iniquities. For as high as the heavens are above the earth, so great is his love to those who fear him (Psalm 103:3–4, 8–11).

Nowhere in the Bible does compassion intersect as beautifully with the righteousness of God's judgement as in this psalm of David. In his healing ministry Jesus revealed the very heart of God. Jesus' healing was not a dispassionate demonstration of his power; he responded with his entire being to the one who came to him to seek healing. The Greek verb translated as "moved with compassion" referred to the entrails of the body.

> When the Gospels speak about Jesus' compassion as his being moved in the entrails, they are expressing something very deep and mysterious. The compassion that Jesus felt was obviously something quite different from superficial or passing feelings of sorrow or sympathy. Rather it extended to the most vulnerable part of his being. It is related to the Hebrew word for compassion, *rachamim*, which refers to the womb of Yahweh. Indeed, compassion is such a deep, central, and powerful emotion in Jesus that it can only be described as a movement in the womb of God (Nouwen et al 1983, 16).

Compassion gives birth to acts of mercy and grace. God's kingdom broke into history not as a doctrine, but as an encounter between Jesus and those who came to him for healing. Healing, then, was a practice and not a philosophy. For the Israelites, the healing practices of Jesus were culturally meaningful expressions of the themes of God's kingdom.

JESUS' HEALING PRACTICES
AND THE KINGDOM OF GOD

Jesus expressed the themes of God's kingdom in the actual practices surrounding his healing encounters. He demonstrated the power of God's kingdom in the words of power that he spoke in the healing encounter; he expressed the compassion of God's heart in his healing touch; and he proclaimed his authority by his teaching. He taught not only in his conversations with those who watched him heal but also by choosing the social context in which to heal. Finally, Jesus sometimes used cultural practices already associated with healing. The practices demonstrated the immanence of God's kingdom in a given culture at a given time in history.

The Word of Power

In every recorded instance of Jesus' healing, he spoke a healing word. The word of God was for the nation of Israel a demonstration of God's power. God created by his powerful word. The Law was a powerful expression of God's will and character. The prophets were empowered when the Word of the Lord came to them. When John wished to express the deity of Christ, he called him "the Word" (John 1:1–18).

When Jesus most wanted to demonstrate his power, he healed by the power of his word *alone*. When he confronted Satan, he *commanded* demons to leave. In contrast to Jesus' healing of sickness, he never touched those possessed by demons in the act of healing them, emphasizing the power of his word. Jesus never struggled with the demons. In fact, Jesus engaged in dialogue with demons only once, in the account of the demon-possessed man of the Gerasenes (Luke 8:26–39). Even in that account the demons never challenged the power of Jesus' word or his authority to command. At the end of his ministry, Jesus *commanded* Lazarus to return from the dead. Jesus demonstrated his power over geography by healing at a distance on the basis of his word alone. Unlike the Old Testament prophets and his own followers, Jesus never prayed for another's healing. In contrast his followers healed only in Jesus' name or acknowledged Jesus' power through prayer.

The Healing Touch

If the word of Jesus proclaimed his power, his healing touch gently whispered his compassion.[3] Most biblical accounts of healing involve touching. Touching the person in the act of healing communicated compassion in three ways. Touching first of all brought the sick into community, powerfully signifying that they were not alone in their illness. A healing touch, more than any of the other senses communicates, "We are together in this. I am here with you."

Touch communicates not only belonging in community but also the sharing of life. When a father blessed his son, he laid his hands on him. Samaritan converts received the Holy Spirit through the medium of the apostles' prayer and their laying on of hands (Acts 8:14–17). Jesus often touched the affected part of the sick person's body as part of his healing; at other times he reached down and lifted the sick to their feet, giving a strong physical expression to the transfer of healing power. The most expressive demonstration of this transfer of the power and warmth of life is in three accounts of bringing the dead back to life. Both Elijah and Elisha prayed and brought young men back to life again (1 Kings 17:21; 2 Kings 4:32–35), but with an extraordinary expression of the sharing of life. They both lay full length upon the bodies of the young men they healed. In one instance the restoration of the young man was explicitly linked to the warming of the dead body by the body of the prophet. Paul also lay upon the body of Eutychus in bringing him back to life after his fall (Acts 20:10–12). The touch of a healer communicates healing power.

Finally, in the cultural context of Israel, touching a sick person communicated a full identification with that person's suffering in order to bring about full restoration. Many of the people healed by Jesus were ceremonially unclean because of their deformities, the presence of decay, or the flow of blood or other bodily fluids. Because of their uncleanness, they were cut off from temple worship and therefore from the presence of God. Additionally, because those who touched them would share their uncleanness until they undertook a ritual cleansing, many of the sick were also cut off from the community of Israel. The touch of Jesus or his followers, then, powerfully symbolized their identification with the weakness and suffering of those who were both physically disabled and also cut off from God's presence and the community that gave them identity. Jesus' identification with them in their distress is the heart of compassion; his healing them is the heart of restoration.

The healing touch restored the sick in every aspect of their lives. They were restored in their bodies – the flow of blood ended, the decaying flesh was restored, the useless and deformed limb was knit together again by quickened nerves, muscle, bone, and sinew. They were restored to the community of Israel, no longer scorned and feared. They were restored to God, once more able to worship him, not only in the temple but in his incarnation. In Christ's healing they experienced shalom and salvation. Christ's healing so truly images salvation that the New Testament writers often used the same word for both.

The Healer

Jesus' acts of healing, whether directly or in his name through his followers, established his divinity. Jesus was keenly aware of the social context in which he healed. He understood the suffering of the sick who came for healing and also knew the hearts of those who observed. He intentionally selected the time, place, and method of many healing encounters to communicate truth about himself. He wielded God's power and exercised God's authority, not delegated to him as a prophet but as his own.

To proclaim his moral authority over the religious leaders of Israel and his Lordship over traditions signified by Sabbath prohibitions, he purposefully healed on the Sabbath. Jesus confronted the hypocrisy and pride of the Pharisees and demonstrated that the Law was intended to promote goodness and compassion, not harsh judgement (Brown 1995). By his healing ministry, Jesus declared himself Lord of the Sabbath (Matthew 12:1–14).

To proclaim himself as the Messiah, he explicitly linked his healing acts to the fulfillment of Old Testament prophecies (Matthew 12:15–21). To proclaim his victory over Satan and his followers, he publicly cast out demons (Luke 4:31–36). To proclaim himself as God, he, in healing, also forgave sins (Mark 2:1–12). To proclaim his triumph over death and decay and his sovereignty over time and times, he raised others from the dead (John 11:38–44) and was himself resurrected.

The Immanence of God's Healing Kingdom

Just as God became incarnate in Jesus in order that men and women may be restored to him, so God's kingdom must break into history and culture for it to become real. Before Jesus, God had revealed his presence through nonhuman and often fantastic forms. People knew of his holiness, glory, and power but only a relative few understood his compassion and mercy. In the same way, God's healing kingdom must be incarnated in culture and history for us to grasp it.

Jesus and his followers often used culturally familiar symbols and acts in their healing encounters. Biblical healing sometimes involved anointing with oil (James 5:14), bathing (John 9:7), the application of a poultice (2 Kings 20:7) or spittle (Mark 7:33; 8:22–26), or obedience to the command of the healer. Naaman was told to bathe in the Jordon to cleanse his leprosy (2 Kings 5:10–14), Jesus told people to rise off their mat (John 5:1–14) or stretch out their hand (Mark 3:5). He told ten lepers to go and show themselves to the priests, but they were not healed until they were on their way (Luke 17:11–14).

Even stranger to us are the accounts that seem to involve magical properties attached to objects. In a seeming contradiction of the first commandment, God told Moses to fashion a bronze snake to save the people of Israel from his judgement. Moses instructed them to look at the snake in order to be healed from the venomous bites of snakes sent by God to punish them (Numbers 21:8). A dead man thrown in haste into Elisha's tomb was restored to life when he touched Elisha's bones (2 Kings 13:21). The Bible records people who were healed as they touched the robe or clothes of Jesus (Mark 6:56) and Paul (Acts 19:11–12). Sick people were set in Peter's path so that his shadow would fall on them (Acts 5:15).

These healing practices and symbols would not seem as strange to those who encountered them in their context. The practices paralleled cultural customs associated with healing outside the Israelite and Christian communities. How should we understand and interpret these practices?

One option is to assume that they represent specific practices that Christian healers should continue to use. If these are accepted as models, however, significant problems arise. First, we can discover few cues concerning when these practices should be used and when they should not be used. Sometimes we can discern why Jesus may have differed in his healing practices. When he told the lame man to pick up his mat and walk on the Sabbath, for instance, it was probably to confront the hypocrisy of the Pharisees (John 5:1–14) who were sure to challenge the arrogance of a man toting his sleeping mat through Jerusalem. In other instances, we might infer that Jesus used one practice rather than another to test and strengthen the faith of the person being healed. With the exception of the passage in James concerning anointing with oil, all of the healing practices are anecdotal and never presented as a model to be emulated.

Another problem arises when the healing practice is separated from its historic and cultural context. The practice or symbol also becomes separated from its association with God. Healing power becomes a virtue of the object or practice. Many years after the Exodus, Hezekiah destroyed the bronze snake because it had been enshrined in the Ark of the Covenant as an object of worship (2 Kings 18:4). Separated from its historic context it had become an idol, not a symbol of God's grace.

Some suggest a second model of interpretation – that biblical symbols and practices associated with healing were appropriate only in a pre-scientific culture during the ministry of Jesus and the establishment of the church. They have been supplanted by Christian health and medical ministries based upon scientific medicine. This interpretation also raises problems because it ignores the fact that the *practice* of scientific medicine is also a cultural expression of a dichotomistic worldview. For all its benefits, scientific medicine is not transcultural.

Though many groups that focus upon miraculous healing ministry as a central function of the Christian community mimic or alternately reject the practices of healers in the Bible, I believe there is another interpretation. Healing practices and symbols in the Bible may not be prescriptive models but rather show that healing must be appropriately expressed in culture to proclaim the imminence of God's kingdom. Even culturally familiar healing practices and symbols may be transformed by their association with God as the healer.

Christian healing ministries in one culture, then, may legitimately use a different mix of symbols and practices from another. Likewise, practices and symbols may change in a single culture over time. The major criterion is not the intrinsic nature of the practice but whether or not it is transformed into an authentic proclamation of God's kingdom and points toward God as the healer.[4] This criterion may be used equally to evaluate biomedical practices as well as African traditions.

Separated by a great desert from the revelations of the God of Israel and the home of Jesus the healer, other peoples, who shared the continent of Moses' birth and Jesus' childhood exile, struggled to understand health, healing, and disease from God's revelation of himself in the created order. From their observation of God's creation, these men and women discovered that fullness of life was rooted in their relationships to divine powers, community, and the environment. Even without the special revelation of biblical events, they too came to understand that disease was rooted in the alienation of individuals and peoples from God and from one another, and that healing involved the restoration of these relationships. They intuitively understood that disease and evil were close relations. They recognized restoration could not happen without healing power and looked to healers who commanded a power greater than their own. They knew that true health and healing happened in community.

Even today their traditions strongly influence their beliefs and practices concerning health and healing. They pursue the curative power of biomedicine but many also discern that its practice is both rich and impoverished. In the next several chapters we will explore the nature of healing practices in Africa and try to discern a way ahead.

Notes

1   The Hebrew word, *rp'*, translated as "heal" in this verse as well as in most places it appears in the Old Testament, signified the fullness of God's restorative work. "In every instance *rp'* is used with reference to restoring a wrong, sick, broken, or deficient condition to its original and proper state. Consequently, I believe that 'restore, make whole,' not 'heal,' should be recognized as the common semantic denominator of biblical Hebrew *rp'*.... All the semantic streams attested in the OT flow freely from this one source: the 'healing' of a sick body (2 Kings 20:5), the 'repairing' of a broken down altar (1 Kings 18:30), the 'restoration' of a drought-stricken and locust-eaten land (2 Chron. 7:14), the 'making wholesome' of undrinkable waters (2 Kings 2:21–22),... and the 'recovery' of a mildew infected house (Lev. 14:48)" (Brown 1995, 28–29).

2   Yahweh forbade Israelites from going to the gods of the surrounding nations for healing (Brown 1995; Avalos 1995). These prohibitions and penalties that seem on the surface to pit belief in Yahweh against physicians (as in the death of Asa, King of Judah for consulting "only doctors" and failing to consult God (2 Chron. 16:12–13)) are best understood in the context of idolatry (Brown 1995). God was not forbidding medical care; he was forbidding the Israelites from seeking healing from the gods of the surrounding peoples. In the healing of Hezekiah, Isaiah combined a common medicinal treatment, a poultice of figs that would draw infection out of a boil, with the word of the Lord that Hezekiah would recover. In fact, in Exodus 21:19 one who injures another in a fight is mandated to provide medical treatment (Brown 1995).

3   There is no record of Jesus or his followers using touch diagnostically either in a biomedical sense or in sensing imbalances in vital energy. The healing touch of Jesus was rooted in the significance given to it by the culture in which he healed and not a philosophy of disease and healing that equated illness to the imbalance of inherent life forces. My use of "healing touch" in this context, therefore, should not be confused with the practice of healing touch as an alternative medical treatment.

4   I am assuming in this criterion that practices in any culture that are intrinsically harmful to physical health cannot at the same time be authentic representations of God's kingdom or point to God as healer.

Chapter 8

Healing in Africa:
Longing for the Kingdom of God

♦ ♦ ♦

Rev. Oscar Muriu, the pastor of our church in Nairobi, says that wherever he goes in Africa, he discovers a longing for the Kingdom of God among its peoples. Essential characteristics of God's Kingdom of shalom are shadowed in the holism of African traditional beliefs concerning health. Though covenants of health in the shadow "kingdoms" of African tradition are often shrouded with fear, the longing for healing and restoration is enlivened with every sickness or misfortune. Themes that emerge from traditional patterns of healing in Sub-Saharan Africa reflect the desire for healing that may only come fully through the powerful restoration of men and women in God's Kingdom.

♦ ♦ ♦

THE PRESENT USE OF TRADITIONAL
HEALING PRACTICES

Obw'effumu: si bwa ddogo.
Sickness from a spear-wound and witchcraft are not (to be treated) alike.
(Lugandan proverb)

Like the Hebrews, Africans have different traditional classifications of disease. These fall roughly into three categories; "natural" diseases or injuries that have no spiritual significance, "natural" diseases that have spiritual causes, and diseases that have only a spiritual cause (Wessels 1989; Jansen 1981).

Distinguishing between the three is not a straightforward diagnostic task. The symptoms of the disease sometimes are the distinguishing characteristic. Yoder, for instance, found six traditional classifications for diarrheal disease among Swahili-speaking women in Lubumbashi. All six classifications involved frequent stools but, beyond that, each disease had its own distinguishing symptoms and aetiology. A child with a rash or "wound" of the anus had a different disease from one with a sunken fontanelle and tongue clacking. A clinician would recognize these symptoms as a later stage of a diarrheal disease involving an inflamed anus and dehydration, but for the mothers the diseases were very different. As (from a medical perspective) the disease became more severe, the mothers were less likely to use oral rehydration or sugar-salt solution and more likely to turn to traditional herbal remedies. Their ideas about the causes of the diseases also moved further from a naturalistic explanation (Yoder 1995).

Healers use factors other than symptoms to distinguish between "natural" and "spiritual" diseases. In Zimbabwe, the distinction between "normal" diseases with a natural cause and "abnormal" diseases with a spiritual aetiology depended upon their severity, length, and frequency of occurrence seasonally and by gender and age (Patel 1995). Severe mental disorders were almost always classified as abnormal. Often, then, the same disease entity, from a biomedical perspective, may be attributed sometimes to natural causes and treated biomedically, and other times to spiritual causes and treated with traditional practices. The classification depends not only upon the characteristics of the disease but on the context in which the disease occurs (du Toit 1981a).

Different diseases require different healers. The wife of an Ethiopian church leader experienced no conflict in combining traditional and modern treatments. "When I am sick, I go everywhere; to the nganga when I'm bewitched through a foot-trap, to the prophet if I wish to find out who poisoned me, and to the mission hospital for normal symptoms of illness" (Daneel 1970, 35).

Many Africans fear condemnation in speaking openly about use of traditional healing practices to Christians, and especially to missionary health workers. Bishop Milingo expressed the depth of that feeling. "They (missionaries) have never accepted mashawe (spirit possession) as a disease worth healing, since they call it by their own name as hysterical and psychosomatic disease, and they therefore consider anyone engaged in fighting it as an imbecile who chases the wind" (1984, 73). Du Toit (1981b) quoted a Zulu medical doctor: "The African has, therefore, always presented two faces, viz, one for himself and his own and another for the minister and the Church in order to avoid some terrible disaster such as excommunication. In the main, when he is sick, the African, Christian or otherwise, seeks the help of the diviner and herbalist." Christian health workers, therefore, find it difficult to accurately assess how often their patients turn to traditional practices for healing.

Because biomedicine has traditionally refused to consider spiritual aspects of disease, few Africans accept it unconditionally as the only option for healing.

> This is not to say that there are not secularized Africans, those who have left the old spiritual heritage behind without embracing a new one. Such people exist but they are looked upon as rather anomalous by the majority who have adopted and adapted parts of a more secular Western culture, but have not bought it wholesale. Even those Africans who have become quite Westernized still have loyalties which stretch into the spiritual at both ends of the spectrum, at the level of their traditional faith and at the level of their adherence to an imported or missionary faith. Thus the traditional African worldview, which is still highly relevant today, is a deeply spiritual one with strong supernatural and experiential elements (Kailing 1994, 490–491).

A survey in Botswana found that there were 339 "modern" health workers in the country in comparison to 3,143 traditional healers (Saayman 1992). In a survey in Burkino Faso, the proportion of people seeking only modern treatment ranged from a high of 53.5 percent for respiratory disease to none for neurological disease. Only in cases of diarrhea, respiratory disease, and stomach pain did more than a third of those interviewed report that they had sought modern treatment alone (Carpentier et al 1995).

Other factors contribute to the decision to consult traditional healers. Those who have the least education will consult the traditional healers more often (Carpentier et al. 1995). People also go to traditional healers more often because the cost is often only a fraction of the cost of scientific medicine and the traditional healers are more accessible (Carpentier et al. 1995; Tsey 1997). Additionally, African governments are increasingly accepting traditional healing as a valid alternative to scientific approaches and are licensing the practitioners, giving them greater credibility. Traditional healers, particularly herbalists, are increasingly modeling their practices after scientific medicine with professional societies, clinics, office hours, and set fees for services (Tsey 1997.)

Christians (Gehman 1989) and Muslims (Carpentier et al. 1995) consult traditional healers less frequently than those who ascribe to traditional beliefs. During times of crisis, however, when medicine has no satisfactory answer or cure, African Christians are most likely to turn to traditional beliefs and practices (Gehman 1989). Traditional approaches to health care in Africa are alive and well among many Christians as well as those who own no Christian belief. People seek traditional approaches to healing to balance the powers of disruption at work in their lives.

HEALING: RESTORING THE BALANCE OF POWER IN RELATIONSHIPS

Restoring the Balance of Powers

The African primal world can be conceived of as a universe of distributed power, perhaps even of fragmented power; it is as much a universe of conflict as the rest of the fallen world in that it is a world not of one Centre, God, but many centres... (Bediako 1995a, 99–100).

Power is the key concept behind an understanding of healing in Africa. When key relationships are disturbed, the fragmented powers are also disturbed. Treatment must restore the balance of power between the sick person and the antagonists of health (Dube 1989). "The concept of 'power' resonates strongly with traditional African conceptions. It is the essence inherent in all medicines and in the symbols of magic ritual. It is also the characteristic par excellence of the ancestors, witches, and alien spirits" (Hammond-Tooke 1989, 62).

Healing power is also central to the ministries of the indigenous or independent churches in Africa. The centrality of healing ministry is one reason why independent churches are growing rapidly across Africa. The specific practices of indigenous churches vary widely from place to place and from one leader to the next but they most often retain traditional African ideas of disease aetiology. "In the independent churches every activity and every aspect of church life is harnessed to healing from a complex of sin, illness, and evil magic or witchcraft. God is a God of power who enables the believer to 'live in strength.' Sickness and weakness have no place because they are directly linked with powers of evil" (Shorter 1985, 169).

For many Africans, any source of power to heal is good because healing itself is good. If suffering is caused by powers that are evil, then restoring the balance of powers to bring about healing must be good. Because the power to heal is good, many Africans feel little internal dissonance in seeking it wherever it may be found.

Patterns of traditional healing reflect concerns about power.

- Power is invested in the person of the healer. Some patients are willing to travel over 500 kilometers to visit healers who are known to have power to heal the disease they are suffering (Carpentier et al. 1995).

- Medicines have power. In many African languages, the most common word for medicine, such as *dawa* in Kiswahili or *mgota* in Pogoro, refers to any substance with power. "Medicines" therefore may encompass poisons, insecticides, and chemicals as well as medicines. The concept denoted by the most common word for "medicine" is not the intent of its use, but the power that it carries to transform. This power may be inherent to the substance itself, but it may also be infused with the power of the healer (Green 1996).

- Charms and magic have power. Some objects have power inherent in themselves as well as power derived from the healer. "The art in the medical-magic profession consists of the ability to control and channel these forces that exist in all objects" (du Toit 1981a, 166).

- Symbols and rites are invested with power.

- Distance has power. Healers and healing substances from afar are often thought of as having greater healing power than those that are local. Even though the Tswana were opposed to the Christian message of the earlier medical missionaries, they accepted their medicine because the healer as well as the medicines came from elsewhere and were therefore more powerful (Fako 1981).

- Power is released by unity of mind and spirit in community. Healing is usually a community experience.

- Words of blessing have power, especially when the blessing comes from those who themselves are powerful.

Power Strategies in Traditional Healing Practices

The strategies of healing in Africa, whether traditionally or in the independent churches, reflect the understanding that diseases and physical evil are caused by an imbalance in powers associated with key relationships. To heal the disease, the healer must redress the imbalance of power, either by decreasing the evil power or countering it with healing power.

- *Remove the source of the evil power.* This is the healing strategy behind exorcism as well as hunting down and destroying witches, either through exile or killing. Healing practices that involve the removal of some evil substance from the body, or that involve purging or bleeding, also work on the assumption that the source of evil can be removed. Some Christians believe that confessed witches may be restored, but many share the more common view that evil is an essential aspect of their nature and that they must be rooted out and destroyed (Daneel 1990).

- *Confront and overwhelm the evil power.* Sometimes the source of the evil power cannot be destroyed, but the power itself can be managed and balanced so that it is no longer strong enough to harm. Charms, symbols, and "medicines" protect from evil magic on a daily basis but provide no long-term immunity (Jansen 1973). Through manipulation of powers, sometimes the person is able to send the disease back to the one who had caused it (Bosch 1987). Miraculous healing also involves a confrontation of the powers of evil and of good. Christian healers appeal to the power of God in confronting demons or ancestral spirits. Traditional healers may appeal to any of a number of powerful, personal forces in their practice.

- *Appease the powers that are causing the suffering.* Ancestral spirits are easily offended and, because they cause trouble when they are angry, healing often requires that they be appeased through sacrifices and other rites. Africans must sometimes also appease living relatives or enemies that have pronounced a curse upon them or employed a spiritist to rally an attack against them. Diviners not only "diagnose" the problem and prescribe treatment, but also specify the behavior that caused offense – behavior that the sufferer is expected to change for healing to be complete. The goal of appeasement is to have the offended person withdraw the curse or attack.

- *Manage the powers to protect from attack.* In traditional practice, many day-to-day activities – the naming of children, forms of address and greeting, the pouring out of a libation, the spoken invitation to ancestors to join with the living in the functions that mark community – represent attempts to prevent the powers from falling out of balance and causing trouble and sickness.

As in many other parts of this analysis, lists imply a neatness that rarely exists in reality. Traditional practitioners do not use linear processes to unravel the tangle of relationships that represent fragmented powers. Context is vitally important. Traditional healers view one's body, mind, soul, and spirit as an integrated whole in contextual relationship with social connections. When faced with similar symptoms in different contexts, a traditional practitioner is likely to make differential diagnoses and prescribe different treatments.

Traditional Approaches to Reconciliation as a Means of Healing

Harka tchabsu dadhabdu / dhungadhu.
The hand that you cannot break, kiss!
(Oromo proverb)

Healing through the confrontation of powers is dangerous. Not only does it risk losing all or raising the level of the conflict, it also destroys community. Many of the traditional practices of diagnosis and treatment, therefore, focus upon a process of reconciliation.

> One woman was dying of heart failure. There was no visible improvement; she was still very ill. Suddenly she requested to be discharged. Asked why, her answer was that a neighbor man came to request her to come home to settle a problem between their households. (Her neighbor) feared that her sickness was seen as a result of this dispute. If she died before settling the dispute, the other household would be left under a very serious curse forever and ever! So, despite her serious condition, she was allowed to go, realizing the social consequences if she did not go. She returned peacefully two days later after settling the dispute (Byaruhanga-Akiiki and Kealotswe 1995, 83).

> A young man named John came to Vanga Hospital suffering from tuberculosis. John began treatment but continued to get worse even though the antibiotic treatment was appropriately matched to the tuberculosis bacilli. A student nurse who spoke with John finally discovered that he had been placed under a curse from an uncle who felt John had been ungrateful for his assistance in school. The hospital staff prayed for John to be released

from the curse, and the counselor helped him forgive the actions of his uncle. It was only after that happened that the antibiotic therapy became effective against the tuberculosis (Dr. Dan Fountain, quoted in Backus 1996).

Hamen malla ajjesse; mallicha ajjesse; ammo nagaan waan inni ajjess dhabe.
Evil kills your son; it kills your horse; but peace has nothing to kill.
(Oromo proverb)

Almost any health professional in Africa could tell stories and anecdotes that reflect the insights of these accounts and proverbs. Broken relationships break a person's and a community's health. How are relationships put right again? Reconciliation in Africa is so important that societies have assembled a peace-keeping and peace-making mosaic. Among the key pieces in this traditional mosaic are confession, the sharing of meals, cleansing, formal covenants, the role of the intermediary or peace-keeper, and compensation.

Confession

An honest confession and expression of regret is often enough to restore a relationship, especially when it was strained by a modest offense due to simple human weakness or oversight, and caused no great harm to the individual or to the community (Ambe 1992). Confession is frequently required as a part of reconciliation for more serious offenses but is often not sufficient in itself (Shenk 1983).

Sharing meals

Our family, like many others, enjoys picnicking. Once, when we anticipated traveling with an African colleague, I suggested that we picnic by the roadside along the way. She was not enthusiastic about the idea so I asked why she hesitated. All she would tell me was that "it was not polite" to eat without offering food to others who would notice a picnic and stand around, once we stopped.

I later recognized that she had politely discouraged me from putting her in a position of vulnerability. For her to eat in front of others without inviting them to share would be excluding them from communal relationship. The sharing of food is a strong expression of community. Strangers must be invited to share in a meal, not because of the nutrition, but because it is a way to signal their inclusion into the community, even if only for a period of time.

I was listening to one of the health workers (in northern Cote D'Ivoire) do a practice teaching session about nutrition. She opened with the question: "When someone says they've eaten well, what do they mean?" and divided us up into smaller groups to discuss it. The woman I was with said the most important factor of having eaten well is that you've eaten in a group and then, secondly, that you've eaten meat. The process of eating in community is even more important to satisfaction than the food itself! (H. Long 1997).

Ceremonies such as funerals, weddings, or puberty rites usually are sealed with a meal that signifies not only the solidarity of the community but also community acceptance of persons in their new roles. Washing hands before the meal symbolizes cleansing and confession of those things that would prevent community, the meal celebrates community, and, among some peoples, washing after the meal symbolizes thanksgiving and anointing, or blessing (Shenk 1983; Christensen 1990). An offender may also prepare a meal for the person or family they have offended. The preparation of the meal signals the offender's desire to be restored; accepting the meal signals forgiveness.

> *Waraana garaa jiru buusa hinqalani.*
> After an injury to the heart, an animal is killed and shared to make peace.
> (Oromo proverb)

Cleansing

Many ceremonies involve ritual cleansing. Cleansing most often involves washing, sometimes with water that has been blessed by the healer. In some traditions, cleansing is also expressed through spitting. "In southern (Tanzania) also men become mvelu, pure, by confession; 'speaking out' is a condition of efficacy in sacrifice and the officiant blows out water as a symbol of bringing up all the anger that was in his heart" (Taylor 1963, 194). Among the Kamba, people would also spit to show that they were harboring no evil when they said something that could be interpreted either negatively or positively (Gehman 1985).

Formal covenants

Formal covenants, often solemnized by ceremony, represent another approach to reconciliation. Shenk (1983) listed seven types of covenants common to many peoples in Africa.[1] Formal covenants are both prophylactic and curative in their intent. A formal covenant prevents the destruction of relationships that leads to death, disease, and misfortune; a formal covenant may also codify the reconciliation of a previously broken relationship. Covenants in Africa have often failed. They may be defeated by witchcraft as well as by the other forces that threaten to tear apart a sense of community (Shenk 1983).

Intermediaries and peace-keepers

> *Owu ne yen reko, opatafo ne hena?*
> Death is fighting with us, who can play the role of a peace maker?
> (Akan proverb)

The peace-making intermediary is a key personality in traditions of African health and healing. The intermediary may be an ancestral spirit who intercedes on the behalf of his or her still living relative with powerful spirits or even to the high god. Intermediaries are also essential to the reconciliation of relationships among the living. Intermediaries may be traditional healers but they may also be elders, or others who fill a recognized ceremonial role. Intermediary peace-makers permit those who have been alienated from one another to address the problem without risking a confrontation. Intermediaries may take the initiative in addressing conflicts within the community or between community or family members, particularly if they have the potential to become so intense that they alienate others.

Compensation and reparations

> *Ti ndu mbiliri oli karii.*
> The cow with pointed buttocks (thin) is compensated with a heifer (fat).
> (Lugbara proverb)

Compensation is an important component of reconciliation in most African cultures. The Truth and Justice Commission, the official government body examining the injustices during the apartheid period in South Africa, published the "Policy Framework for Urgent Interim Reparation Measures." On page 1, the policy framework acknowledges not only the physical losses of those affected by apartheid but also the destruction of human dignity through "human rights violations and state neglect." It acknowledges that reparation is required not only as an exercise of justice to correct abuses in the past but as a necessary instrument of national reconciliation that discourages vengeance and retaliation. The policy calls not only for reparation in physical goods and services but also in symbolic interventions, including proper burials, provision for public confessions and apologies, and victim-offender mediation.

Deciding upon compensation, therefore, is not a matter of law alone but is "person-oriented" (Shenk 1983).

> Kapundwe's dog was found eating Busangu's sheep. The evidence indicated that the sheep had died naturally, and only then did the dog begin to eat their flesh. Nevertheless, Kapundwe gave Busangu a sheep in restitution. Then he gave him a second sheep, then a third. Then 100 francs. Why the apparent over-compensation? It was because Busangu said, "I feel badly about my dead sheep." Kapundwe and Busangu both realized that the pain from the loss of the sheep could become malevolent; it could develop into bitterness. Neither wanted that to happen. The giving of compensation needed to continue until Busangu was at peace (Shenk 1983, 20).

The goal of compensation and reconciliation in Africa is ultimately not fairness but the restoration of fullness in relationship. The amount of the compensation is often, therefore, not proportionate to the amount of the loss. Reconciliation is complete only when the offended person can say "I no longer hold these words (of cursing or bitterness) in my heart" (Christensen 1990). Westerners would suspect that this system would be constantly abused. Is it not equivalent to awarding "punitive damages" where the plaintiff sits as judge and jury? Not exactly; the community brings pressure upon all parties in the dispute to reconcile their differences.

> *Kan hilolle harre dha / kan hinaraaramne jini dha.*
> The one who refuses to fight is an ass; the one who
> fought and refuses to be reconciled is a fool.
> (Oromo proverb)

> *Garaa duude mannaa / karraa duude wayya.*
> Better a blocked road than a blocked heart.
> (Oromo proverb)

Persons who have suffered loss are also under community pressure to reconcile with those who have hurt them. Hidden bitterness is dangerous to the health of all in the community. It is the root of sin and death. It not only poisons the heart of the person who holds it but may express itself in the sickness and destruction of the one toward whom it is directed.

The Restoration of Right Relationships is the Heart of Healing Practice in Africa.

As in Hebrew culture, the essence of healing in Africa is the restoration of the balance of power in relationships. While power can be balanced with a contrary application of power, reconciliation that leaves no reservoir of bitterness to overflow later is the best way to restore relationships. According to Christensen, the process of peace-making and peace-keeping, symbolized in the soré plant, is the central theme of the Gbaya society. While the form of peace-keeping differs from one people to the next, the themes that emerge from this analysis parallel the healing themes among many African people.

The soré tree is a common softwood that grows on the savannas of Cameroon. It is a very useful tree to the Gbaya people. It produces a soft, moist, "cool" wood. It does not have the stateliness of the forest hard-woods and rarely attracts lightning. Between the thin bark and the wood is a "slippery" substance. Bad things slip off the soré bark, and it is used to calm and cool those who are feverish. As it cools, it cleanses. The Gbaya use the young leaves to wipe the dirt off their bodies. They use the older, mature leaves for wrapping fresh meat. The plant is strong; it can be broken or cut down and will grow back again. Children enjoy the fruit of the tree.

The physical characteristics of the tree are reflected in its ceremonial significance. It is the "soré-cool-thing" – a root metaphor for peace and life among the Gbaya.

- Soré is for making things new. When things fall into disarray in the community, household, or the life of the individual, soré makes the way clean. A new village is formed around a soré tree. The binding of its leaves together symbolizes peaceful relationships as well as a binding of the evil forces that led to the disruption.

- Soré is for cooling a fight. When a calm person of dignity throws soré between two combatants, they are faced with a choice. If one crosses the soré to continue fighting, the soré becomes the threshold of judgement, and the person will die. If the combatant crosses the soré in peace, the soré is a gateway to reconciliation and life.

- Soré brings reconciliation between warring villages. When thrown between warring villages, soré symbolizes the need for a mediator to right the wrongs that led to the fighting. Women of peace in the warring villages will "cool" the warriors by sprinkling them with water from a soré branch.

- Washing in soré water cleanses from *simbo* (the sin of transgressing a taboo). Hunters who transgress the taboo of killing a leopard, for instance, return to the village with a soré leaf in their hands to signify that they are ceremonially unclean. They are confined in a "cold house" with soré branches across the threshold. To leave the house before being invited would cause death. When the priest comes to take them for washing, however, it is transformed into a gate of peace. The priest immerses the hunters in a pool of water that has been cleansed by soré leaves. As the hunters return, they are anointed with soré medicine to cleanse them of the dirt of the taboo.
- Soré brings blessing. When the woman-peace-thrower washes hunters and their weapons with soré water, she pronounces a blessing, not only so that the hunt will be successful, but so that the hunters may live in peace with one another, protected from quarrels that could cause death and injury.
- Soré cools *dua* (witchcraft). The diviner will throw soré at a person to declare his or her innocence from charges of witchcraft. A person who holds to a soré branch while undergoing a trial by ordeal declares his or her innocence. Soré cools the vengeance of the family of the one who was hurt by witchcraft. If a person meets death because of a false accusation of witchcraft, the family that made the accusation may dress one of the young girls of the family in soré leaves and present her as compensation to live as a part of the family that suffered the loss.
- Soré breaks the strength of evil. Throwing soré at a tyrannical or mean person will deplete that person's strength but not cause death. Soré may be tied to the tail of a dangerously unruly cow or rubbed on a bully to restrain the evil forces behind the aggressive behavior. The properties of the soré are transferred to the bully or cow.
- Soré cools the anger and sorrow surrounding death. Soré may be rolled up in a new woven mat by the husband of a woman who died young, and sent to her family. The priest will place soré at the threshold of a woman's home whose son died during the initiation rites. In both cases the soré is meant to fill the gap caused by that person's death and bring comfort.

The ceremonial significance of soré encompasses many of the healing themes of this chapter. The seen and the unseen are united in soré. It is used medicinally as a balm but its symbolic significance carries even greater power. The chief name of Jesus among the Gbaya is "Jesus, our soré-cool-thing." The richness of reconciliation as an act of healing is a bridge to understanding the healing work of Jesus. It transcends the "miracles of healing" by pointing to the essential characteristics of Jesus' healing ministry.

Jesus: Our Soré-Cool-Thing

Paralleling the Hebrew and Greek languages, the Zulu word for "spirit" is *"umoya,"* also meaning wind or breath. The *umoya* of the South African Zionist churches shares many healing parallels with that of the Gbaya. Like soré, the Spirit cools.

Spirit becomes a benign and benevolent influence, life-giving and health-bearing. Because of their association with movement, air and breath are considered among the "cooling" elements that counteract and neutralize "hot" and dangerous states, such as those produced by sorcery or passion (Kiernan 1990, 105).

Jesus Christ is indeed our Soré-cool-thing. The longing for the kingdom of power and healing that Pastor Muriu reported is fulfilled in the person of Jesus Christ. The healing themes that occur over and over again throughout Africa meet together in his person. He cools the heat and pain of sin and cleanses men and women of its stain. He stands between sinners and God as soré stands between antagonists.

> Because God is the All-Present who exists eternally for others, every sin which attacks the life-force of another despoils him. He is the Author of the moral law because he is the Victim of every breach of it. Every conflict is against him; all the brooding anger from the heart of man, let loose in the world as an independent force of destruction, falls upon him. At the heart of the totality stands the Cross, cosmic because it is the Creator who hangs upon it. There the love of God bears the sin of the world and every curse dies out on him. God forgives the transgression and antagonism of our race, submitting to the evil of it until it is swallowed up and submerged in fathomless love. The shadow menaces him and is dispelled by his perfection; the weight tramples him down and is carried by his strength; the heat of enmity is assuaged in the coolness of his peace, and its filthy contagion cleansed by his blood. In the midst of the world, man's eternal Neighbour has died for him and risen again (Taylor 1963, 194–195).

HEALING IN COMMUNITY

Wifwila pa bengi bamwalawila.
The one who encounters problems in a crowd will be helped.
(Kaonde proverb)

Dhukkuba dhokffatte / qoricah male duute.
She hid her sickness and died without medicine.
(Oromo proverb)

Bisa nwile ulabulwa ng' hungu.
Hide a sick person and you'll be betrayed by funeral lamentations.
(Sotho proverb)

Sickness and healing in Africa are communal experiences. Neither sickness nor healing can be private matters. Missionaries who have been hospitalized in Africa, or Africans who have been hospitalized while visiting a western country, soon recognize the vast differences between African and western approaches to illness. Westerners living in Africa soon are exhausted from the steady stream of visitors to their hospital room; Africans visiting in the West become depressed by loneliness if well-meaning friends cut short their visits or visit infrequently "so that they can really rest." Those who try to hide their sickness cannot be healed.

Illnesses hidden from the community cannot be diagnosed and treated. A medical practitioner and patient cannot alone come to the right diagnosis of sicknesses that are caused by another person or spirit. Everyone who knows the sick person must be involved in the diagnosis because only together can they unravel the web of relationships to discover the cause of the illness.

Hiding an illness may be motivated by shame or guilt that will eventually affect others.

Dhukkubi funyann qabe / hidhi hinhanqaatu.
The disease of the nose will not stay away from the lips.
(Oromo proverb)

Because disease or misfortune may be a punishment or curse for wrongdoing, the sufferer who tries to hide it may be motivated by shame or guilt. The sickness then is likely to spread, not because of contagion, but because of association of the family or community with a shameful act. Without confession and restitution the strength of the curse or punishment becomes greater and more widespread. This is particularly true if the one who suffers from a shameful illness is a leader.

In John Mananke's Zionist community of healing in Zimbabwe, the ordinance (or sacrament) of communion is an important aspect of healing in community. Prophets screen those who enter the building for the communion service. They observe the face, eyes, and bearing of those who come. If they sense a person is hiding an illness or concealing bitterness, they will bar that person's entry. The man or woman will instead be escorted to a courtyard to confess. There they wash one another's hands and return to communion the following day after they have been cleansed from hidden sin (Shenk 1983).

Hiding an illness brings no relief from the expectations and obligations of society.

> *Azo 'aa amvu ku ni ni.*
> Only sickness does not dig.
> (Lugbara proverb)

Only the sick are excused from performing the tasks and obligations that they must otherwise accomplish. Those who hide sickness will either be criticized for not contributing a fair share to community life or will wear themselves out and possibly worsen the illness by attempting more than they can physically accomplish. The sick person is under a social obligation to reveal the sickness and seek help (Jansen 1973).

The one who hides illness will not receive instrumental assistance from the community or family.

The family and wider community usually mobilize resources to care for one of their number who is ill. This includes help with daily tasks, transport, food, and money from family members and community contributions. Those who hide their illness or misfortune forfeit the practical help that the family and community can give.

The one who hides illness does not receive the emotional support of community and friends that is essential to healing.

> *"Omulwadde taggya mutwe wansi."* nga tewannajja gw'aya gala.
> "The patient cannot raise his/her head from the pillow," the
> nurse says, if a welcome visitor has not yet arrived.
> (Lugandan proverb)

> *Moeng ngaka, o sidila babobodi.*
> Like a doctor (herbalist), a visitor's arrival helps the sick to heal.
> (Sechuana proverb)

The emotional support of friends and family speeds healing and lessens the experience of pain for anyone who is ill, even in highly individualistic cultures. In the strongly relational cultures of Africa, the healing force of many visitors is even more important. Visiting not only gives emotional support but signals that the sick person has open and free relationships with community and family members. Close relatives who consistently fail to visit the sick person may fall under suspicion of having contributed to the illness or of harboring anger, envy, or bitterness.

Those who suffer from chronic conditions that are most commonly attributed to the work of witches or other enemies may join a "community of affliction" (Shorter 1985) or the healing center of an independent church. These centers of healing are built around an outstanding traditional healer or a charismatic church leader and provide a sense of belonging that transcends the sick person's own family and community.

The one who hides an illness cannot experience the healing power of community.

The community, particularly within the tradition of the independent churches, not only mediates healing through emotional and instrumental support but also focuses the collective power of their own life force and spirituality on healing the patient. The sequence of a Zionist healing service illustrates the importance given to the collective spiritual power of a group of people.

Zionist healing services begin with instruction from the minister who builds the solidarity and emotional power of the healing band through highly emotional and interactive preaching. Following the message, the benches or chairs are pulled to the side, the children may be dismissed, and the doors and windows closed and fastened.

> Members of the congregation press back against the walls of the room leaving a clear place in the center. While a hymn is begun with the theme of sickness and health, men and women, who are officially designated as healers, trot around forming an inner circle and they are usually led by a prophet if one is present ... The *thandazo* (healer) is empowered to lay hands on the sick, to pray over them and bless them.
>
> These (healing) powers reside in most of the initiated and healthy members of the congregation. Only the uninitiated (non-Zionists) and the unhealthy or inactive are excluded from participation in the healing circle (Kiernan 1990, 93–94).

The circle rotates with dance and song. Unlike the practices of traditional healers, dance and music is always accompanied by simple words normally directed toward Jesus and not sung in unison but with each person following his or her own melody. The music and song, accompanied by the increasingly strong beat of the drums, combine to build and communicate a sense of power.

> The desired culmination point is the full presence of the Holy Spirit. To reach that aim the spirit is approached through music and dance. The most suitable part of the music for the Holy Spirit is the rhythm because in Zulu thought the Holy Spirit and rhythm are both imagined as carriers of numinous power.
>
> Dance is directed toward the supernatural forces, especially to the Holy Spirit. Furthermore dance creates power itself... Because the (inner healing) circle is normally small, power is concentrated in the middle of the circle. That is the point where we normally find the patient kneeling (Balzer 1989, 178–179, 177).

> Individual healers step from the circle, place their hands on the patient's head or shoulders, or on the region affected, and pray vigorously and ecstatically over him or her ... Quite often the touch of the hands is supplemented by pressure from the healer's staff laid on the affected part of the sick person. Whether hands or staff are employed, two distinct types of action are involved: forceful pressure and brushing off. The first symbolizes the communication of strength and resolve. The second is symbolic of the removal of unclean and undesirable elements. Thus, unfit members are excluded and periodically brought back into the healing community until they are cured and fully reabsorbed (Kiernan 1990, 95)

Community and Shame: The Problem of AIDS

In light of the importance of community as a healing power in Africa, why do numerous proverbs warn those who are sick of the consequences of hiding their illnesses? Why would anyone wish to hide an illness? If an illness springs from shameful acts, communities may turn their collective power against the sick person. Persons with AIDS (PWAs) often hide their condition because, while they need the support of the community, they also fear their reaction.

A research project in Western Kenya to determine community based resources and barriers for home care for PWAs illustrated this dilemma (Kiiti et al. 1996). Field workers in a local Christian hospital developed in-depth relationships with twelve PWAs and followed the course of their lives over eight months. The needs of these six men and six women, average age 28 years, frequently approached desperation. They and their families had often spent all of their resources in treatment and in search for a cure. Eight of the ten who were or had been married also had infected spouses. Eight of the twelve had children; a total of thirty-three children who would be orphaned. The chief remaining caregiver for four of the PWAs was one of their children under the age of thirteen. They needed and longed for the support of the community to help them with physical, social, emotional, and spiritual needs.

In focus groups, community members identified several resources that they make available to the sick. These included visitation, medicines (traditional and modern), assistance with household tasks, literature, support, comfort, and love.

Fear, however, stood between the PWAs and the care of the community. The PWAs feared that if the nature of their disease were known, they would be even more isolated and shamed. Many community members believed that AIDS was a curse resulting from the immorality of the sufferer. Additionally, some of the PWAs felt that they would be shamed because they would have no food or beverage to serve their visitors. Because community members felt that care of the sick was first of all the responsibility of the family, the PWAs feared bringing shame on their families by admitting to the need for help. Finally, many community members also feared contracting AIDS by visiting in the home of a PWA. Some felt so strongly that they urged the field worker, who for most PWAs had become their most important friend, to visit them only in the cover of darkness.

There was some hope of overcoming this barrier of fear. The youth of the community, teachers, and youth leaders not only identified more comprehensive church and community resources but said they could mediate between PWAs and community members. Though even some of the medical staff of the Christian hospital responded to PWAs with condemnation and fear, the field workers who befriended the PWAs in the study became advocates and intermediaries to churches, hospital staff, and community leaders.[2]

In becoming mediators, the field workers stepped well beyond their service role and into the role of healers. A priest is one who mediates between people and their gods. Many African healers are in that sense also priests, but their priesthood is shadowed by the spirits. True healing is found only in the kingdom of God, but diviners sometimes lead their patients toward a kingdom of shadow rather than light.

Notes

1   A *friendship covenant* represents a formal commitment to friendship similar to
the one between David and Jonathan (1 Samuel 20). A friendship covenant is
often witnessed by tribal elders.

A *blood brotherhood* involves the sharing of blood or of a joint sacrifice. It
may be voluntary but it may also be imposed by elders who fear that two
adversaries would fight and destroy the community. Among the Gbaya, warring men may eat one another's blood in a covenant meal to symbolize the
establishment of a peaceful relationship (Christensen 1990).

A *kinship covenant* recreates harmony when there has been a quarrel
between kin. It is especially important that a quarrel between parents and
children be reconciled since the life of the family and community flows
through the progeny, and to break that link brings death.

A *covenant of adoption*, often involving the sacrifice of an animal, is, for
many peoples, the only way to incorporate a stranger into the tribal community.

Among some people, the establishment of the *marriage covenant* involves a
formal opportunity for guests to discuss, confess, and reconcile any griev-
ances that may have arisen throughout the marriage negotiations. To begin
marriage without harmony among the members of the families may be dangerously destructive.

Because land is the physical representation of a people's wealth and identity, the transfer of land from one person and family to another is potentially
disruptive. The Kikuyu sometimes established a *land covenant* involving the
sacrifice of a goat and the sprinkling of its blood and entrails along the
boundary of the transferred land, marking the covenantal acceptance of the
transaction.

Finally, two warring tribes could end their hostilities through a *peace covenant*, often involving restitution and sacrifice.

2   An educational project subsequent to the study helped to break through the
barrier of fear and bring additional resources of local and church communities to the care of the many persons affected by AIDS.

Chapter 9

Healers: The "Priests" of the Shadow

♦ ♦ ♦

While in Kenya I read an interview with a herbalist who was aggressively mar-keting the "chameleon" drug for the treatment of AIDS. How deeply the remedy may have been rooted in African tradition was not apparent in the interview because the herbalist chose to explain the efficacy of the medicine using a biomedi-cal model. It seems that the medicine contained earths of different colors and con-sistencies. When eaten, according to the herbalist, it eventually found its way into the blood. Once in the blood, the medicine changed the white blood cells to a color to match its own. Because the HIV virus lowers immunity by attacking white blood cells and these cells were now red or brown, the HIV virus no longer could have any effect. People affected by HIV were spending large sums of money to purchase this substance, hoping that it would restore them to health where west-ern methods had no answers.

♦ ♦ ♦

TRADITIONAL HEALERS

Classification

Though traditional healers are increasingly forming occupational groups, there is no single "College of Traditional Healers" that establishes and promotes specialties and subspecialties.

The variation across Africa can hardly be overstated. For example, the branch of the Traditional Healers Association for just one village of about 2,000 people in Ghana was comprised of twelve healers but with many others in the village who refused to join the association (Tsey 1997). These twelve people, half men and half women ranging in age from around 35 to over 70, represented three distinctive categories of diviners (those who *primarily* diagnose and treat disease by spiritual power) as well as several categories of "naturalists" (those who *primarily* treat disease through herbs or medicines). Even within this one village, however, it was impossible to discriminate too closely. The diviners also used herbal medicines, and the "naturalists" believed that many of the diseases they treated had a spiritual origin.

Multiplying the variation in that one village – representing only one tribal tradition in only one African country – by the number of different cultural traditions in the different countries of Africa would result in a number too large to be helpful to anyone. To even attempt to describe the variations would be an impossible task.

Among the myriad of healing traditions throughout Africa, however, there are a number of common paths to healing that transcend the specificity of differing traditions. In this chapter, then, I will concentrate on the broad similarities across the continent, recognizing that I am losing much of the depth and richness of the variations.

- *Diviners*

  Diviners consult the spirit world to discover the cause for an illness or calamity. They may discover the cause of an illness through symbolic magic such as "casting the bones" and reading them; or through possession by a spirit medium; or both. People consult a diviner when they feel that the disease has a spiritual origin (Jansen 1981).

  The diviner then tells the patients the course of action they need to follow to restore the balance of spiritual power to their lives. The diviner, therefore, often promotes reconciliation between people, including ancestors. Diviners often create and empower charms and medicines. In much of Africa, diviners are referred to as *ngoma* (the Bantu word for "drum"), but the word is extended to those who use it in healing rituals. They have also been referred to as "witch doctors," a classification that normally does not signify a witch who is a doctor but one who fights against the evil works of witches and sorcerers. Though sometimes witches may also be diviners (Gehman 1985), witchcraft and sorcery, because they are evil, are not regarded as healing practices. Diviners and herbalists are sometimes involved in "public health" tasks such as the siting of a new village or the isolation of people with infectious disease. According to Chavunduka, traditional healers, in these cases, may integrate their "naturalistic" and spiritual understandings of health to suggest that a village be sited on high ground and near sources of clean water.

- *Herbalists*
  Herbalists, often called *nganga*, are trained in the use of herbal remedies. They master traditional wisdom and knowledge concerning the medicinal and ceremonial use of herbal medicines.[1] They may also be diviners.
- *Traditional birth attendants*
  These are mostly women, seldom men, who assist mothers in childbirth and provide advice before and after the birth.[2]
- *Prophets, exorcists, and prayer healers*
  These represent classifications of healers within African churches. Prophets most closely parallel the role of diviners in traditional practice.
- *Other classifications of healers*
  - Bonesetters, who repair fractures in both people and animals;
  - Rainmakers, who strive through magic and sacrifice to restore prosperity through hastening the coming of the rains;
  - Suckers and "surgeons" who use horns or surgery to suck or to cut out harmful substances from the body (Kealotswe 1989); and
  - Peace-makers, such as the Gbaya "woman peace-thrower," who serve in a ceremonial role of reconciliation.

Many others, not generally regarded as healers, are important to healing practices. Elders, parents, and community leaders have special power to bless or to curse; to reconcile and make peace. Pastors and elders often are regarded as commanding spiritual power to heal through prayer and the laying on of hands.

For the rest of this chapter, I will focus upon traditional healers who retain a spiritual, immaterial dimension in their healing work. Diviners and prophets in the independent churches certainly fall into this category, but so would many of the other traditional healers as well. It is impossible to create a neat, mutually exclusive taxonomy. The practices of many herbalists, traditional birth attendants, and bone-setters, for instance, while not as explicitly "spiritual" as the diviners (perhaps not involving spirit possession or trances) nevertheless are rooted in the world of spirits. Because of the great diversity across Africa, the remainder of this section is unavoidably ambiguous and imprecise when applied to a particular setting.

"Calling" and Training

There are three primary ways people are called to become traditional healers (Tsey 1997). First, they may informally learn some healing skills from a close family member and later begin to use them. Secondly, they may undergo a formal apprenticeship to another healer, often a close relative. These first two roads to healing practice are more common for those who practice herbal medicine than for diviners.

Finally, a person may be called to the vocation from the spirit world. A person called to healing work often becomes sick from an illness that shows no response to biomedical interventions. When a diviner is consulted, he or she reveals that the sick person is possessed by a spirit who is calling him or her to become a healer. "The 'calling' is generally accompanied by a sense of fear ... because one of the constraints placed upon the individual who has been called is the belief that failure to proceed with training might lead to either madness or death" (Cheetham and Griffiths 1989, 308). Among the dozen healers that Tsey (1997) interviewed in his Ghanian village, every one of the five who said that they were "called" to the healing role also said that they would not have chosen it without the "call."

In other instances, the spirits might communicate a call through dreams rather than through sickness (Byaruhanga-Akiiki and Kealotswe 1995). Diviners most often learn their craft as an apprentice to another diviner or herbalist, and, in some cases, through the instruction of guiding spirits, often the spirit of an ancestor. Their success in the craft depends upon their own skills of listening, discernment, and presentation as well as the knowledge and reputation of their master and the power of the possessing spirit.

The calling and training of many of the prophets within the independent churches have strong parallels to the calling and training of the *nganga*. Many prophets are also called to their ministry through an illness caused by possession by a spirit, sometimes equated to "the Spirit" and other times an ancestral spirit who mediates to "the Spirit." During their apprenticeship to a senior prophet, they learn how to interpret dreams, have visions, diagnose diseases relationally, predict outcomes, and prescribe treatments. They may also offer sacrifices to ancestral spirits (Oosthuizen 1989).

Healers as "Priests" of the Shadow

Are traditional healers evil? Most Africans outside the Christian community would answer "no." Traditional healers help to maintain balance within the network of relationships comprising a community. From a traditional perspective, they contribute to healing.[3] Christians find the question harder to answer because of two confused and overlapping sets of moral criteria. The first set of criteria focuses upon the results of the interventions. Many traditional interventions have a therapeutic effect, but others cause or aggravate sickness and injury because they are physically destructive. This is usually not an intended outcome. Traditional healers who set out intentionally to destroy rather than heal would at best lose their livelihood and at worst be identified as witches, not healers. Most injuries or sicknesses caused or aggravated by traditional healers are rooted in their lack of understanding of the physical and biochemical processes of the body rather than their intent.

The second set of moral criteria relates to the essential nature of the healing practice rather than the results. Christians who apply this set of criteria hold the *nganga* who brought relief to a person through the apparent mediation of ancestral spirits as guilty of greater sin than the traditional midwife who caused a woman's death because she did not have the technical skills to manage a complicated delivery. From this perspective, it is the fallen nature of men and women, as mirrored in an African worldview, that darkens traditional healing interventions. Traditional healers are "priests of the shadow" in so far as their practice is shaded by the same shadows that affect African perceptions of health and healing.

Traditional Healers and the African Worldview

The practices of the traditional healers emerge naturally from the world view that they share with the people they serve.

Personal attribution for disease

The diagnostic practices of both the traditional healers and many independent church prophets focus upon the social context of the disease as much as upon its symptoms. As a healing practice, divination assigns a personal cause to the disease or misfortune. The prescription to emerge from divination often involves restoring the balance of power in key relationships.

Centrality of power

Diviners cultivate an aura of power. Personal power is first dependent upon their position as mediators to the spirit world. Diviners demonstrate their power in the number and nature of the spirits they are able to call to do their bidding. The healers' clothing, the trappings of the therapeutic setting, and command of the rituals communicate power arising from access to special knowledge and mystical ability known only to them.

The diviner also establishes power through command of the patient. The diviner is highly directive and speaks with certainty about the diagnosis and treatment (Mkhwanazi 1989). Through ritual and command of spiritual powers and medicines, diviners induce altered states of consciousness in the patient and onlookers, including disassociation, glossalalia, fainting, and trances. "The main theme in Xhosa medicine is power versus weakness. A good healer has the charisma of manipulating this power. The Xhosa healer knows how to suggest to his patients that his omnipotence is a reality" (Jansen 1973, 139).

The adherents of many of the independent churches in Africa believe that their leaders command the power of God to heal.

> Power, and not prayer, is the emphasis; and power – even when it is the power of God, or the power of the Holy Spirit – can be 'stored away' in people, especially in the founders and prophets who control the churches (Shorter 1985, 168).

Because the prophets attribute their power to heal sometimes to God, more often to Jesus, or, most often, the Spirit, they claim that they are better able to discern the causes of an illness than those who draw upon lesser powers.

> Much emphasis is put on "the Spirit of power" and/or "the spirits," which could either be the Holy Spirit or the ancestors. These metaphysical contacts give the prophet a specific position as he/she is considered to understand the victim's/patient's problem much better than any western doctor

and better even than the diviners. The prophets' supernatural contact with "the Spirit" and/or ancestral spirit(s) gives them special insight into the nature and cause of illnesses, according to their own testimony and those whom they treat. Prophets are thus considered to be more convincing in their diagnosis and procedures than is the western trained doctor (Oosthuizen 1989, 83).

Non-linearity of time

The diagnostic practice of taking a history assumes a linear concept of time and causation. The modern physician views disease as the consequence of a linear series of events and exposures. To correctly diagnose the disease demands not only physical examination but retracing the process back through the clinical history.

Traditional practitioners do not use linear processes to balance the "fragmented powers" that cause disease and misfortune. Context is everything. "[Traditional healers] view one's body, mind, soul, and spirit as an integrated, indivisible whole in contextual relationship with social connections and the physical and spiritual universe. When one is sick there are many factors involved. The *why* and *how* of the sickness has to be probed and interpersonal relationships which include horizontal and vertical relationships are explored" (Byaruhanga-Akiiki and Kealotswe 1995, 69).

For the diviner and his or her patient, diagnosis is not a deductive conclusion but a progressive revelation. The healer, sometimes in a trance, suggests what the problem may be and remains carefully attuned to the patient's response. Eventually, through this unhurried dialogue with the patient and through the healer's own knowledge of the social setting, as well as any insight that might actually come from the spirits, the diagnosis is progressively revealed. The process is mosaic, not linear (Jansen 1973). When faced with similar symptoms in different relational contexts, a traditional practitioner is likely to make differential diagnoses and prescribe different treatments.

Traditional healers rarely carry out a physical examination to determine the source and nature of the disease. For instance, the Xhosa word for "examination" comes from the same root as a hollow reed or wind instrument and probably originated from seeing modern doctors use stethoscopes. It is never used in reference to traditional healing.

Identity dependent upon community

The traditional healer does not isolate the patient from his or her community in the diagnostic and treatment procedures but builds upon community understandings. First, other members of the person's family (or in the case of the independent churches, other church members) are often present during the diagnostic interview and healing sessions. They, as well as the patient, contribute to the process of the discussion and may combine the powers of their own life forces by participating in the interventions. Because traditional healers use the patient's vernacular in describing the problem, they not only make the problem understandable but also establish a sense of belonging (Jansen 1973).

Continuity between the physical and spiritual dimensions of disease and healing

The diviners, simply by consulting the spirits, define a continuity between the physical and spiritual worlds. Their treatments retain that continuity. "Spiritual" healing is decidedly physical in its dimensions. The diviner may give the patients medicine or refer them to a herbalist. An ancestor may be appeased through physical sacrifice, or a living enemy compensated through a gift. Just as there is little concept of physical healing without addressing the unseen dimensions of power and relationship, there is little concept of "inner healing" that is not accompanied by physical acts, ceremonies, or substances. The therapeutic interventions of traditional healers make use of all of the senses of the patient, giving a sense of wholeness and continuity in every area of life (Jansen 1981).

Fatalism

The traditional healer frames healing interventions within the patient's limited sense of dominion and command over the future. Diviners rarely give a negative prognosis without also suggesting a way to escape that is within the person's capability to respond. Because of the power of the body to heal itself, patients often assign natural progress in healing to the interventions of the diviner (Jansen 1973). As patients assign efficacy to the diviner, their own level of hope and confidence in the diviner grows – which is also good for future business.

The diviner also limits healing interventions to the patient's ability to conceptualize the future. Jansen reports that among Xhosa healers there is no concept of disease processes requiring multiple visits. Patients are more likely to attribute failure to the inadequate power of the healer than to the process of disease. Consequently they visit multiple healers, rather than making multiple visits to the same healer. Since this is true, traditional healers rarely diagnose a chronic disease. Instead they focus on immediate relief of a symptom and identify it as a discrete illness episode rather than explain the patient's present condition as part of a longer disease process (Jansen 1973).

A sacramental world view in dynamic balance with a practical approach to life and living

> *I nya mini ku, midri koyo ya?*
> You won't stay to eat; do you use a rattle?
> (Lugbara proverb)

> *Lubaale aliirana*
> The witch doctor profits either way (if the patient lives or dies).
> (Lugandan proverb)

Many traditional healers earn their livelihood from their practice. While many Africans seek their assistance, they also recognize the profit motive at work. These two among many proverbs highlight negative characteristics of traditional healers.[4] Traditional healers, like other "professionals" in a service industry, adapt their practices to maintain their clientele. Shorter describes the work of a healer who he calls *Maji-ya-soda* (a pseudonym), reputed to be the most famous in southwestern Tanzania at the time he wrote the book.

Shorter describes Maji-ya-soda as "a professional healer of great dedication, gentleness, and assurance" (Shorter 1985, 175). Maji-ya-soda thrived in Tanzania in the late 1960s but the early 70s brought a time of societal change and he became perceived as a political threat. The people surrounding his community practice were dispersed and resettled in new villages. At the same time, the water spirits, who defined Maji-ya-soda's practice, "abandoned him." In 1979, the promises made to the people by the government in the early years of the decade had failed to materialize, and the people became increasingly restless and uncertain. Maji-ya-soda persuaded village leaders to approach the government on his behalf. Finally he received permission to treat cases that had not been treated successfully at the dispensary.

> Adaptable as ever, Maji-ya-soda produced a streamlined version of the water-spirit ritual. Initiation now took one night instead of several days. Clients paid new and higher fees in cash, instead of in labor or kind, and

such practices as binding initiates with ropes and mats during their ordeal were discontinued. By the early 1980s Maji-ya-soda's clientele were more numerous than they had been at any time ... Several of Maji-ya-soda's junior mediums ... had moved to new villages elsewhere and were practicing water-spirit medicine with Maji-ya-soda's approval and under his control. A new and improved model of the water-spirit structure had now come into being (Shorter 1985, 179).

Shorter never questions Maji-ya-soda's sincerity of belief in the spirits, but also demonstrates how he adapted his rituals to the characteristics of a changing market. In further recognition of changing cultures, traditional healers in numerous countries are forming associations, one of the first steps in creating a professional identity (Chavunduka 1995).

The clients of traditional healers recognize that healing is their business and often a good one. Clients also know that traditional healers often fail to deliver what they promise. In modern African comedies, the audiences laugh heartily at portrayals of diviners as clowns, complete with gaudy costumes and exaggerated gestures. A Westerner sitting in the audience and laughing along with the Africans may find it hard to believe that traditional healers are taken seriously. Beneath the laughter, however, lies a core of belief and fear that leads many in that same audience to seek the care of a diviner in a time of crisis. The traditional healers promote this belief through market oriented strategies, often intuitive but sometimes intentionally planned (Twumasi 1975), and also through their sincere conviction that spiritual reality underlies their practice.

BIBLICAL PERSPECTIVE ON TRADITIONAL HEALERS

Shadow is a mixture of light and darkness. The work and person of traditional healers embrace some of the aspects of health and healing that motivate the African search for what is, in fact, the kingdom of God. Traditional healers recognize the healing power of community; they know that the boundary between what is physical and seen and what is immaterial and unseen is not a solid but only a porous membrane; they recognize that there are healing powers external to the body of the patient; they sense that sickness and health often have moral dimensions; personally, some of them reflect genuine gentleness and concern in their healing practices.

There is also much in the work and person of traditional healers that blocks the light and warmth of God's revelation. Instead of the loving gracefulness of God's kingdom, the clients of diviners often feel a shiver of dread. When the practice of traditional healers is compared to the healing ministry of Jesus, the outlines of that chilling shadow are revealed.[5]

Jesus did not use healing to accumulate power. Jesus normally did little to draw attention to his healing ministry. In fact, he often discouraged people from saying who had healed them. While the miracles that Jesus performed were signs that he was the Messiah, he never tried to trade on them to increase his power. Jesus attributed his healing power directly to God his Father. Traditional healers, too, will often attribute their power to a spiritual force but, at the same time, by word, rite, and trappings encourage their clients to identify them with the power they command. Jesus' extrasensory knowledge about those he healed did not arise from a trial and error dialogue, or from a seance, but rather his own power (Shorter 1985).

Jesus used no mediating spirits. In biblical accounts of healing, neither Jesus nor his followers ever went into a trance or were possessed by a spirit in their healing ministry. Neither Jesus nor his followers depended upon a mediating spirit in appropriating God's power. Jesus in fact denied the temptation to prove himself to others by drawing upon the power of angels or mediating spirits. He refused Satan's temptation to throw himself off the pinnacle of the temple to be saved by angels and refused to command angelic spirits as allies in defeating those intent upon his death.

Jesus did not depend upon magic to manipulate the spirits but upon simple words and deeds that were in themselves unremarkable. Jesus offered no charms or spells nor did he perform any rituals in his diagnosis and healing. "Magic is always fraudulent, since it invests ritual actions with a power they do not possess. It is also the enemy of all true religion since it is based on self-interest and not on the abandonment of the will to God" (Shorter 1985, 146).

Jesus' healing could not be explained as a placebo effect, in some cases because either the person was unaware of his intervention or suffered from a condition not normally affected by mind-body mediation. He healed the centurion's servant from a distance without ever being in his presence. Congenital blindness and deafness, a visibly atrophied hand, or the restoration of a severed ear do not represent conditions that are successfully mediated by the strength of the person's belief in the power of the healer.

Jesus did not attribute blame for the conditions he healed to other people or to the people he healed. He healed unconditionally. Affixing blame for sickness upon other people invites either the destruction of community through mutual recrimination or the blaming of the victim.[6] Neither Jesus nor his followers demanded that the sick person fulfill any ritual conditions as a price for healing.

Jesus did not heal everyone in Palestine but, in his healing ministry, he never failed. There was no power that he did not overcome, whether that power was demonic or natural. Traditional healers often fail; Jesus never failed.

Jesus was truly holistic in his healing practices. Though as a man Jesus did not have a scientific knowledge of the body and its functions, he did nothing in his healing ministry that harmed the physical functioning of the body. The holism of many traditional healers is compromised by their lack of understanding of the physical functioning of the body. Therefore they may prescribe either harmful treatments or, alternately, useless treatments that delay medically sound interventions. Healers who set themselves and their traditions in opposition to scientific medicine and discourage people from consulting biomedically trained clinicians are particularly likely to cause harm.

Jesus demonstrated compassion. Not all traditional healers pursue riches as carelessly as the herbalist selling the chameleon drug; many are motivated at least in part by the desire to alleviate suffering and bring health. Even that, however, falls short of compassion. Traditional healers, much like the priests of the Old Testament, have no basis in their worldview to assign meaning to suffering except as a punishment or as a victim.

> What is left of compassion, as a personal quality, if it is detached from passion ... Human beings are called not only to share Christ's sufferings but even to complete them, to make up in their own sufferings what is needed "to be undergone by Christ for the sake of his body, the Church." Human suffering is then far from being useless. Pope John Paul II has written: "To a suffering brother or sister Christ discloses and gradually reveals the horizons of the kingdom of God." Moreover, when suffering is accepted and its saving role understood, there is even joy in suffering. "It makes me happy to suffer for you," says St. Paul. It is not because suffering is enjoyable in some inverted or perverted way, but because weakness – in God's disposition – becomes a source of ultimate strength (Shorter 1985, 16).

Traditional healers cannot help those who suffer from sickness, disability, or injury to construct a transcendent meaning for their suffering.

African traditions tolerate ambiguity but they cannot understand the essential paradoxes of the Christian faith – strength in weakness, leadership in service, life through death, or joy and salvation through suffering. Traditional healers do not enter into the suffering of another or bear suffering on their behalf. Some may be merciful and kind but they cannot follow the paths of African tradition to true compassion any more than the Hebrew people could follow the Law to a true understanding of God's grace and character without the person of Jesus Christ and the revelation of the new covenant.

African healing traditions also cannot present true hope. Every person Jesus healed during his ministry in Palestine is now dead. All those who have experienced healing through traditional healers in Africa are also now dead or will be soon. Because nothing in the worldview or work of the African healer permits reconciliation between the distant high god and his created beings, the 'hope' of healing is doomed to eventual failure. Death is not the gateway to new life but only to a new dying as the spirit fades from memory into a nameless and terrifying void. Reconciliation with God is possible only because of the passion of Jesus.

HEALERS IN THE INDEPENDENT CHURCHES

Is the shadow cast by those elements of darkness in the African worldview at all diminished in the independent churches that continue to embrace traditional perspectives on health, disease, and healing? Yes, it is diminished but not fully overcome.[7]

The parallels between the prophet-healer and traditional diviners are strong.
- Both may call upon the powers of ancestral spirits in helping them diagnose the problem, though prophets may identify the spirit presence as the Holy Spirit (Kiernan 1990).
- Both assume that the illness is caused by a moral failing or witchcraft, and the diagnosis involves the attribution of blame and responsibility (Kiernan 1990).
- Both dress distinctively so that they may be identified as healers (Oosthuizen 1989).
- Both retain symbols of their authority, such as a staff (Oosthuizen 1989).
- Both may depend upon dreams, visions, and possessions in divining

the cause of a disease and its treatment (Oosthuizen 1989).
- Both use symbols (holy water, cords, candles, etc.) in their healing encounters (Oosthuizen 1989).
- Both use words as healing tools but the prophet uses prayers, delivered either by him or her or by other members of the Zionist band (Oosthuizen 1989).
- Because sickness is associated with moral failing the sick person may be marginalized from the community or Zionist band until the diagnosis is complete and the person has recovered. Healing often marks a return as a fully accepted member of the community as well (Kiernan 1990).

Not all of the shadow is gone. The parallels between the traditional diviner and the prophet/healer in the independent churches are not just in form but sometimes in substance. Some of the practices of the prophet/healer are rooted in the same non-biblical worldviews as the diviner. There are some key differences as well.

First, the prophet does not minister alone but in partnership with a preacher/teacher. In order to minister effectively in Africa, African church leadership must include the roles of the "mediator" and the "medium" (Taylor 1963). The "mediator" provides the link to God, administering the sacraments of the church and acting as the father or elder to the people. The "medium" must interpret the Bible in the struggles of everyday life, speaking God's word to the brokenness of his people. These two roles reflect the practical, seamless spirituality of Africa as well as the essential message of the gospel. God must be immanent in the everyday life of the African peoples but not recreated in an image shaped by their needs and traditions.

The healing ministry of many independent churches depends upon the complementary roles of preaching and healing. Zionism combines a "biblical revivalism with African traditional practices in relation to illness and misfortune ... Preaching properly culminates in healing, while healing in the absence of preaching is rendered ineffectual. The one is incomplete without the other, because the power released in healing is generated in the course of preaching" (Kiernan 1990, 153).

These two functions are embodied in two separate roles. In a healing encounter the minister draws unifying themes from the Bible and directs the content and emotionalism of his preaching to the creation and empowering of community. The prophet then diagnoses the disease and prescribes treatment.

Unlike the prophet, the diviner has no such counterpart. The minister not only incites the band of Zionists who will participate in the healing but also draws their attention to the source of power and the written basis of their faith. Unlike traditional healers, who have no source of outside authority for their practice, the dynamic complementarity of the healing and preaching roles in independent churches sometimes permits healing ministry to respond to the instruction and authority of the Bible. The following statement (translated to English) was drafted and signed by eleven bishops of the independent churches in Western Kenya[8] (where the prevalence of HIV infection is just under 50 percent in antenatal women) after they participated in a workshop designed to help them reflect biblically on AIDS. It illustrates the corrective influence that the ministerial function may have in healing ministry.

> We, the Nyanza Luo Bishops of African instituted (independent) churches in Nyanza recognize that HIV/AIDS is destroying our families and threatens the very survival of our families, future generations, and our society. We recognize that some of our traditions contribute to the spread of HIV/AIDS. We are now closely examining these traditions in light of Scripture and in light of the present situation of HIV/AIDS. We affirm that HIV/AIDS is neither a curse nor witchcraft, but is a disease that is spread primarily through sexual contact and also through blood and from an infected mother to her infant. This disease is spreading very rapidly through our society because our families are breaking apart and are under severe stress through:
> - Sexual activity of our youth before marriage
> - Unfaithfulness in our marriages
> - Some of our cultural practices, including sexual cleansing[9] and wife inheritance.[10]

Recommendations

> Since there is not yet a cure for HIV/AIDS, and while it is our prayer that a cure will be found, we recognize that God calls us to obedient living and to a lifestyle of faithfulness. God promises blessing to those who follow his laws. Even if a cure is someday found, the root problem will remain. We call our churches to a lifestyle that brings God's blessing of life. We therefore commit our churches and clergy through our teaching and our own lifestyles to obedience and make the following recommendations:
> 1. Church leaders must strongly teach that HIV/AIDS is caused by the HIV virus, and not the result of a curse or witchcraft.

2. We must do all in our power to encourage our youth through instruction and example to abstain from sex before marriage. Parents should be good role models for their youths and provide biblical instruction on morality at an early age.
3. Church leaders should teach both their polygamous and monogamous members to remain faithful to their wives and husbands, and set an example in their own marriages.
4. From henceforth, members will be encouraged to marry one wife/one husband.
5. Members are encouraged to have an HIV test before marriage.
6. We affirm that widows and orphans must be supported by the extended family; while we reject physical cleansing and inheritance rituals that facilitate the transmission of HIV/AIDS.
7. We commit to developing skills to provide counseling to families which are in difficulty.
8. We commit to opening discussion on the needs of our married people to fulfill each other emotionally and physically within marriage.
9. We affirm that the Bible states that what God has joined together, no man should separate. We encourage husbands to avoid separation due to employment, since it may lead to mistrust and immorality. Transfers should involve both husbands and wives.
10. We must avoid some activities surrounding burial rites that encourage sexual activity at night.

We commit our churches to this task and extend our challenge to the wider church (HIV/AIDS and Traditional Culture 1996).

Several things are remarkable about this statement.
- The workshop in which it was developed was done at the request of the Organization of African Instituted (independent) Churches and the bishops of Western Kenya, not imposed from the outside.
- It had broad representation of the independent churches led by charismatic men who normally do not work together.
- They framed health in a covenant perspective explicitly linking experience of God's "blessing of life" to obedience to his Law.
- The bishops explicitly rejected the traditional beliefs concerning the etiology of AIDS and publicly labeled it as incurable.
- The bishops took positions contrary to some of the blend of custom and Christianity that characterizes the syncretism of many independent churches.

The prayer healers/prophets in these churches would be less likely than the ministers to publish a statement such as this one. The tension between the roles of the prophets and preachers is a healthy one in independent churches.

Finally, despite syncretism, many independent churches elevate Jesus Christ to a position of worship, power, and authority. As Christ is elevated to a position of authority and honor above the ancestors, and as ministers who have received some instruction in God's Word complement the work of the prophets, independent churches move their congregations closer to understanding that Jesus is the only source of healing power.

> When you heed the things of God,
> you need not wear an amulet
> to make your marriage fruitful.
> A woman is struggling with a difficult labor,
> and suddenly all is well.
> The child, placenta and all, come forth
> without an operation. He is the Great Doctor!
>
> O Jesus you have swallowed every death
> and every kind of disease,
> and have made us whole again.
>   (Kuma 1981, 11, 15)

Notes

1   As I mentioned in the previous chapter, I will not in this book be able to explore the wide and extremely productive area of the medicinal use of herbal remedies. While many herbalists will cite biomedical reasons along with traditional ones in explaining the efficacy of the medicines, their craft is more closely tied to traditional worldviews than to naturalistic ones (Gehman 1985).

2   The work of traditional birth attendants often combines aspects of herbal and spiritual healing with skills specific to the birthing process. Once more I am constrained by the length and flow of the book as well as the tremendous variation in natal practices throughout Africa from exploring the work of traditional birth attendants in any detail.

3   The illness and even death that sometimes accompany their healing practice would traditionally not be attributed to the interventions of the healer that negatively affect health. What we would understand biomedically as ill effects of treatment interventions might be attributed to failure on the part of the healer but not to intention.

4   The first proverb chides a guest who refuses hospitality by asking if he or she

is a healer and therefore rich enough to have better food than what is being served. The last observes that traditional healers, unlike workers whose wage is tied to their productivity, take their fee no matter what the outcome.

5   Some may feel I am judging unfairly in writing this section, especially since I am not African myself. That concern may arise from a misunderstanding about the nature of evil. In comparing ourselves to Christ, everyone of us will find evil in our lives and practices. The light of Jesus reveals evil in each one of us and enables us to see those areas of our daily lives that fall into its shadow. In contrasting the work of traditional healers with the healing work of Jesus Christ, I am not stepping beyond what is biblically legitimate.

6   One exception to this is Paul's warning to the Corinthians that their dishonor of the Lord's Table was the cause of sickness, weakness, and death among members of their congregation. For a fuller discussion of illness, death, and God's judgement in the New Testament, please refer to Chapter 5.

7   For the remainder of this section I will focus upon the practices of the Zionist churches. The Zionist churches grew out of the Christian Catholic Church that originated in Zion City, Illinois. The Zionist churches, concentrated largely in southern Africa, form the largest of the three major traditions of independent churches in Africa that also include the Ethiopian (*Amatopi*) and African Apostolic Churches (*Abapostoli*) (Oosthuizen 1989). There is tremendous diversity in the practices and doctrines of the independent churches and certainly not everything in this section will apply to all of them. The principles, however, are more broadly applicable.

8   Church of Christ in Africa, Coptic Orthodox Church, Legion Maria of Africa Church of Mission, Nomiya Lup Roho Church, African Israel Nineveh Church, New Sayun Church of God, Church of Peace in Africa, Episcopal Church of Africa (not the Anglican Church), Musanda Christian Church of Kenya, Sayun Church of God, Church of Mercy, and the Organization of African Instituted Churches (OAIC).

9   The belief that a widow must be sexually "cleansed" through intercourse, necessarily involving the exchange of sexual fluids, with a male relative of her late husband before being accepted back into the husband's clan and receiving their protection and support.

10   The biblical tradition of a widow being taken as a wife by her late husband's brother for her own protection and to bear children to maintain the name and family of her late husband. If, as is often the case, the woman's husband died of AIDS and the woman is HIV+, the HIV infection will spread throughout the family. As in the custom of sexual cleansing, a woman who refuses, along with her children, loses the support of her husband's clan.

Chapter 10

The Healing Drama

◆ ◆ ◆

He [the healer] dipped a branch deeply into one of the buckets of holy water and sprinkled the crowd energetically ... Immediately after the sprinkling, shouts and screams were heard in different sections of the crowd and struggling people were carried forward to the altar. In some cases there was a total surprise. Friends or relatives who had never been afflicted with spirits, or had anything to do with them, were found to be possessed.

One of (the victims) was summoned to the healer, a young woman in a yellow frock. Holding her by the hair, he drenched her with holy water from a bucket in his other hand and the woman began to scream and go into convulsions. (As the demon refused to exit in a fifteen-minute dialogue with the healer), he poured more water on the trembling woman until she was completely drenched.

The final capitulation of the spirit was greeted with cheers and clapping from the audience and the woman was told to go home with some of the holy water in a bottle for her to drink from time to time, as a medicine (Shorter 1985).

◆ ◆ ◆

For those who live in myth, the meaning of the symbol can only come true as the symbol itself is enacted (Taylor 1963, 150).

Spiritual truth in Africa is incarnated in symbol and ritual. Though healing powers may operate in the unseen world, healing acts belong to the world of concrete experience. Healing acts in Africa, whether done in the independent churches or by traditional healers, are usually highly emotional group activities, dramas of broken relationships and the struggle between good and evil.[1]

The healing drama unfolds in two interwoven acts: 1) the cause of the illness or misfortune is revealed, and 2) the treatment for the illness or misfortune is prescribed.

ACT 1: REVEALING THE CAUSE OF THE DISEASE

The process of divination usually follows a definite sequence. First, the diviner or prophet asks about the symptoms of the patient. The nature of the problem permits the diviner to concentrate the next step of the diagnosis on a limited set of relationships. For instance, in many African traditions, infertility, repeated miscarriages, or complications of pregnancy may be traced back either to witchcraft or to the alienation of another woman within the extended family, who may or may not still be living (Daneel 1970).

Secondly, the diviner probes deeper into the patient's life to try and discover the root cause of the problem. Because most diviners are part of the communities they serve, they often have some knowledge of their patients and family relationships. Twumasi (1975) reports that diviners in Ghanaian villages would hide in the dark to secretly listen to village gossip related by groups of men. They also would invite children to come to their home or shrine to eat and would encourage them to talk about what they have heard their parents say about themselves or others. As the diviner probes more deeply into possible causes for the problem, he or she watches the reactions of both the patients as well as the group who participate in the healing session. Family members often participate overtly, suggesting possible causes for the problem but, if not, their emotional and physical responses to the probing suggestions of the diviner guide the direction of the diagnosis (Kiernan 1990).

Finally, many diviners and prophets from the independent churches maintain that they receive insight directly from God or the spirits while in one of several altered states of consciousness.

- *Possession*. Both diviners and prophets often claim to be possessed by spirits. When this happens, many but not all also fall into a dissociative trance or spell, often accompanied by trembling, or other bodily manifestations of the spirit's presence, and glossolalia (speaking in tongues). Diviners often distinguish between the different natures and kinds of possessing spirits (ancestral, morally neutral, or evil) whereas many prophets of the independent churches regard all possessing spirits as evil, with the exception of the Holy Spirit.

- *Interpretation of dreams.* Both diviners and prophets interpret the dreams of the supplicant and his or her close relatives. Sometimes they maintain that God or the spirits reveal the diagnosis in their own dreams even before the healing session (Shorter 1985; Chavunduka 1995; Oosthuizen 1989; Zvanaka 1997).
- *Throwing the bones.* Normally, only diviners (not prophets) "throw the bones," tossing down bones, slabs, pebbles, or other objects. The diviners then "read" the patterns made by the objects and make a diagnosis (Chavunduka 1995; Daneel 1970; Kealotswe 1989). Diviners throughout Africa use rattles, mind-altering drugs, incense, and many other methods of discerning the reason for an illness or misfortune.

ACT 2: TREATMENT INTERVENTIONS

In the first act, both the prophets of the independent churches and the traditional healers follow essentially the same script. In the second act, however, the plot line diverges for these two groups. Many independent churches have already rejected some traditional healing practices and underlying values as contrary to Christian belief.

1. Once a diagnosis is made, the diviner will normally accede to the demands of the afflicting spirits who may be aggrieved. Most prophets of the independent churches, however, refuse to treat the afflicting spirit with any respect. Instead they identify it as a demon and bind and/or exorcise it in a power encounter (Zvanaka 1997). At the same time, many of the prophets instruct church members not to confront other extended family members who choose to appeal to the afflicting spirits.

2. Diviners turn to mediating spirits as the source of healing power. Most, but not all prophets, turn toward God or the mediating persons of Jesus or the Holy Spirit as superior sources of healing power.

3. Some diviners use sorcery to counteract the acts of sorcery or witchcraft. Prophets of the independent churches normally reject the explicit use of evil powers to confront evil powers.

4.   The Bible provides the authority for the work of the prophets and ministers. A 'prophet' operating without the constraints of the institutional authority of the church would be little different from a diviner (Kiernan 1990, 164).

Nobody can hope to cover the entire scope of the interventions that blend together throughout Africa in the second act of the healing drama but, to understand how Christian health care may become more relevant to the cultural context of Africa while retaining biblical integrity, it is important to understand the nature of traditional interventions.[2] These overlapping interventions include 1) medicines, 2) charms and rituals, 3) powerful words, and 4) exorcism.

Medicines

In many African languages, the word for "medicine" refers to any powerful substance. In a generic sense therefore not all "medicines" are good or are used for healing purposes. Witches, for instance, often give their clients a poisonous "medicine" that may be secretly administered to their enemies. Some of these substances have only ascribed power but others are biochemically toxic.

Whether good or evil, the strength of a medicine depends upon its innate characteristics, the method by which it is administered, the quantity, and the power ascribed to it by its context or the person prescribing its use.

Innate characteristics

Many herbal medicines have innate medicinal characteristics. The dispensary of every herbalist contains well-known herbs and compounds of widely accepted efficacy and others that are uniquely his or her own. Many herbal medicines have measurable biochemical effects; others do not.

Other medicines draw their power not from their biochemical efficacy but their appearance and source. The Bomvana, as well as other African peoples, consider bitter, dark-colored medicines as stronger than sweet or light-colored ones (Jansen 1973). Prophets of some independent churches in Botswana will not use roots or herbs in their pure form. They consider the roots as devilish because they are hidden underground. They reject the use of raw herbs because they resemble the medicines of traditional healers (Kealotswe 1989). The power of these substances must somehow be transformed to be acceptable. They accept cow dung, for instance, as an important cleansing agent because it combines the medicinal qualities of all the plants eaten by the cow or oxen (Kealotswe 1989).

Method of administration and quantity

The power of medicines also varies according to its mode of administration and quantity. Herbalists administer some of their strongest medicines by scarification in which the medicine is rubbed into cuts made in the skin. Injections parallel this traditional practice and are often considered the most potent of the methods of administration (Jansen 1973; Spring 1981). Also, if a little bit of medicine is powerful, more must be more powerful. As a result, in a problem not at all unique to Africa, some patients will take larger than prescribed doses of either herbal or manufactured medicines, sometimes endangering their health (Shorter 1985; Jansen 1973).

Attributive powers

Finally, medicines may be common elements imbued with the healing power of a natural object, spirit, or of God. Water is a good example because even ordinary water that has been sanctified by the blessing of a minister is a powerful symbol in the Zionist churches. The healing power of the water "... is derived only from the spoken word delivered in a public manner by one with a socially recognized position whose power is based on the social support of a believing community" (Kiernan 1990, 109).

> First of all, water is imbued with the power of the spirit. Whenever possible, baptisms are conducted in flowing water where movement emphasizes its power. The candidates for baptism may be immersed numerous times and thrash about during the baptism to demonstrate that they are being empowered by the Spirit.
>
> Secondly, unlike medicinal substances that derive their power from the characteristics of the earth, water has no power of its own. As a cooling medicine, water derives its power from the word of blessing spoken over it by the minister. The herbs and roots of the earth are "hot" and dangerous medicines; sanctified water is a cooling medicine. Though water is also used externally in ceremonial cleansing, its medicinal use in its pure form depends more upon its cooling characteristics, like *soré*, rather than its cleansing properties.

Finally, when mixed with ashes and salt, water is a cleansing agent. As a prescription for illness and especially for stomach pains, the salt or ash solution washes out the insides. It expels harmful substances in the stomach by causing vomiting; and so drives out the evil spirits that are causing the affliction. In addition to causing vomiting, the ashes are a cooling substance that can help to neutralize "hot" emotions or substances.[3]

By attributing power to ordinary substances and using them in healing sessions, the independent churches enthusiastically re-interpret the sacraments. Pogoro Catholics in Tanzania, for instance, permitted the people to use herbal medicines not tainted with divination but banned most traditional medicines as sinful. But what, then, to do about common substances imbued with power not by divination but by church tradition? Because Pogoro Catholics believed that symbols of God's power such as holy water, ashes, and oils for anointing are able to transform, they created a new category of medicine called 'medicines of the Church.' These substances were thought not only to have healing properties in themselves but also gave those who used them favor for protective care of intermediaries to God such as angels and saints (Green 1996).

Charms and Rituals

Traditional healers and prophets use a staggering number and variety of symbols and rituals in addition to medicines. Symbols and rituals can be fully understood only within their own particular context, a task well beyond the scope of any one book. Within each healing encounter, however, objects and rituals symbolize to the senses what is taking place in the unseen world. The symbolism of healing rituals may be exceedingly rich in meaning as the following examples from the Zionist churches illustrate (Oosthuizen 1989).

- The basic uniform of the Zionists consists of a long flowing outer robe for men and a tunic and skirt for the women. Cords, sashes, and ribbons may be worn about the waist or draped over the shoulders. During the healing service, a prophet may designate one of these items as a protection against illness. The pastor's wife will make the item on her sewing machine, and the garment may be publicly blessed by the pastor and given to the person with the blessings of the congregation on a Sunday morning.
- The staff of the Zionists is a weapon, following the traditional Zulu

practice of warriors' carrying their spears with them whenever they left their homes. While the Zionist is not allowed to use his staff in fighting, it has become instead a spiritual weapon. Touching and prodding a sick person with the staff drives away the evil causing the sickness. The most powerful staves are cut from a tree growing beside the waters. Like a reed, the staff is therefore imbued with the "cooling" quality of the water below and the air and wind above, symbolizing the spirit.

- Additionally in the Zulu creation myth, because the man and woman originally emerged from the reeds, reeds have remained identified with the source of life. A father is called *umhlanga*, a bed of reeds, because his children are broken off from him and share in his life. The staves used in the healing encounter are stored together during the week in a corner of the minister's house, symbolically linking their owners in the life and identity of the Zionist band. When they are distributed to members at the beginning of a healing service, the members symbolically "come out" from the minister. As the meeting continues, the staves come together again in a circle of joint worship and healing, symbolizing equality within community. After the service, they are again stacked together, symbolizing the unity of the healing experience and promising it again in the future.
- Strips of blue or green cloth may be attached to the staff or to another stick and waved above a person, band, or house as a flag. The flags symbolize protective power over the homes of Zionists, preventing the attack of mystical forces of evil. Like water, other ordinary objects may be sanctified by prophets for protection (Daneel 1970).
- Sanctified needles worn by healers in their lapels may be used to puncture the skin or nasal cavity to remove evil blood and water.
- Inhaling the smoke of sanctified newspapers assists in driving out evil spirits and protecting the person from future possession.
- Some women wear ribbons and sashes around their abdomens to stimulate fertility. Some prophets indicate that they can determine the gender of the child by a prescribed pattern of knots in the cloth.

These final examples illustrate the danger of symbolism. The bronze serpent originally symbolized God's power to heal Israel but later was destroyed when it became the object of worship. Likewise African Christians may assign power to the symbols themselves, so that they come to be no more than another "medicine of the church," different in form but not in meaning from the amulets and charms of the diviners.

Powerful Words

Words hold the power of life and death and of health and sickness. I previously discussed the destructive power of words spoken explicitly as a curse or with the evil power of anger or bitterness. Words are also powerful agents of life and health.

Blessings

The water of the Zionists derives its power from the blessing spoken over it by the minister. In many African traditions, words of blessing transmit the life force from one person to another. Blessings are passed from those who are older to those who are younger. Among some groups, including the Maasai, spitting is a symbolic blessing and transfer of life force from one person to the next (Brodeen 1995). Many greetings and words of farewell throughout Africa are in the form of blessings, often very practical and to the point.

Magic

Similar to the practices of the peoples bordering ancient Israel, the right words spoken in the right circumstances by a person who is in relationship to powerful spirits have the power to manipulate the spirits to do the diviner's bidding (Vanderhoof 1994). Diviners demonstrate their command of secret knowledge and power through magical words, songs, and glossolalia.

Written words

These also may take on a magical power. For example, the emphasis upon the Qu'ran as the literal Word of Allah in Islamic Africa lends a magical value to portions of the Qu'ran written in Arabic.

Morimen (among the Mende of Sierra Leone) are specialists who use their mastery of Arabic to help clients pursue love affairs, cure barrenness, divine the future, gain employment, win court cases, harm enemies, pass school exams, defeat witches, drive away demons of magic and so forth.

A moriman evokes a verse's power by writing it on paper, rolling it and tying it with string and putting it in an amulet pouch. Alternatively, he may write the verse on a special length of board with a piece of burnt wood and then wash off the words with water to make a black potion (*nesi*, 'holy water'). The moriman blesses the amulet or liquid and gives his client instructions for its use. The client may wear the amulet or bury it, or he may drink the nesi or rub it on himself (Brodeen 1995, 24).

Preaching

The Zionist prophet is empowered by the words and emotional intensity of the minister (Kiernan 1990). In Zionist services the minister's preaching before the healing service fulfills two roles. First, in reading the Creed, the Ten Commandments, and a Psalm, the preacher focuses the congregation upon God as the source of power. He also uses the techniques of preaching, particularly call and response, and the repetition of simple themes to build emotional power among the members of the congregation (Kiernan 1990; Daneel 1970). In a healing service, the preaching is centered upon the generation and release of power rather than upon instruction.

Prayer

"Prayers of Protestant origin walk so delicately amid their 'ifs' and 'maybes' that they lack the ingenuousness of all sincere prayer" (Taylor 1963, 168). Prayer is an essential component of healing among independent churches. Their prayers are not characterized by 'ifs' and 'maybes' but are confident, repeated affirmations of God's healing – simple down-to-earth petitions like most of the traditional prayers of Africa (Mbiti 1992). Prayers have two purposes in the healing service. The first is communication of expectant petition to God, but the second is directed toward the development of group identity and emotional power. In healing sessions in a closed room, the volume of prayers, dancing, songs, and instruments can be deafening (Kiernan 1990). The cacophony alone acts as an expression of community power and unity.

Exorcism

Many illnesses are attributed, both traditionally and in independent churches, to possession by outside spirits. When possession is diagnosed as the problem, diviners discern how the sick person has offended the spirit and how to appease and pacify it. The "prescription" often involves an animal sacrifice.

Unlike sacrifice in the Old Testament which was a symbolic expiation of moral guilt before God, sacrifices in Africa are normally directed toward the appeasement of disgruntled ancestral or created spirits. The sacrifice is less symbolic of repentance than of renewed hospitality and compensation to an important and powerful person whom the victim had somehow offended.[4] Once the spirit has received adequate honor and recognition, the spirit leaves the person voluntarily. The diviner avoids confrontation by acceding to the demands of the spirit.

Unlike the diviner, the prophets of the independent churches confront evil spirits in a display of power and forcibly exorcise them. Exorcism is also common in Pentecostal churches and is encountered occasionally in Catholic and Protestant churches as well.

Exorcism Rites

The rites surrounding exorcism vary widely. Some are violent and heavily dependent upon ritual.

> Special sessions are held to free people from drugs or alcohol addiction. (In these circumstances) the prophet/prayer healer is active while the congregation sings to the accompaniment of drums and rhythmic instruments. Staves (are) put against the person, hands laid on the person, who is forcefully hit (often manhandled) on the body in order to get the evil forces out; loud, fast praying and shouting, which often ends up in glossolalia are all part of the whole procedure (Oosthuizen 1989, 88).

Others carry an almost circus-like atmosphere. In the story at the beginning of this chapter, Shorter (1985) described one healing service of a noted healer that had about 10,000 people in attendance. Before the drama started, the healer had said that those who were possessed by evil spirits would begin to shake when they were sprinkled with holy water.

The spirits in the next woman refused to leave when confronted with the name of Jesus, some even denying any knowledge of him.

> Again, there was the same reluctance of the spirits to depart and repeated drenchings with holy water. The crowd followed the dialog with laughter and amusement. The spirits begged to be allowed to stay, but one by one they departed, the whole process taking nearly half an hour ... There were several more successful exorcisms of this kind, while volunteers continuously fetched water to replenish the holy water buckets (Shorter 1985, 192–193).

Former Archbishop Milingo's beliefs surrounding exorcism more closely parallel the beliefs of the Pentecostal evangelical churches than those of the independent churches (Kailing 1994). Like the Pentecostal evangelicals, Milingo emphasizes biblical belief, repentance, and reconciliation with God, not just healing. Unlike most Pentecostal evangelicals, Milingo believed some ancestral spirits to be morally neutral, though he did feel that all spirits of possession were evil and in the service of Satan.

Bishop Milingo maintained that healing, including exorcisms, required first of all repentance and then reconciliation with God. He felt that prayers would not be effective if 1) the afflicting spirit was there because of the active or tacit invitation of the possessed person, or 2) the possessed person harbored bitterness toward God and did not desire a true reconciliation with him.

> We have often obliged some of our patients to bring all the utilities and all the medicines they were given by the medicine men … We shall replace them with the power of the Lord and with some sacramentals like holy water. One woman has refused to bring the utensils and the medicines, and the spirits have also forbidden her to enter the church. She has to make a decision between Jesus and Satan, but she is so afraid of the threat of death from Satan that she does not reflect on the victory of Jesus over sin, death, and Satan himself (Milingo 1984, 41–42).

> It is now a common practice during healing sessions to prepare the petitioner for reconciliation with God and with their friends … There have been cases where healing did not take place just because someone believed that God had not been fair with him or her. There have also been cases in which the petitioner hated God – the source of goodness … Hence such petitioners should first ask pardon from God so that they may be forgiven and, in turn, forgive God. One cannot ask a favor from someone with whom one is in a state of enmity (Milingo 1984, 26).

After preparing the "patient," Milingo would begin a healing service that he outlined in seven steps.

1. The congregation invited God's presence with prayers of praise and thanksgiving. Unlike the almost violent manifestations of God's presence among the Zionists, Milingo believed that God signaled his presence through "a profound silence, and the gentleness and relaxation" reflected in the face of the sick (Milingo 1984, 27).
2. He called upon the saints and angels to be mediators to God on behalf of the ill and possessed.

3. He called upon the diseases and possessions to reveal themselves. Many of the sick felt their pain more severely during this time as the diseases revealed themselves through fits and possessions.
4. As Milingo prayed for healing, centering on the power and person of Jesus Christ, the intensity of the response increased. Many of those afflicted by evil spirits rolled on the floor screaming, and some lost consciousness.
5. To symbolize the presence of new life among those who were healed, Milingo would sprinkle them with holy water and lay his hands on them as he prayed for the coming of the Holy Spirit to bring new life.
6. Just prior to the end of the service, Milingo would raise the crucifix and ask Jesus to seal the work of healing with his blood.
7. Milingo ended the service with prayers of thanksgiving to the Trinity, to angels, and to the saints.

The practice of exorcism varies widely throughout Africa from one church group, prophet, or preacher to the next. All exorcisms involve confrontation between the alleged powers of light and darkness.

The Debate over Exorcism

There is considerable debate concerning the role that exorcism should play in Christian healing. While admitting that the practice of exorcism was often therapeutic for the person who evidenced possession, Shorter also concluded that mass exorcism was ultimately a destructive practice.

> Popular or mass exorcism ... runs the risk of causing people to demonize their experience of suffering to an exaggerated degree. Fear of the devil replaces the love of God and a morbid interest in demons is encouraged. People are diverted away from prayer and the sacraments which are regarded as being not sufficiently powerful for the exorcist's purposes. The identification and exposure of devils is not a substitute for the practice of love, service, and justice in community. The whole phenomenon may become a dangerous aberration (Shorter 1985, 198).

Shorter also warned that exorcism only mimics the practices of the diviners without sufficiently challenging or transforming them. He also questioned the 'magic tricks' of the exorcists that seem designed to entertain rather than instruct, and questioned whether or not these 'shows' challenged people with the need to examine their own behavior and be transformed by Jesus Christ (Shorter 1985, 199).

Others object to exorcism because:

1. In externalizing evil, it does not challenge people to examine their own lives.
2. By struggling with the spirits, exorcists show them too much respect, emphasizing their power and increasing fear.
3. Participants attribute power to the instruments and rituals rather than to God. In the end, because the practice of exorcism so closely parallels traditional beliefs and practices, the people are unable to recognize the kingdom of God as distinct from their own traditional beliefs and practices (Daneel 1990).

Those who support the practice of exorcism argue (Daneel 1990; Milingo 1984):

1. The Bible accepts the reality of evil spirits and both Jesus and his followers practiced exorcism. It is a practice rooted in the Bible and the traditions of the church, not just in African thought and practice.
2. It is most often a healing force in the lives of those who experience it. It is often accompanied by pastoral care.
3. It is performed in the name of God and depends upon his power rather than manipulative techniques. It establishes God's authority over the powers of evil and the authority of his servants over the work of witches, wizards, and sorcerers.
4. It can extend God's grace to wizards, witches, and sorcerers who would otherwise be permanently cut off from the family of God.
5. If the church fails to effectively address a belief so deeply rooted in the daily lives of many Africans, they will continue to seek assistance from diviners and others who share their belief in evil spirits but not in the salvation of God. The practice of exorcism becomes, therefore, an essential expression of God's kingdom in Africa.

In my reading I did not find even one African author who recommended that exorcism be totally excluded as a part of the healing practices of African churches.

Direct and Indirect Interventions: The Subplot

While ritual and symbolic interventions hold the center stage of the healing drama, another more subtle subplot is taking place. In many cases some of the most effective healing interventions are rooted in the process of diagnosis and treatment. The following account illustrates how indirect interventions also contribute to healing.

Johane Manami, a Zionist prophet in the healing city of Moriah headed by the preacher Mutendi, pronounced the following diagnosis for a Zionist evangelist whose wife was mentally imbalanced. The diagnosis was not made quietly in a consulting room but publicly in a healing meeting with other church members, supplicants, and junior church officials, one of whom interpreted for the prophet who spoke in tongues. The others in the room responded with prayers and affirmations.

> Finias, God says that He has witnessed the malevolent spirit in your wife and that the spirit comes from her deceased relatives. He says, "I see the members of her family at home, kneeling before the spirits and then calling her name. Your wife must tarry here a while so that my servant (Mutendi) can pray for her and touch her with his staff. Then you will receive sanctified water for your use at home." God says, "You have too many thoughts, Finias; you must stay at home, filled with only one thought, and pray fervently. Your in-laws are at loggerheads with you because of the bride-price. For this reason your wife is possessed by a malevolent spirit. You have thought that the spirit was sent by your enemies, but now you know that it comes from your in-laws. Take your wife to her house at a later stage, and leave her there a while. If you take her home directly from here, the spirit will have even greater power in your wife than is the case today. Her parents must also do something so that the spirit can leave her. Therefore she must stay at home until she is back to normal. I [God] shall accompany you to the house of your in-laws. My servant too will guide you and your wife" (Daneel 1970, 37–38).

The diagnosis is virtually indistinguishable from one that a diviner might have given (Zvanaka 1997). The woman's condition was the result of an evil spirit sent against her by her own family members who were dissatisfied with the bride-price. The prophet progressively revealed the diagnosis, beginning with the broadly applicable revelation that she was possessed by an evil spirit and then explaining why and how that possession happened. The prophet pronounced the diagnosis and treatment while he was possessed by "the Spirit" and speaking alternately in tongues.

The direct interventions included:

1. A firm instruction to Finias to pray for his wife
2. A healing appointment with Mutendi for prayer and healing intervention through the touch of his staff
3. Sanctified water for continued use at home

A clinician might question the efficacy of the direct interventions but would probably see the value in the indirect ones that, if followed, would provide an extended period of recuperation, assure continued care for Finias' wife, strengthen their marriage, promote the reconciliation of extended family relationships, and reinforce hope for recovery. The indirect interventions included:

1. A prolonged, indefinite rest in the supportive environment of Moriah
2. A prolonged period of rest at Finias' household, accompanied by an instruction to Finias (a Zionist evangelist) to remain at home with his wife and be more single-minded in her care
3. An instruction to Finias to take his wife to her parents' home for a longer visit, indirectly enlisting their help in reconciling the strained relationship with other in-laws
4. An assurance of God's presence in his wife's illness as well as the continued guidance of Mutendi as his servant
5. An implied assurance that, given an indefinite period of time, his wife would return to normal

Healing Themes in the African Drama

The drama of healing is repeated thousands of times daily throughout Africa in as many variations. What links these repeated dramas together and gives them healing power?

Transcendence is made real in ritual and symbol. The "world in between" is brought near. The power of God and the spirits to heal is revealed and faith, even though it be misdirected, is strengthened. Faith promotes healing.

The diagnoses are delivered with authority and fit the worldview of the sick person. Illness is made understandable. It is named in the mother tongue of the person who is sick. Naming the cause of the illness implies authority over it. Additionally, the authority of the practitioner in identifying the cause of the illness builds confidence in the healer's interventions.

The healing interventions fall within the bounds of the person's limited sense of dominion and concept of the future. The healing interventions are usually affordable, accessible, immediate or short-term, and do not require frequent repetition.

There is always hope for recovery. No diagnosis is ever hopeless. There is always something the person can do that brings hope of restoration.

The 'treatment plan' builds community. The family of the affected person is involved in the diagnosis and normally plays a key part in the healing interventions. The diagnosis and intervention often involves an indirect confrontation and reconciliation with those who have become alienated from the ill person and his or her family. Strengthening individual relationships, rebuilding social networks, and restoring community peace affects not only the health of the sick person but the health of the community as well.

In some cases the medicines and the treatment interventions, particularly those involving dressings, nutrition, birthing practices, or manipulation of the affected part of the body, have specific and measurable medical value.

HEALING IN AFRICA AND LONGING FOR THE KINGDOM OF GOD

Pastor Muriu maintained that Africans are searching for the kingdom of God. How does the search for healing reflect the search for the kingdom?

Search for the King

Reflecting the search for a king, Archbishop Milingo maintained that the Christian God presented in many churches did not have the immanence even of the African high god.

> The God who is said to be in the Holy Heaven, who is at peace with himself and does not care what is happening among the people on earth, is certainly not an African God. The distant God is the one whom Africans miss in their churches on Sunday. He is far from them. He is a special God who remains in the Church as preached by Western Christianity (Milingo 1984, 75).

Africans search for a God whose kingdom embraces not only the heavens but the earth, not only the spiritual but the physical, a God whose kingdom is not distant but is immanent in the lives of his creatures. In Christian health care in Africa, Christian medical practitioners often separate the realm of healing from its king. In our health ministries, we preach God as the one who gives hope for the future but science as the sovereign of the present. In healing ministry, our message belies our belief. In our practice, we communicate that God's realm begins where the reign of science ends. Our challenge is to understand and practically communicate God as the king of a healing kingdom that embraces and integrates faith and science in everyday life and ministry.

Quest for the Power of the Kingdom

When John the Baptist's disciples questioned whether or not Jesus was the Christ, Jesus pointed to what he did. His powerful acts of healing constituted the key evidence that he was indeed the Christ (Matthew 11:1–6). He healed and preached with quiet authority and great power. Traditional healers carefully cultivate belief in the powers that they possess or are able to command. Their power to heal is derived at least in part from faith. Not so with Jesus. His healing power was not derived from faith; rather, faith grew and flourished as a response to his power to heal.

When we, as Christian health workers, isolate the King from the realm of science, we also misattribute the power to heal to the manipulation of nature and not to the Creator. We carelessly root out the faith that traditional healers work so diligently to cultivate. Traditional healers practice so that people will attribute healing, no matter how it happens, to the powers that they purport to control. When those who are healed through our ministry attribute their healing to power that we "control," we point them away from God and toward science. In so doing we point them away from faith. Actually, they are right and we are wrong. Instead of denying God's power in healing, we must affirm it, pointing not to science derived from God's creation, but to the Creator. Our healing ministries do not simply "buy us the right" to proclaim the message of the gospel; our healing ministries are an integral part of our good news because, like Christ's resurrection, they too are an expression of the power and victory of God's kingdom.

Longing for the Community of God's Kingdom

Africans also long to experience the sense of individual fulfillment and identity that emerges from immersion in a loving, giving, and caring community. The practice of scientific medicine is modeled on western beliefs concerning privacy and individualism rather than African beliefs concerning community. The patient is examined alone; she is given an individualistic diagnosis and prognosis alone; she is often hospitalized alone. Health workers give little attention to healing interventions directed toward the person's community or family relationships. Merely restoring a sick person's ability to live in alienation from others is not to heal. It is also, in Africa, ultimately self-defeating because alienation eventually exacts an even greater toll.

Traditional communities in Africa are the instruments of both healing and wounding. Those who are sick usually experience the care and concern of their family and local communities; but many become sick because they fail to satisfy the sometimes unknown demands of the same community.

In traditional thought, the concept of an interdependent community is bounded by ethnicity. There is nothing that effectively transcends ethnic communities to bring peace. One of my Somali friends characterized Somali culture with this saying[5]: "My clan against your clan; my family against your family; my father, brothers, and I against your father and brothers; my brother and I against my father; me against my brother." The Somali nation bears witness to the power of community identity to divide.

In contrast, the church is pictured as the Body of Christ in which there is "neither Jew nor Greek, slave nor free, male nor female" (Galatians 3:28). The African church has not fully grasped the power of these words and is often fractured along the same fault lines of ethnicity as the continent.

In sickness and disability, however, churches of Africa are able to experience the essential paradox of strength and weakness that is the key to community within God's kingdom. Communities of affliction must turn to God and to one another in their weakness; and discover a strength of unity and belonging that transcends the divisions of African society. God chose the weak and lowly things of the world to shame the strong and noble (1 Corinthians 1:27–29). The unity and power of God's kingdom is often modeled better in a meeting of Christians affected by AIDS than a consultation of denominational church leaders. Those who know that they have lost their lives are in the best position to discover God's life, not only for them as individuals but as a community united and made strong by him.

How can the enterprise of Christian health and healing activities in Africa become a living, practical expression of God's kingdom in day-to-day ministry so that people are drawn to the light of God rather than trapped in shadow?

First, Christian health practitioners need to understand and desire to embrace a biblical model of healing. They must open their minds and hearts to new directions and perspectives that transcend the boundaries of their own training. I briefly outlined biblical models for health and healing in the first two chapters of this book.

Secondly, they must understand how traditional African perspectives and practices on health and healing bear the image of biblical understanding and also how these traditional understandings and practices, many of them bearing strong parallels to biblical perspectives, have been nevertheless darkened by sin.

Thirdly, Christian health practitioners must be able to relate biblical teaching and African traditions regarding health and healing to the scientific perspectives of medicine that have guided and informed their practice. In the next two chapters, I will turn to this task. In the first of the two chapters, I will present a conceptual framework integrating biblical teaching, African traditions, and scientific medicine so that they may be considered together rather than in opposition. In the second of the two chapters, I will fill in some of the gaps in this model with insights from scientific medicine and public health.

Finally, Christian health practitioners must recognize some practical ways to begin to change their health and healing ministries – an extremely difficult task, given the urgency of medical and health needs that drain the increasingly scarce resources and already depleted personal reserves of health workers. The prayers of many Christian health workers focus upon God's daily renewal of personal strength, compassion, and love to minister gracefully to just one more person in a never-ending procession of suffering people – while at the same time trying to balance the complexities of rising costs in a time of shrinking resources. I approach this daunting task in the last chapter.

Notes

1   Once again, I cannot represent the tremendous variations throughout Africa or even the various types of traditional healers within a single cultural group. In this section, for instance, I do not highlight the work of traditional healers that relate to "natural" diseases or events. Some herbalists, bone-setters, and traditional midwives, for instance, practice without any explicit reference to personal etiologies of disease or the spirit world. Most often, however, traditional healers whose practices appear to more closely parallel the practices of

scientific medicine infuse their healing interventions with meanings derived from a decidedly non-scientific holism.

2   In the section to follow, I attempt to build an overall picture of the nature of healing practices rather than develop a rigid system of analysis and classification. It is impossible to impose mutually exclusive categories upon healing interventions. The least satisfactory way to understand and appreciate a complex mosaic is a minute examination of each individual piece.

3   The practice of expelling evil substances and spirits is a common one. Bleeding an afflicted person or "magical" surgery in which the traditional practitioner retrieves a foreign substance from the body of a sick person are both concrete representations of the expulsion of evil influences from the body.

4   Some apparent sacrifices among the Zionists have yet another significance. In some exorcisms, a chicken is sacrificed over a dinner plate so that the plate is covered in its blood. The plate is then broken and thrown away to demonstrate not appeasement but the final breaking of fellowship with the spirit (Daneel 1990).

5   The system of kinship among the Somali is greatly simplified in this saying.

Section II

Chapter 11

Medical Science and Shalom

◆ ◆ ◆

An elder approaches the council and looks for a place to sit. He carries his stool –
a unique seat by western standards. This stool has only three legs. Besides that,
instead of standing straight up and down, the legs run diagonally from the edge of
the seat. They cross in the middle where they are bound together with strong cord.
If that binding force collapses, so does the man. Likewise, if one leg is missing, the
man falls to the floor. But today, his stool has all three legs tied tightly together,
and the seat supports his weight.

I often think of such a villager and his stool when I consider the three-pronged
approach needed by Christian health workers in Africa – the three "legs" of med-
ical science, traditional wisdom, and the teachings of Scripture, all bound tightly
together by the strong, strong truth that God is the only Healer.

◆ ◆ ◆

INTRODUCTION

If a young Hebrew or African man, childless, rejected by his community,
and suffering in poverty, claimed on his deathbed that he possessed *sha-*
lom or wholeness, his friends would think that he had lost his mind. In
neither Hebrew nor African tradition was *shalom* or wholeness an ethereal
concept. In their understanding, shalom was not an inner peace in the

face of disintegrating prosperity, community, and health. Shalom was material and physical. Public health and medical practitioners would concur. A dying young man is not a healthy young man.

In this chapter I will narrow my focus. Because I intend to show how health sciences complement the understandings of the Bible and culture, I will focus on the area where they most overlap – the health of the human body. Hebrew, African, and scientific approaches to health converge in the importance of the human body to the experience of shalom in this world. Illness and disability limit the experience of shalom. A sick, dying, or physically or mentally disabled person may enjoy a full, happy life and close, intimate relationships but she cannot enjoy the fullness of shalom. We know this intuitively. How many parents, spouses, or siblings of a disabled person long for that person to remain eternally impaired? None. We long to see the fullness of that person's personality and emotions without the limitation of the disability.

There is no record in the Old Testament of the restoration of the lame, blind, or deaf. However, in response to a question from the imprisoned John the Baptist, Jesus cited his restoration of these disabilities as primary evidence of his authenticity as the Messiah (Matthew 11:1–6). Jesus' healing ministry was the pledge of full restoration one day.

Sickness limits the experience of shalom. After a long period of illness, we find that restoration to physical health restores our spirits and souls as well. God created us to be embodied. We cannot be disembodied and also whole beings as God created us. In God's eternal kingdom, we do not learn how to cope triumphantly over sickness and death but are separated from them forever.

Healing and restoration are signs of God's kingdom. All healing is mediated by physical or biochemical changes. When Jesus restored a withered hand, physical changes occurred. Flesh, muscle, and tendons were restored; the circulatory and nervous systems began to function; the biochemical and electrical processes within the brain that controlled the coordination and movement of fingers were reactivated.

DIVINE REVELATION, TRADITION, AND SCIENCE BOUND TOGETHER BY SCRIPTURAL AUTHORITY

In previous chapters, we saw how God's revelation of shalom and the healing power of his kingdom is shadowed in the traditional wisdom of

Africa. Scientific medicine and public health disciplines together represent a third set of insights that must inform biblically holistic health and healing ministry. Scientific medicine and the practice of public health focus upon the preservation of health and healing of disease and injury by understanding and altering the processes that mediate health and disease.

As mentioned earlier, some peoples of East Africa customarily sit upon a stool with three legs. The legs run from the edge of the seat diagonally, crossing in the middle where they are tied together. If the cord or fiber that binds them together breaks, the stool becomes useless. Also, if the stool had only one or two legs, a person sitting on it would lose balance and fall. However, a three-legged stool holds his weight. Christian workers who approach health and healing ministry in Africa with the tools and insights of only medical and public health science, only traditional wisdom, or only the teachings of the Bible will also lose their balance and effectiveness. The weight of ministry requires the balanced strength of all three legs.

But even this three-legged ministry will collapse in a disastrous heap if there is nothing that binds the legs together. The legs will slide away from one another. The cord that binds these three legs together and defines their relationship must be the authority of the Bible and the centrality of God as the only Healer.

Does tradition insist that ancestral or totemic spirits be consulted in diagnosing a problem? A relationship of faith to Jesus Christ from whom all healing springs must supplant these spirits in an integrated Christian ministry.

Does the culture of scientific medicine so dominate the ministry that all traditional belief and practice is uncritically lumped together as superstition? That culture, rooted in scientific arrogance, must be transformed to a culture of humble learning and personal respect in an integrated Christian ministry.

Is God's revelation placed in opposition to medicine so that consulting a physician is regarded as a violation of faith? That interpretation must be changed so that medicine is accepted as an expression of God's healing power in integrated Christian ministry.

The binding force of scriptural authority and the power of God assures that revelation, science, and tradition remain, each in its proper place. For a three-legged stool to bear weight, the legs must be attached to the seat of the stool in a triangular configuration, each playing its own role. All three legs are required but *no one leg can take the place of another* without the stool becoming unstable.

When I first tried to describe this concept to a visiting physician, he concluded that I was suggesting that traditional belief and practice were equal in importance to God's revealed truth and the insights of medicine. When bound together by the authority of scripture, the question is not one of relative importance but of relative position. We easily understand how traditional belief would have to cede to medical science or God's revelation.

One missionary physician told me that to treat some gynecological problems, the people would traditionally pack the vagina with a poultice of herbs and donkey dung, a healing practice that made sense within their worldview but that often introduced severe infection. Many traditional practices carry the potential of physical harm, however well intentioned they might be. Almost all Christian health workers are able to tell stories of repairing physical damage done to the body through traditional medicine. Science is better equipped than tradition to understand how medicines interact biochemically with the human body. Medicines and procedures developed through scientific inquiry are often better than those developed traditionally.[1]

Science has been poorly equipped, however, to understand how to right broken relationships that lead to disease and ill health. The missionary physician who told of the traditional treatment in the previous paragraph also told of reconstructing a stomach that had become so scarred through repeated ulcers that the opening to the intestine had finally fused together. When he explored the reasons for the ulceration, the patient, and eventually also the physician, attributed it to powerful but evil people who had been progressively moving the markers that demarcated the sick man's land. The man was a victim of others more powerful than he. Medical science had no tools to understand either the magnitude of the crime within a rural African setting or its solution.

The Law of Moses helped them understand the crime. Moving a boundary stone was as deserving of God's curse as murder, incest, or even bestiality (Deuteronomy 27:17). Depriving a person of the land that God had given to the family was a violation of the covenant relationship. This destroyed the integrity of the community, and eventually the well-being of the landholder and his family. Mosaic law offered no clue, however, to how the problem should be approached within the traditional culture of this African man. Even seeking the help of a witch to place a curse upon the perpetrators of the crime gave no certainty that he would regain his lost land. Righting this health problem would have required a knowledge of traditional wisdom.

How does traditional wisdom inform biblical revelation? Though I cannot remember who related this exchange to me, I clearly remember the impact in helping me see the Bible through different eyes. A missionary told the story of Joseph and his brothers to a group of rural African men for the first time and asked them what lessons they learned from it. The missionary intended to teach them that *Joseph's obedience* brought *him* great blessing from God. After considerable discussion, the men concluded that *Joseph's continued loyalty to his family*, despite the treachery of his brothers, resulted in the survival of the *entire clan*. Neither interpretation of the story challenged its authority but both were shaped by the worldviews of the interpreters. In fact, the meaning that the African men gave to that story probably fits better with an understanding of the Abrahamic covenant than the individualistic interpretation.

Later, as I wrestled with how to challenge a widely shared belief that AIDS was the result of a curse, I realized that never once in my Christian life had I received biblical instruction about blessings and curses. I came to recognize that tradition informed biblical revelation not by challenging its authority but by raising new questions and opening my mind to new, legitimate interpretations.

Bound together by the authority of God's Word and sustained by his healing power, each leg of effective health and healing ministry complements the other in its uniqueness.

DIVINE REVELATION, TRADITION, AND SCIENCE REPRESENT COMPLEMENTARY PATHS TO UNDERSTANDING

Divine revelation stands in a category by itself. Because revealed truth is not derived from observation, the key questions are ones of authority and obedience. The Hebrews who obeyed God's laws concerning diseases and ceremonial cleansing were spared many of the diseases that afflicted the Egyptians and other countries about them. The Israelites did not have to know how their obedience related to the spread of infection for them to be healthy.

The limitations of this approach are clear. If health interventions are based on authority alone, they are limited in their effectiveness by the knowledge and character of the authority figure. Claiming divine authority for a diagnosis or prescribed treatment is obviously not sufficient to establish its effectiveness. Accepting the word of the wrong authority can be dangerous and even fatal. Secondly, even if the revelation is from our God who is in fact all knowing and of perfect, loving character, the revelation may be misinterpreted. Thirdly, exclusive dependence upon divine revelation to address issues of health and healing often leads to passivity or fanaticism. There is no path to knowledge in areas where the authority is silent.

Unlike divine revelation, traditional and scientific approaches to health are both rooted in observation. Scientific observations are specific, not general. Findings are expressed in probabilistic statements that become part of the scientific literature reflecting and shaping theory; not in pithy, authoritative sayings that become part of oral tradition, reflecting and shaping worldview. Tradition and science follow different paths to understanding. I need not look beyond my own family to begin to understand the complementarity of the two approaches.

My wife, Kendra, and I learn about the world in two distinctly different ways. I am analytic. In order to *really* understand something, I need to be able to analyze it – to take it apart and understand how its constituent pieces relate to one another. Kendra, on the other hand, is contextual. For her to *really* understand something, she needs to see it in its context.

The differences became obvious when we studied Bengali together. I quickly developed a better understanding of the grammar of the language. I would ask my teacher questions like, "How would I say, 'If the villagers decide together that they did not want to participate in the program, what steps might we take to persuade them to reconsider their decision?'" It is not so much that I would ever actually say that awkward sentence, but that Bengali grammar was, for me, a puzzle to be solved. Alternately I might ask how the religious vocabulary derived from Arabic reflected a different worldview from the religious vocabulary derived from Sanskrit.

However, Kendra would ask, "When it's time to leave the home where I have been a guest, what kinds of things should I say?" At the end of our three months of training, I could (given enough time to think about it) construct grammatically precise sentences with a very limited vocabulary.

Kendra knew how to carry on a conversation in the situations she most often encountered in daily life. Even if she did not always get the verb tenses or word order quite right, she was able to communicate and to build relationships. In part because of her learning style, Kendra profited more from our three months of language study than I did.

On the other hand, when Kendra was struggling with her thesis, I was able to devise conceptual models to explain her findings far more quickly than she. Because of my analytic learning style, I was able to organize findings particular to a specific context into paradigms that could be applied in diverse settings.

Traditional wisdom is contextual. Wise people observe associations between events and derive lessons from them. Whether or not the lessons can be applied outside their setting is not an important question. To derive these lessons, the learners do not need to know how a behavior is tied to a particular outcome. The Lugandan proverb, *"Ombuiri kisaka: ekivaamu kye kikulya"* (The human body is like a thicket: what comes out of it can devour you) captures a medical and social truth. Wise observers noted through the years that exposure to bodily excretions could make others ill. They also noted that bad behaviors that come from the body could cause harm. What happened inside the body was hidden from their view, however, as a thicket hides a wild animal.

Traditional wisdom is not limited to proverbs and oral tradition. Complex systems of health and treatment may emerge that organize traditional wisdom into unified abstract systems of medical thought and practice such as Ayurvedic medicine or homeopathy. The Office of Alternative Medicine (OAM) in the National Institutes of Health (NIH) in the United States divides sixty-one alternative medical practices into seven categories. Under "Alternative Systems of Medical Practice" the OAM lists fourteen complex systems of medical practice rooted in traditional wisdom (National Institutes of Health 1995).

Whether in the form of a proverb or alternative medical system, traditional wisdom is based upon associations observed within a limited context. Traditional practitioners, therefore, may prescribe the right precaution for the wrong reason, or, alternately, the wrong precaution for the right reason. Community members who avoided bodily secretions of sick people because they believed in the wisdom of the proverb would contract fewer infectious diseases than those who ignored this advice – even if they did not understand how disease and excretions were related to one another.

In some parts of Africa, on the other hand, people had long noticed an association between the amount of liquid consumed and the volume and frequency of diarrhea – a correct observation. They also wanted to decrease the severity of the diarrhea – a worthy end. So when their children had diarrhea, parents stopped feeding them breast milk, water, or food – a deadly solution.

Traditional wisdom is also its own judge. The tradition dictates the criteria by which the fit of the diagnosis and effectiveness of the treatment are to be evaluated. This practice easily leads to a closed system in which every event has an explanation within the system itself. When traditional wisdom becomes encapsulated in a self-contained system with few external referents, learning and progress either stop or move very slowly. Because the traditional management of diarrhea was never analyzed, intervention by intervention, by criteria external to its context, the deadly nature of withholding fluids never came to light. Deaths were attributed to forces operating in spite of the traditional practice, not because of it.

Science is analytic. Like tradition, science is based upon observation. Unlike tradition, however, science limits itself to those aspects of the world that can be measured. Science also has developed strict rules of inquiry to identify associations that are likely to be real and exclude those that are false.

Medical researchers focus upon the processes of life and disease within the body. They strive to understand how the body functions and how these functions may be altered through health related interventions. In order to do this, medical scientists must break the functioning of the body into its constituent processes and parts. Why do they follow this path to knowledge?

First, the physical functions that maintain life in persons and animals can be examined, manipulated, and measured. Of the components that blend together to form men and women in their wholeness, only the body is material. Additionally, processes of the human body share many similarities with the bodily processes of other animals. Medical scientists can learn much about how human bodies function and how these functions can be manipulated by examining what happens in animals.

Second, the body is not simply a throw-away container for the soul. The health of the body and the health of the person are intimately linked. Additionally, the body is the means whereby men and women relate to the physical world, including one another. Effective medical and surgical interventions that emerge from medical research improve the total quality of life even though their focus is highly constrained.

Third, though medical and surgical interventions could be developed through trial and error alone, they are developed more effectively from in-depth understandings of bodily processes and structures.

For all of its power to do good, scientific medicine has its dangers. First, if clinicians permit the limitations of this approach to knowledge to define the limitations of their practice, they become technicians and not healers. Clinicians who limit their knowledge and interventions only to what can be physically measured and manipulated never actually treat people but only a series of illnesses and injuries. They suffer the same limitations as healers that I suffered as a language student – able to construct grammatically complex sentences correctly but unable to communicate effectively. I concentrated upon getting the mechanics of the language right but lost sight of the fact that the purpose of language was to communicate. In the same way, clinicians may concentrate on the science of medicine and forget that the purpose of medicine is to heal.

Complex interactions are often overlooked in the modern practice of medicine. Medicine often attends only to the most proximate cause of an illness or injury, ignoring the extended web of causation. Scientific medicine provides a wide range of tools to combat an infection, fewer to address a compromised immune system that failed to protect the person against the infection, even fewer to address the fear that weakened the immune response, and none to address the interpersonal conflict that led to the pronouncement of a fearsome curse. Scientific medicine is only beginning to understand the mechanisms of the mind-body relationship, and most clinicians are ill equipped to understand those interactions.

Finally, scientific medicine can create a culture in which its unique strengths and analytic approaches to learning become the exclusive evaluative criteria by which health interventions are judged. Among clinicians, the word "unscientific" is an epithet rather than a description of complementarity. Faced with the sometimes destructive consequences of indigenous healing practices, they come to regard all traditional wisdom as superstition. In denying the validity of other paths to health knowledge, they secularize their ministry and constrain God's revelation to their personal lives and "spiritual" ministries, never permitting it to inform their practice.

All three legs to the stool are needed to bear the weight of health and healing ministry. Each of these paths to insights in health and healing ministry has strengths and limitations inherent to its underlying presuppositions and methods of inquiry. The Christian health practitioner must learn from each of them.

Miraculous healings by God, traditional practices, and scientific medicine all share some common characteristics.

1. They all relate to the created order.
2. They all reflect the power of God to heal.
3. They complement one another.

1. *Miraculous healing, scientific, and traditional medicine all relate to created order*

In examining how science, tradition, and revelation contribute to understanding and maintaining bodily health, or how healing is mediated by physical changes, it is hard not to fall back into a dualistic worldview. In health and healing ministry, the science of medicine is often set in opposition to holistic or spiritual healing. The very English vocabulary of "natural" and "supernatural" or "miraculous" and "ordinary" presumes this dualism. In the West, we put great emphasis upon *authenticating* miracles, a task that would be meaningless to the Hebrews or within many African traditions.

> The term *nature*, which implies an autonomous, self-sustained universe, is not found in Hebrew thought. Rather, the word used for this world and its order is *bara'* (created). The term, in fact, is a verb and implies an origin in, and continued dependence upon, God. To us, some events may seem ordinary and others extraordinary, but all are due to the active, sustaining hand of God. In the biblical sense, no birth of a child is "natural," nor any divine healing "unnatural" in the sense of being contrary to the divinely created order.
>
> We first need to see all healing as God's work. If we place too much emphasis on "miraculous" healing, we are in danger of reinforcing secularism. To overstress the miraculous implies what is not miraculous is natural and can be explained without God (Heibert 1994, 234).

As long as we conceptually divide God's work into the miraculous and ordinary, the natural and supernatural, we are fated to place spiritual and physical health ministries into two distinctive categories and struggle to define their relationship to one another. One is material; the other immaterial. If we define health and healing ministry as an expression of God's character and power in his created order, we escape the trap of that definition. All healing becomes divine healing.

Positive and negative emotions and states of mind affect physical health because cultures, emotions, and the pressure that the blood exerts against the walls of a blood vessel are all linked in God's created order. Satan, demons, and angels are a part of God's created order. Medical interventions that alter the biochemical, mechanical, or electrical processes of the body also affect the immaterial heart and soul.

Recognition that all healing interventions fall within the created order also provides a new set of evaluative criteria that transcend medicine and tradition. Traditional healing practices that are harmful to the body usually fail not because of the intent of the healer but because of his or her incomplete understanding of the created order. Science gives us effective tools for understanding the material rules that underlie God's created order. Recognizing the limitations of science, however, frees health practitioners to be learners who recognize that scientific tools are only one set that they must master to be effective in health and healing ministry. Understanding of God's creation may be broadened and deepened by those who have structured their understanding with a different set of tools.

When clinicians identify with others as fellow creatures who are seeking to understand the Creator and the rules of his creation, they are free to ask new questions and find new patterns of ministry. Instead of struggling to define the relationship between medical and spiritual ministry, Christian clinicians can ask how their practice of medicine affects the immaterial reflections of God's image in their patients. As they seek to understand disease and health, they can search God's created order not only for a pathogen or pattern of exposure to harmful substances but also for a broken relationship, fear, or stress. Instead of condemning all traditional belief because of the areas that remain dark and destructive, they can rejoice as they listen and acquire understandings of God's created order that science cannot deduce.

2. All Healing an Expression of God's Power

All healing comes from God. Healing practices, whether they are a direct intervention of God or mediated by the created order, are all empowered by him.

First, God may choose to heal a person by directly intervening in his creation. These are the healing miracles in which God's power is not mediated by "natural" processes in ways that we can understand. Jesus' healing ministry did not amaze the Hebrews just because it was "supernatural" but because it was also the promised sign of the powerful coming of God's kingdom. Jesus demonstrated God's power in his healing ministry.

Can the forces of Satan command healing? It seems so. The Israelites were surrounded by other nations with priests and healers who served gods other than Yahweh. God forbade Israel to turn to these gods for the promise of shalom (Brown 1995). The priests of these gods apparently commanded some healing power, perhaps exercised directly and perhaps mediated by the belief of the person who came to them for help. The same is true of traditional healers, including those who use divination and who, wittingly or unwittingly, call upon powers of darkness in their healing. Again, whether their healing power is direct or mediated, it is often effective.

In alerting his disciples of the end of the age, Jesus acknowledged that the false "christs" will perform great signs and wonders (Matthew 24:24) apparently including healing (Revelation 13:12–14). Even if evil forces can sometimes heal in order to deceive, the power they command still comes from God. As part of the created order, Satan and his angels have only the power that God has delegated to them and that he has not yet chosen to take away.

Secondly, most healing is mediated by the restorative power that God created within the processes of the human body. The motto of Tenwek Hospital in Kenya is "We Treat. Jesus Heals." What does that motto mean? What about a little girl who comes to the outpatient clinic with bacterial pneumonia? If the doctor gives her a course of antibiotics and she recovers within a week, where is Jesus in that process? If the child had received the same antibiotic from the chemist in the village pharmacy, she probably would have recovered just about as quickly. The truth of the motto lies not in the faith of the child, her parents, or the caregiver. It does not even lie in whatever prayer she received, for she would have probably recovered without prayer. A dose of antibiotic is neither Christian nor pagan. The healing was not a direct and instant intervention of God. The truth of the motto lies in an understanding of God's healing power.

Dr. Paul Brand regards the healing power that we commonly experience each day as even greater evidence of God's might than his direct healing interventions.

> Even for us Christian physicians, I think it is a necessary discipline that we foster that sense of wonder and appreciation of the human body. I find that to some Christians, the idea that God had to work out the details of all these wonderful systems of chemistry and physics somehow detracts from their concept of his omnipotence. They like to think of God waving a wand or speaking a word and everything happens without anything that would correspond to what we would call careful planning. To me, the idea of God having to sit down and think out how to make blood clot at once when it spills yet never clot inside the system does not detract from my concept of his greatness, but enhances it. (Brand 1995, 44)

The effectiveness of all healing or preventive interventions depends upon the healing power that God designed in the human body as part of his created order. Jesus created the healing process in the body (John 1:1–3) and sustains it by his power (Hebrews 1:3). The "natural" healing powers of the body are derived from his power in the design and sustaining of his creation. Jesus' creative and sustaining word is no less a word of healing than the words that he spoke to the sick crowded about him in the towns and fields of Galilee.

Finally, treatment itself is an exercise of the dominion and authority that God gave to men and women as their creation gift. Healing interventions, whether they emerge from traditional wisdom, public health, or scientific medicine, are effective when they either strengthen the healing power of the body or weaken the destructive powers of disease and injury opposing it. Effective healing interventions have two things in common regardless of their source. First, the intervention emerges from some level of understanding about the working of the created order. The understanding may be general and contextualized or highly specific and scientific. Secondly, the intervention must alter some aspect of the material or immaterial processes that affect the health of the person. The power to understand and exercise dominion over God's created order was given to us by him.

The three legs of effective health and healing ministry in Africa – revelation, traditional wisdom, and science – represent three distinctive paths to knowledge, all relate to the created order, and are all expressions of

God's power to heal and sustain health. Finally, they represent interdependent approaches to health and healing interventions.

3. *Miraculous healing, scientific and traditional practice may complement one another*

How can health workers in Africa combat childhood deaths from acute respiratory diseases?

Health is not built, nor disease and injury treated, through a single intervention. Lowering deaths from acute respiratory disease in Africa requires multiple interventions involving the insights and methods of medical and public health science, biblical revelation, and traditional wisdom and values.

The matrix in Figure 1 illustrates how a health issue may be approached holistically. I have extensively modified a matrix originally developed to examine the range of interventions in injury prevention and treatment (Haddon). In designing interventions in regard to acute respiratory infections, for instance, the Christian health worker must consider three basic dimensions of health and disease.

A health worker developing interventions to reduce mortality from pneumonia must first consider the time line of the illness. An intervention may be directed toward: (1) preventing acute respiratory infections (primary prevention or promotion), (2) treating acute infections when they occur and preventing progression into a more serious condition (treatment and secondary prevention), and (3) helping the child back to full health once the acute infection itself has been addressed (rehabilitation or restoration).

The health worker must also consider the target of the intervention. Will it be directed toward individuals, communities, or organizations and institutions? In addition, the health worker should consider the nature of the intervention itself. Will the intervention be drawn largely from science, from relationship to God through revelation, or from tradition?

Interventions in acute respiratory infections may be directed toward individuals

Interventions at different stages of the disease episode may be rooted in science, biblical revelation, and cultural traditions.

1.   The intervention might address issues of personal hygiene and care. Respiratory infections may be prevented, for instance, by avoiding

Table 11.1

Units of Intervention in Biblically Holistic Health and Healing Ministry

UNITS OF INTERVENTION	SEQUENCE OF INTERVENTIONS		
	Primary Prevention and Promotion	Treatment and Secondary Prevention	Rehabilitation and Restoration
Relationship to Self (Individual)			
Hygiene and personal care			
Caregiving			
Risk behaviors			
Identity, worth, and efficacy			
Relationship to Others (Community)			
Family			
Community (Church)			
Population groups			
Government and regulatory agencies			
Caregiving organizations and agencies			
Relationship to the Environment			
Patterns of exposure to harm			
Economic structures and employment			
Cultural practices, values, and beliefs			

the spread of the pathogens through the air or through unwashed hands. This primary prevention intervention is rooted in the scientific understanding of disease.

2. The intervention may be addressed toward caregiving. Prompt recognition, diagnosis and treatment of pneumonia with antibiotics is a treatment intervention rooted in science. In a communal setting a person other than a parent, perhaps an older sibling or grandparent, might be the primary caregiver. A health worker could train that person to help the sick child recuperate. This intervention would combine scientific knowledge with traditional practice in the restoration of the child's health.

3. The intervention might be addressed toward behaviors that either put the child at risk or strengthen her resistance. If a child is approaching the age to be weaned during the season of the year with the most respiratory infections, a health worker might encourage the child's mother to continue breast-feeding until the risk of infection has decreased. This would probably strengthen the child's resistance through the milk itself and the continued warm intimacy with the mother as well as decrease the risk of infection by limiting exposure to other infected children. In cultures where outside pressures are causing mothers to wean their children at progressively earlier ages, the health worker might also appeal to traditional understandings of how breast-feeding and the welfare of the child are related.

4. The intervention may be addressed toward issues of worth, identity, and efficacy. Parents who had already lost one child to respiratory infection, for instance, might become passive in the face of another seriously ill child, feeling, perhaps, that the child's disease is a punishment from God. Those parents may need, first of all, a restoration of a right relationship to God and an understanding of the significance of their behavior to the health of their child. Secondly, they may need specific instruction in how to care for sick children and the assurance that they are able to do it. These interventions integrate the insights of science, biblically based spiritual understandings that challenge traditional belief, and the reinforcement of traditional understandings of parental responsibility.

Interventions may be directed not only toward individuals but also toward groups and structures associated with communities.

1. Some interventions may be directed toward nuclear or extended families. To be effective in a communal setting, for example, efforts to control infection through frequent hand washing require the understanding and cooperation of the entire family, particularly those who are primary care givers to younger children.

2. Community interventions are also important. In urban settings, many parents do not have extended family members living nearby. Both father and mother often work to pay school fees and maintain the family. When a child is sick, this pattern is disturbed. Churches may need to organize to provide for some of the needs of families with sick children, particularly if the sickness is chronic or severe. If the child requires hospitalization, the church community may need to help with the costs of treatment. These interventions spring from biblical teaching as well as African traditions of mutual support.

3. Some interventions, particularly those using mass media, may be addressed to population groups at risk. Educational campaigns to help parents distinguish between a cold and a more serious infection requiring referral might be organized through elementary schools or maternal and child health clinics.

4. The spread of respiratory diseases may be affected by the rules and policies of governments and regulatory agencies. If elementary schools, for instance, continue to accept all the students that somehow manage to drag themselves through the door each morning regardless of their health, respiratory diseases may spread rapidly. The schools may need to develop policies regarding when a child may be sent home for illness, inform the parents, and then enforce those policies.

5. The care-giving institutions may themselves be the target of interventions. Outpatient clinics in urban areas, for instance, might need to add evening or early morning hours if children are to have access to care. A hospital may need to change visiting rules to permit parents to remain with young children who must be hospitalized. To broaden its ministry a larger Christian hospital might wish to train counselors who are equipped to comfort seriously ill children in ways appropriate to their age.

Interventions may be directed toward the environment.

1. Children living near industries that pollute the air are more suscepti-
    ble to respiratory infection than those living where the air is clean. It
    is appropriate for Christian health workers to address interventions
    toward environmental factors that affect health.
2. Issues related to economic structures and employment also affect
    child health. Lower paid workers who have neither insurance nor
    money are more likely to delay care than those who have greater
    financial resources.
3. Finally, patterns of cultural practice and tradition may affect the
    health of a child with a respiratory infection but interventions are
    impossible to design without knowing what beliefs exist.
    (a) Are there herbal medicines in traditional use for respiratory
         infections? Are they medicinally harmful or helpful?
    (b) Are respiratory infections associated with disturbances in any
         particular set of relationships? How should Christian health
         workers respond in diagnosis and care?
    (c) What practices of prevention and care for the sick now exist?
         How may the helpful ones be strengthened through new under-
         standings? How may harmful ones be weakened while still pre-
         serving the healing intent?

I have shown how the matrix may be used as a planning tool in order to
illustrate the complementary nature of interventions directed toward the
multiple aspects of shalom and springing from God's revelation, science,
and tradition. The use of the matrix also illustrates some of the other
important principles of this chapter.

*   As a planning tool, the matrix is specific to a particular problem but
    encompasses all the relationships that comprise *shalom*. While I chose
    to use respiratory infections in the illustration, the matrix could also be
    used to explore other problems such as violence and even poverty.

*   The idea of the matrix is not to fill in every cell with one intervention
    from the Bible, one from tradition, and one from science. Choosing the
    appropriate interventions is far more important than having all of the
    cells filled.

*   The matrix demands synthetic, multidisciplinary thinking. It cannot
    be completed within the bounds of a single discipline or approach.
    Interventions that depend upon the resources and evaluative criteria of a

single discipline cannot be holistic in a biblical sense. Any approach that depends wholly upon a single set of understandings will be bound by the limitations of these understandings and cannot be holistic.

• Fielding biblically holistic health programs requires the diversity of skills, gifts, and cultures that comprise the Body of Christ. Biblically holistic programs must transcend multiple boundaries. *Christian physicians cannot practice biblically holistic health care alone; neither can pastors nor priests.* No one person, regardless of his or her profession, can practice biblically holistic health care. The practice of such care requires an interdependent community of co-workers who together are empowered by God for ministry.

In biblical health and healing, health science is but one of the three legs that must bear the weight of ministry. The implications of this approach are eminently practical. Scientific medicine must take its place as a servant of healing ministry and not its master.

Notes

1   I am in no way intending to discount the great potential of traditional medicines as biomedical cures. Quinine is just one of the medicines that originated in the study of traditional practices. These studies should be encouraged and continued. We should also recognize, however, that assigning value to traditional medicines based upon their biochemical properties reflects a scientific rather than traditional worldview. The "power" of a medicine from a scientific worldview depends only upon its physical properties, a far more narrow perspective than the concepts of "power" in African traditions.

Chapter 12

Witch Doctors, Alternative Medicine, and the Common Grace of Health and Healing

◆ ◆ ◆

Imagine the following scene in the camp of the Israelites during Joshua's campaign to capture the lands of the Canaanites. Spies have just returned from a Canaanite city.

"The plague in the Canaanite city has ended," Othniel reported to the others who had met together to discuss strategy.

"Are you sure?" asked Zelophehad. "Surely Yahweh would not bless our enemies. You must be mistaken. The last scouting party said that the plague was great. The people were weak and rarely left their dwellings. We could have taken the city with little fighting."

"That has changed," said Othniel. "And let me tell you what else I saw. I saw men and women outside the city and they buried their waste just as we do. I also saw a group of those who were sick in a camp outside the city gates. Those who brought them food and drink washed before going back into the city again."

"Has Yahweh become the God of the Canaanites?" Zelophehad asked. "They are following our Law. Or has Yahweh taken away the plague because of sin in our own camp? I do not want to fight another Ai."

"No, I saw their worship," replied Othniel. "They continue to sacrifice to their abominable images. But the plague has also stopped. Could it be that their gods have stopped the plague?"

Eleazar the priest, who had listened to the conversation in thoughtful silence, now spoke and there was a note of alarm in his voice. "No, do not even say those words. Stone images do not heal. If the plague has stopped, Yahweh stopped it. But I am disturbed. Why would Yahweh bless those who do not worship him? There must be sin in our camp. We must call the people together and examine them."

◆   ◆   ◆

HEALTH, HEALING, AND COMMON GRACE

This highly unlikely debate never took place – at least not among the Israelites. If we could have traveled through time to participate in the discussion, we would have been tempted to interrupt and say, "Yes, the blessing of Yahweh did stop the plague, even for the Canaanites, but not because Yahweh became their God. It is because they followed a law that Yahweh gave to protect you from sickness in ways you do not yet understand." We might then launch into a lecture on the germ theory of disease and how even unknowing obedience to the laws of God was protecting the Canaanites. If we could put ourselves in the place of these Israelites, but with our medical knowledge of today, we would not doubt Yahweh's work as healer or the exclusivity of his relationship to us, his people.

Though the ancient Israelites probably never debated this issue, modern Christians do. Increasingly health and medical researchers agree that spirituality, measured by practices such as prayer and meditation, participation in religious activity, and sincere belief, contributes to the maintenance of health and promotes healing.[1] Our first response is to rejoice that health and medical research appears to support the message of the Bible; but there is a catch. The beneficial effects appear not to be tied to Christianity alone but to spiritual practices that span a broad range of religious belief.

We feel trapped. We dare not deny the authenticity of the research but we are also reluctant to admit that God would bless both Buddhists and Christians who meditate daily. We ask, like the imaginary Israelites, "Why would God bless with health those who do not worship him?"

In fields such as psychoimmunology evidence continues to mount for the link between spirituality and health. Research will continue to reveal the complexity of the interactions between emotions, belief, mind, and body. As Christians, we should welcome this empirical affirmation that God has created us as more than physical beings. This growing body of evidence, however, is not now and never can be effectively marshaled as an argument for the truth of the gospel of Jesus Christ.

Why did the Canaanites in our imaginary account escape disease? They lowered the rate of infection by properly disposing of wastes and by isolating contagious persons. Why does "religious practice" promote health and well-being? God created each one of us as whole beings so that the activities and emotions that accompany many expressions of spirituality also promote well-being. The link between spirituality and health is one of common grace rooted in the way we are created.

THE HEALING POWER OF PRAYER: GOD OR SCIENCE

God hears those who come to him in Jesus' name and responds as a loving father. But the very act of praying may hasten healing even if it is not directed toward the true God. Can we separate these two sources of God's healing power? No, not with certainty.[2] To suppose that we can is to revert to a dichotomy between body and spirit, the natural and supernatural, that poorly reflects the way we are created and the way that God heals.

God's sovereignty is the ultimate confounding variable in any study on spirituality, health, and healing. Because God may respond to the prayers of both Christians and non-Christians alike with restoration or death and because God created us so that many spiritual disciplines enhance the healing power of the body, scientific study may only illumine Christian belief (just as Pasteur's discovery of germs illumined certain aspects of the Old Testament Law) but not establish its truth.

Therefore we cannot argue that because some intervention has a healing effect, the theological or philosophical body of thought in which it is rooted must also be true. Just because an African recovers after a witch doctor's healing interventions lift a burden of fear does not mean that the witch doctor's beliefs are true, good, or godly.

Just as the just and the unjust have learned to harness God's gift of rain to grow food, the just and unjust can also discover and apply God's common grace of health and healing. In the remaining portion of this chapter, I will show how traditional religious belief and practice promotes health and healing.

COMMON GRACE IN HEALTH: PRINCIPLES OF HEALTHY LIVING ASSOCIATED WITH AFRICAN BELIEF

People who find meaning in their lives are healthier and cope better with bad events than those who cannot.

Nothing happens by chance in traditional African belief. In sickness and calamity as well as extraordinarily good fortune, entire families and even communities try to discern what lies behind the events they observe. Eventually they arrive at a consensus that gives the event meaning within the context of their worldview. Finding meaning, particularly in the face of traumatic events, is a key element in successfully coping with them.

In general, religious belief is associated with the development of better coping skills.

- Among 850 elderly men confined to a hospital for serious disease, those who used explicitly religious coping strategies were significantly less depressed than those who tried to cope without religious strategies (Koenig et al. 1992).
- Caregivers (caring for patients with cancer and Alzheimer's disease) who indicated a strong religious faith and practice were emotionally more healthy than those who indicated little or no faith (Rabins et al. 1990).
- Though the initial response of religious adolescents to the death of a brother or sister was more severe than the response of non-religious adolescents, their long-term ability to overcome depression and confusion was greater (Balk 1991). Most parents forced to witness the slow death of their child from chronic disease found that the religious beliefs that helped them to cope with the initial loss strengthened in the year that followed (Cook and Wimberley 1983).

Religious belief improves coping skills because it allows people to find meaning in what happens to them. Religious adolescents initially reacted more strongly to the death of their sibling than those without faith because of the dissonance between the harsh reality of their sibling's death and their belief in God. Over the course of the following months, however, they were able to assign meaning to the events surrounding the death of their brother or sister while the non-religious adolescents continued to suffer confusion and depression (Balk 1991).

Most religious patients severely ill from cancer reported that they

gained faith and increased their frequency of prayer and church attendance even though they were not able to rationally reconcile their illness
with God's power and justice. The majority of the patients maintained
that God had a reason for their cancer even though they did not yet know
what it was (Moschella et al. 1997). Meaning sprang from faith rather
than a strictly rational process.

Outward religious behavior alone appears not to strengthen coping
skills in difficult times if it fails to provide a sense of meaning. In a study
of 114 patients with cancer, those whose beliefs led them to new meaning
in life through their cancer were less anxious than those whose religious
behavior and beliefs failed to give meaning to their suffering. In another
study, women who scored high on religiosity were more satisfied with
their lives than those who scored low, but the effect was mediated by their
ability to sense some purpose in their lives (Chamberlain and Zika 1988).

The struggle to construct meaning in life often leads to religious belief.
A group of elderly patients who structured their life experiences into a
coherent story reported that they were better able to face death. Of these
elderly men and women, those who reported that they were "less religious" at the beginning of the study discovered that their religious life
deepened as they constructed their life stories and began to attribute
meaning to the events of their lives (Georgemiller and Getsinger 1987).

In an in-depth study of caregivers who attended their partners dying of
AIDS, Folkman (1997) discovered a constant interplay between the
depressing, tiring, and negative experiences of caring for loved ones as
they slipped inevitably toward death, and the positive, life affirming, and
redeeming meanings that they created out of their experiences. She discovered four processes that contributed to the ability of the caregivers to
cope with their difficult tasks and eventual bereavement.

- *Positive reappraisal:* Caregivers reinterpreted events in order to see
  them in a positive light. One caregiver, for instance, reframed the
  struggle to help the dying person through severe night sweats from a
  sleepless, emotionally, and physically draining task to an expression of
  love.
- *Goal-directed, problem-focused coping:* In order to retain some sense of
  control in a worsening situation the caregivers focused upon the successful mastery of discrete activities and skills, such as learning to
  administer IV fluids. The caregivers constantly adjusted their goals to
  fit the declining condition of the dying person and monitored the

outcomes. Early in the course of the disease, the goals might have been to get the person with AIDS to take all the medicines on time or to eat and drink healthy foods. As the person with AIDS approached death, the goals included things like planning for the funeral service, preventing the person from suffering severe pain, or informing and scheduling visits from family and friends.

- *Spiritual beliefs and practices:* Explicitly spiritual beliefs and practices were most important to those caregivers who were bereaved during the course of the study. They were better able to positively reappraise the person's death and to find continuing hope.
- *Giving positive meanings to ordinary events:* Those who were dying and their caregivers consciously assigned positive meaning to daily events, particularly those communicating love and care, that resulted in a greater sense of control or self-esteem, or that distracted them from the heavy burden of everyday life.

The parallels between these coping strategies and traditional beliefs about disease, health, and healing in Africa are striking. Traditional healers, family, and community members transform life events from disconnected anecdotes into coherent stories that explain the past and also direct and inform events in the present. Traditional healers focus the attention of the sick and their families on accomplishing a healing task within their scope of mastery, increase belief in the power of their interventions, and nurture hope by giving positive meaning to daily events. Once understanding of a particular event is achieved by attributing meaning to it, people and communities also have a better idea of how to control future outcomes.

People who believe that they can change their lives are healthier than those who feel helpless to change.

Africans who go to traditional practitioners for guidance in discovering what has gone wrong to make them ill or bring about bad events are trying to restore some feeling of control.

Helplessness and Disease

People, for instance, who approach breast cancer and melanoma passively, with a sense that there is nothing they can do about it, tend to recover less quickly and die quicker than those who aggressively combat their disease to gain mastery over it. In fact, patients that medical personnel evaluate as troublesome, because they question their treatment and make suggestions, have been shown to live longer than those who are "well-adjusted." Laboratory studies of these people to measure the activity level of natural killer cells demonstrated that the immune system was more actively engaged in the fight against disease among those who fight to retain control than those who accept their diagnosis passively (Levy 1986).

In another study, half of the occupants of a nursing home were told that they had the primary responsibilty of caring for themselves and were given simple daily choices to make. The other half were told that they would be well cared for by the staff and that they should be happy. The actual level of care that both groups received did not differ. Several weeks later, those whose sense of control was enhanced were happier, more alert and active, and in better health than the second group. A year and a half later twice as many (30%) of the men and women in the second group had died than those in the first (15%) (Peterson and Seligman 1987).

Self-Efficacy

Isn't a sense of control illusionary in some instances? Yes, but a certain level of illusion appears to be helpful, giving both a protective and healing effect. A sense of self-efficacy, the belief not only that certain behaviors lead to better outcomes but that persons are capable of undertaking these behaviors, has been identified as a critical factor in adopting and maintaining good health habits (Roskies and Lazarus 1980). Persons with a high sense of self-efficacy are more successful than those with a low level of self-efficacy in quitting smoking, in controlling their weight, in protecting themselves from sexually transmitted diseases and unwanted pregnancies, and maintaining a healthy regimen of exercise (Strecher et al. 1986). Recently widowed women who felt that they exercised control over their bereavement showed a lower level of physical dysfunction than those who felt out of control (Gass 1987). Elderly (over 60 years) men and women who felt that they could effectively deal with stress in their lives also demonstrated less fear of dying than those who doubted their ability to handle stress (Koenig 1988).

Meaning and Control: Patterns of Attribution

People's sense of meaning and control are bound together in how they answer the question of "Why do bad (and good) things happen?" People who attribute bad events to causes beyond their control are more likely to remain passive in situations that they could potentially change. Internal, stable, and global patterns of attribution for bad events are the most debilitating and most closely associated with poor health.

> An internal explanation points to something about the self (e.g., "It's me") and makes loss of self-esteem following a bad event more likely. A stable explanation refers to long-lasting causes (e.g., "It's the way the world is") and is apt to produce chronic difficulties in the wake of bad events. A global explanation specifies a pervasive determinant (e.g., "It's going to undermine everything that I do") and increases the likelihood that bad events will produce widespread problems (Peterson and Seligman 1987, 240).

In a fascinating study, researchers reviewed newspaper reports to collect the responses of thirty Hall of Fame baseball players to good and bad events in their baseball careers. Those who gave internal, stable, and global explanations for bad events in baseball games died earlier than those who did not (Peterson and Seligman 1987). In another study, 172 college students were tested in regard to their explanatory style for bad events, and measurements were made of their health one month and one year afterwards. Those who gave stable and global explanations for bad events were more likely to be sick (from colds, sore throats, flu, etc.) than those that gave unstable, specific explanation (Peterson and Seligman 1987).

These findings help to explain some of the paradoxical findings of some studies on religion and the sense of control. To recognize the hand of God (or spirits) in shaping everyday happenings, good and bad, does not result in passive helplessness if it is combined with a conviction that people can affect God's actions.

Why is this so?

How does this relationship between a feeling of helplessness and poor health work? Why do those who attribute bad events to forces beyond their control, either internal or external, experience poor health? There are several possible reasons (Peterson and Seligman 1987).

- They may become passive in facing illness.
- They may not follow good health behaviors and thus increase the risk of disease and injury.
- They tend to be poor problem-solvers and may not be able to see

possible solutions and courses of action.

- They are more likely to be lonely because they tend to be more socially withdrawn.
- They are more likely to suffer depression.
- They have less competent immune systems.

Control, Christian Belief, and African Tradition

How may these truths be used therapeutically? William Backus (1996), a Christian psychologist, counsels people facing illness to substitute healing beliefs drawn from their faith for the false beliefs that delay recovery and lead to helplessness. The healing beliefs that he prescribes to the sick parallel some of those of African tradition in giving people a sense of control over the course of their disease.[3] (See Table 11.1). The differences in the sense of dominion also become apparent. While the healing beliefs that Backus recommends involve a strong sense of direct personal control, African healing practices depend upon the mediating power of another person or spirit. Sick people, however, maintain some level of perceived control because they believe they can influence those who have the power to heal.

People who have extensive social networks are healthier than those who do not.

When Africans assert that individual health and well-being is intimately bound together with a person's relationship to his or her community, they are affirming one of the best established associations in health research. People who are well connected with others in extensive social networks live longer, become ill less frequently, and recover from illness and injury more rapidly than those who do not (Broadhead et al. 1983; Israel 1985; House et al. 1988). Immigrants from nineteen countries, for instance, who attended church regularly and identified with people from the congregation reported less *anomie* and had significantly lower blood pressure than those who did not attend church (Walsh 1980).

African beliefs associating community divisions and ill will with poor health of its members also foreshadowed the theory of social capital. A community with a high level of social capital is highly interconnected through extensive membership in groups and associations and is comprised of members who trust one another. Communities with high social

Table 12.1

Religious Belief and Control: Pathological Beliefs, Healing Beliefs, and African Beliefs

Pathological Beliefs (Backus: 1996, 92–93)	Healing Beliefs (Backus: 1996, 96–97)	Traditional African Beliefs
Life is hopeless.	I believe that hope is a choice. I choose hope, not hopelessness.	I believe what I have been told – that through powerful people and spirits, I am able to oppose or appease the forces causing this illness.
I am a helpless victim – life and all its circumstances are in charge of what happens to me.	I believe that I am personally responsible for my treatment and for managing it.	I am helpless on my own to fight this illness but with the advice of the traditional practitioner, my family, and community, I have a chance.
If I get a serious illness, the worst will happen and I will die.	I refuse to believe that my diagnosis is a death sentence.	If I faithfully follow the advice I have been given, I will recover unless God wills me to die.
Medical treatments hardly ever work, and they have awful, unbearable side-effects.	I believe treatment is effective against this illness, especially the skillful efforts of scientific medicine *combined* with my strategies for replacing lying thoughts with the truth.	I believe that skills and power in fighting disease come from many different places. If I seek help from many powerful people and do what they say, I will be healed. Powerful diseases require powerful cures that may be more expensive and painful than less powerful ones.
Once you have a disease, there is nothing you can do to help yourself.	I believe my hormones and immune system are on the side of my healing and even now are working to overcome this illness.	I believe that my ancestors and other spirits will intercede to God for my healing and fight against opposing spirits if I do what I must to keep them happy with me and my family.
I'm only going to get worse, and I'll be nothing but a burden to everyone.	I can recover from this illness and live a rich, productive life of service.	I will recover if God wills that I recover.

capital are more prosperous and possess more effective civic institutions than those with a low social capital (Putnam 1993). Evidence also suggests that societies with high levels of inequality in income also have higher rates of mortality not as a function of poverty alone but because they fail to invest in social capital (Kawachi et al. 1997). Apparently, even lonely individuals who live in trusting, involved communities will live longer than similarly lonely people in communities with low levels of social capital.

People who enjoy close, loving relationships with others are healthier and live longer than those who have no close relationships or whose close relationships are dysfunctional.

The greater the intended intimacy of a relationship in Africa, the more powerful the curse that may be uttered when that relationship is betrayed, and the more powerful the blessing when the relationship deepens in intimacy. Curses and blessings are tangible expressions of the power of an intimate friend or family member to bring health and healing or sickness and death. The studies below are typical of findings that are widely supported in health literature.

- In a nine-year study of almost 5,000 people in Alameda City, California, women who experienced a low level of intimacy and had only a few marginal friends were almost three times more likely to die than those who had enjoyed close relationships and had numerous friends who were important to them – no matter what their initial health or other risky behaviors. (Age-related relative risk of death equaled 2.8; for men 2.3) (Berkman and Syme 1979).

- In a study of more than 3,000 men and women throughout the United States, those who had undergone negative life events in the last five years, (such as separation or divorce, serious illness, or financial difficulties), used tobacco and alcohol more frequently, exercised less, slept less soundly, and weighed more than those who had not experienced these things.

- Patients experiencing severe cardiac problems who spent extended periods of time with hospital chaplains (about an hour a day compared to about three minutes) left the hospital between 1.8 to 2.1 days sooner than those who had the shorter visits (Thomas 1997).

People who live their lives free of guilt and fear are healthier than those who do not.

Many traditional healing rituals in Africa are designed either to deliver the sick person from guilt and fear, to reconcile broken relationships, or sometimes to "even the score" by placing a burden of guilt and fear upon a real or supposed enemy. One of the strengths of a properly functioning African community is to relieve stress by defining behavioral expectations, sharing the load of work, and providing physical and emotional support in times of crisis.

We intuitively recognize that we are more likely to become ill when we live with fear and guilt that result in other intensely negative emotions. Clinicians also testify to the destructive power of these emotions and experiences. Dr. Dan Fountain (1994) looks at questions concerning relationships among family members, curses, ill wishes of others, and the fear and guilt that results from them, and he includes such items among the essential questions in a diagnostic interview in Africa.

Medical students in the Family Practice program of the Medical University of South Africa fail their diagnostic role-plays if they neglect to include this relational component in their questioning, even if the rest of their approach is clinically sound (Germond 1994). Relieving fear and bringing about reconciliation in broken relationships is an essential therapeutic tool in many church-related programs and hospitals throughout the world (Allen 1995) but is still ignored or done only haphazardly in many others.

Fear

Just as the fear of dying increases the power of a curse, uncontrolled death anxiety can sicken a healthy person and aggravate the illness of a sick one. Like other negative emotions, living under a burden of fear compromises the immune system and makes sickness more likely.

- In a study of some 1,400 people across the United States, non-religious young people (ages 21–34) were three times more likely to mention death in the interpretation of twelve ambiguous pictures than those who identified themselves as religious (Richardson et al. 1983).
- In a study of 345 people, younger people who were little influenced by religion were most likely to be anxious about death, while older people for whom religious belief was of high importance were least likely to be

troubled by fear of death (Thorson and Powell 1990).
- Terminally ill patients facing their deaths within a few weeks were significantly less likely to fear death than younger and healthier patients. Those who reported the least fear were those with strong religious beliefs, a supportive religious community, and lower levels of pain (Gibbs and Achterberg-Lawlis 1978; Smith et al. 1983–84).

Guilt

- Guilt, whether true or false, compounds the negative effects of fear. Most studies of women who have been victims of rape show that many blame themselves for the assault, attributing it to their own poor judgement or flaws in their character. Women who blame themselves demonstrate higher levels of depression, fear, and sexual dissatisfaction during the months following the assault (Meyer and Taylor 1986). In another study researchers asked women who had been raped about stressful events in their lives prior to the rape. Those who had previously experienced the death of a relative (other than their own child) recovered more quickly from the rape than those who had not, probably because of the coping skills they had learned during that time in facing the loss. Women who had previously been criminally assaulted, however, or who had lost a child recovered much more slowly. The researchers attributed their slow recovery to unresolved feelings of guilt from the loss of their child or their previous assault – guilt that was aggravated when they had to cope with rape (Silver and Wortman 1980).
- Nearly half of 71 mostly single young women attending support groups because of severe emotional disturbances after undergoing voluntary abortion changed their religious affiliation to an evangelical or fundamentalist church. Those who joined one of these churches improved more rapidly than those who did not, possibly because they found a sense of forgiveness for guilt they might have felt in having the abortion (Tamburrino et al. 1990).[4]
- Hospitalized psychiatric patients who believed in individual sin reported a higher level of depressive symptoms than those who did not (Kroll and Sheeham 1989), perhaps because they had no resources to deal with their sense of guilt.

By now, it is becoming obvious that the factors that promote and destroy health are highly interrelated to one another and often cluster together. In a 28-year longitudinal study of over 5,000 men and women in California, frequent attendees of religious services were significantly less likely to die than those who did not attend. Frequent attendees also enjoyed more extensive social networks, smoked less, and less frequently abused alcohol. During the follow-up period, frequent attendees were also more likely than non-attendees to further develop their social networks, to remain married to the same spouse, to quit smoking, and even to increase exercise (Strawbridge et al. 1997).

People who behave righteously are healthier and live longer than those who behave sinfully.

In a survey of mothers and children in Ponea Kriek in Cambodia, World Relief staff discovered that the children of Muslim families were better nourished than their equivalent counterparts in the Buddhist communities (Hanson 1998). Muslim children ate more fruits and vegetables that were rich in vitamins than children in Buddhist families. These differences were due in part to the dietary rules that are a part of local Islamic custom. For these people, as for the ancient Hebrews, dietary customs have a moral dimension.

In a close parallel, researchers find that certain groups, such as Seventh Day Adventists, are healthier and live longer than the general population, no matter where they are found. Seventh Day Adventists, even more than many Christian groups, follow numerous practices that contribute to good health. Every culture regards as morally good many of the habits and behaviors they *perceive* as life giving and sustaining. In the same way they regard as morally bad many habits and behaviors they *perceive* as destructive to good health.

Many Africans, for instance, believe that actions that destroy community and harm relationships are morally evil. Broken relationships, isolation and anomie, jealousy, fear, and guilt also contribute to ill health and retard healing.

In most cultures, good people live longer and better than bad people because the right thing to do and the healthy thing to do are often the same thing. Research makes this connection clear.

In health studies in the United States, church attendance or religious belief and practice are measurable indicators of people who are concerned with the moral dimensions of their behavior. In two extensive annotated bibliographies of over 230 scientific studies examining the linkages between health and faith (Matthews and Larsen 1995; Matthews, Larsen and Barry 1993), higher levels of religious practice[5] were associated with:

- Less involvement in premarital sex
- Fewer sexual partners
- Less frequent oral and anal sexual intercourse
- Fewer friendships with sexually permissive peers
- Lower rates of cervical cancer
- Fewer acts of delinquency
- Higher academic achievement
- Lower incidence of tobacco related cancers
- Lower levels of abuse of all types of drugs
- Lower levels of childhood behavioral problems
- Stronger social networks
- Increased use of seat belts in automobiles
- Fewer illnesses, injuries, and use of medical care
- Generally lower rates of many cancers

When Seventh Day Adventist youth were asked why they abstained from alcohol, tobacco, and drugs, "my commitment to Christ" was the strongest predictor with "I want to be in control of my life" and "concern for my health" almost equally strong (Dudley et al. 1987). The same youth were more likely to come from stable families with strong support networks. Though there are exceptions, health promoting factors seem to cluster around good people wherever they are from.

DO ALL EXPRESSIONS OF SPIRITUALITY
PROMOTE HEALTH ALIKE?

African traditions of health and healing, like those of many different belief systems, have some parallels to the common grace of God discovered in principles of healthy living. Does that mean that biblical Christianity is no better than African traditional spirituality? The earlier chapters of this book give a resounding "No." African tradition must be transformed by Christian belief to reach fully the goals that it promises – men and women living at peace with God, the environment, and one another in a transcendent and loving community characterized not by fear and guilt but by grace. African tradition and biblical Christianity are both rooted in spiritual reality, but one focuses upon often competing powers of dangerously petulant spirits and the other upon the healing and sustaining power of a personally involved good God. Biblical Christianity not only permits a loving relationship to God but also best fits the patterns of community, life-style, and behavior that preserve health and hasten healing.

Some studies illuminate areas where religious belief alone is not enough to affect health status, or may affect it negatively. *That* a person believes is not sufficient; *what* a person believes makes a difference.

Nature of God

Those who believe that God or spiritual forces demand rejection of modern medicine as a test of faith put themselves and others at risk. Even in the United States, perinatal and maternal mortality are greater if parents adhere to a religious belief that, as an act of faith, excludes prenatal and curative care (Spence et al. 1984). Leaders who drive a wedge between the worlds of "scientific medicine" and traditional healing and then demand exclusive allegiance to tradition leave the person vulnerable to many diseases. Like some traditional healers, the leaders and pastors of many indigenous Christian groups in Africa demand that their followers refuse medical care as an exercise of faith, often delaying effective treatment.

Religious belief that fails to intersect the physical world or that promotes self-destructive behavior also reflects a God who is either distant or evil or both, and leads to poor health. The strength of identification of Chinese students in Singapore with traditional Chinese religious values, for instance, failed to affect their alcohol use (Isralowitz and Ong 1990). Young people who were involved in occult religious traditions, embracing a set of values that promoted antisocial behavior, suffered greater substance abuse than those who were not (Tennant-Clark, C. M. et al. 1989). The parallel to the "shadow" of African traditional religions is significant. When traditional practice promotes behavior destructive of community (i.e., engaging a witch to place a curse upon an enemy in an attempt to escape that enemy's power to cause illness), it may promote individual and community "dis-ease" rather than health.

Finally, religious beliefs that focus upon God (or spiritual forces) as a powerful judge may promote greater anxiety and long-term health problems. Christians who are sincerely invested in their churches and religious experience normally are healthier than those who are not (Ferraro and Albrecht-Jansen 1991; Koenig et al. 1994; Koenig et al. 1993; Schwab and Peterson 1990). Reversing the pattern of research findings in Christian belief, young Muslims who were sincere about their religion experienced higher anxiety about death than those who were religiously insincere (Beg and Zilla 1982). One possible reason is the Islamic belief that Allah would determine their eternal destination by balancing their good and bad acts immediately following their deaths, a fearful reckoning for many Muslims.

Christians, who are motivated to good actions by the fear of being punished by a vengeful God, parallel the experience of the Muslim students. In these studies, people who are highly involved in certain Pentecostal expressions, or who depended heavily upon religious broadcasting for religious experience to the exclusion of involvement in church communities, were more anxious, expressed more anger and loneliness, were at a higher risk of alcoholism and reported a generally lower health status.[6] It is possible that the fear, crisis orientation, and anxiety created by some Christian movements and religious broadcasters may contribute to these effects.

Nature of Faith

The effect of religious involvement upon health depends not only upon the nature of belief in God but the mechanism by which faith operates. Numerous studies discriminate between intrinsic and extrinsic faith. The religious activities of the intrinsically religious person spring from a heart of belief. Intrinsically religious people live by their beliefs, regardless of anticipated outcomes and even in the face of difficult circumstances. The extrinsically religious person uses religious practice as a means to an end. They believe that they will better achieve external goals by "being religious" but often have no inner core of belief that guides their practice.

In studies that discriminate between extrinsic and intrinsic orientations to faith, the effects of each often emerge as mirror images of the other. In one study of 309 men and women, for instance, depression increased with extrinsic religious orientation but decreased with intrinsic religious orientation (Genia and Shaw 1991). In a study of coping with breast cancer, intrinsic belief enhanced coping ability while extrinsic belief had no significant effect (Johnson and Spilka 1991). Among Mormon college students, intrinsic religiousness was positively associated with multiple measures of well-being and negatively associated with anxiety while extrinsic religiousness was positively associated with anxiety and negatively associated with ten of the eighteen measures of well-being (Bergin et al. 1987).

In a study of 586 patients who had experienced a negative life event, the researchers tried to deepen their understanding of the aspects of faith that contributed to coping. Like the other studies, they found that four factors (belief in a just and loving God, the belief that God was a supportive partner in the coping process, involvement in religious ritual, and the search for spiritual and personal support through religion) were particularly associated with improved coping skills (Pargament et al. 1990). Prayer also varies in its effect. Prayers of petition and ritual prayers repeated from a prayer book were associated with sadness, loneliness, tenseness, and fearfulness when they were not also accompanied by colloquial prayers for guidance in decision-making and meditative prayer. Colloquial prayer was associated with happiness and meditative prayer with existential well being and religious satisfaction (Poloma and Pendleton 1991).

Simply practicing religion apart from sincere belief may have negative rather than positive effects. As with many of the studies, it is hard to discriminate the direction of causation. Hard times may drive even unbelieving people to the practice of religion in hope that things might get better. If that were so, extrinsic practice could be simply an effect of difficult circumstances. Religious practice from a sincere heart of faith, however, was consistently associated with positive measurements of health and well being.

The implications for African tradition are apparent. Traditional religious practices are so interwoven with day-to-day life, that it becomes hard not to be extremely practical. If my religious practice fails to maintain the health of my children, protect me from my enemies, or bring me wealth, what good is it? Many of the intrinsic aspects of traditional practice in Africa, particularly those that revolve around spirits, bring fear and discomfort rather than peace.

In the imaginary story that opened this chapter Eleazar the priest was puzzled and disturbed when it appeared that Yahwah had stopped the plague in the enemy camp. The parallel question exists today. Does the practice of religion alone enhance health and help fight disease? The answer is not as simple as it may first appear. Just as surely as it is true of Canaanites who bury their excrement, men and women who are empowered by their faith to give meaning and direction to their lives, who find hope and grace instead of fear and guilt, and who live in community with close and loving relationships will be healthier, regardless of whether they are putting their trust in truth or in hopeful fantasy.

African traditions and practices reflect many deep understandings of the common grace of health and healing but they also fail in many ways – often bringing alienation instead of forgiveness, vengeance instead of grace, fear instead of comfort, and passive helplessness instead of enabling dominion. Ultimately belief returns to the questions of truth, power, and goodness. Evil power finally wounds and destroys.

Exclusive belief in scientific medicine ultimately fails as surely as belief in the mediating power of ancestral spirits. Only God heals. Christian health workers in Africa offer medicine in one hand and God's salvation in the other. In the final chapter, I will suggest how we can do better offering both together.

Notes

1   The National Institute for Healthcare Research systematically reviews clinical research in which religious belief and practice is measured as a variable. In a recent annotated bibliography reviewing research related to life satisfaction, religious commitment was reported as a positive effect in 48 (73%) of the 66 studies that measured specific health outcomes. Religious commitment had a negative effect in only six (9%) of the studies and in the remaining 12 studies it was neutral or showed mixed outcomes (Matthews and Larson 1995). Other annotated bibliographies show similarly positive associations between religious commitment and good health outcomes (Matthews, Larsen and Barry 1993; Larsen 1993).

2   Even the strongest among the studies that followed a randomized, double-blind protocol failed to control many variables. In this study the experimenters randomly assigned coronary patients to either an intercessory prayer group or non-intercessory control group. Neither the patients nor the attending staff at the hospital knew to which group the patients had been assigned. The patient and the intercessor never met. Those in the non-intercessory group did not have an intercessor assigned to pray for them. The patients in the intercessory group experienced fewer life threatening events that those in the control (Byrd 1988). Even this carefully designed study, however, could not control for the prayers that may have been offered by friends and family

for either the treatment or control group. Access to prayer is not something that may be controlled like access to an experimental medicine. Some believers would also argue that assigning patients to a no-prayer control group demonstrates how poorly the scientific method is suited to measure the effects of religious belief.

3   I am not equating the content and truth of African belief to biblical truth but only pointing out that both endeavor to restore a feeling of control to the person who is sick. In the last section of this chapter, I examine the contrast between the truth of Christian belief and the harmfulness of some African beliefs and practices.

4   Numerous studies identify other factors associated with church attendance such as the social support that also contributes to relieving stress and lessening fear (Matthews and Larson 1995; Matthews, Larson and Barry 1993).

5   The studies comprising these bibliographies were not screened to omit those that would associate religious commitment and behavior with poor health results and so are representative of a well established pattern of findings.

6   In this study as well as others, it is impossible always to determine the direction of causation. Are anxious and ill people more likely to seek out religious broadcasts and Pentecostal expressions, do these experiences increase anxiety, or is there some interactive effect?

Chapter 13

New Pathways to Health and Healing Ministry

◆ ◆ ◆

A mouse once had a serious problem. As he got older, he could not hear, see, or smell as well as he could in his youth. He could not run as quickly. Yet he still had to leave his safe hiding place to find food. Several times he had almost been caught by the cat. He could see that he would soon either starve or become the cat's meal. He thought about the problem for a long time without a single good idea, so he began to talk to his friends. They were not much help either, but finally one of them gave a suggestion. "Why don't you ask the dog for help. The dog is a big, wise elder animal and the dog is not frightened of the cat."

The mouse had little to lose so he gathered up his few possessions and laid them at the feet of the dog. With the dog looming above him, he gazed humbly at the ground and said, "Oh wise and learned dog, greetings. I have heard of your mercy, power, and wisdom and have come to you for help. Here is my humble gift for you."

The dog looked down at the mouse before him and replied. "Mouse, you have brought little with you, but I am a merciful animal and I will hear your problem." The mouse began to tell the dog of his dilemma but long before he had finished, the dog interrupted him. "I am surprised, small mouse, that you were not able to discover the solution to your problem. You, too, must become a dog, so you can chase the cat and no longer be afraid."

The mouse could not deny that the solution would work but was muddled at how to accomplish it. "Oh gracious and merciful dog, how do I become a dog as you wisely suggest?"

"Ah, mouse," replied the dog, "I am but the consultant; implementation is your job."

♦ ♦ ♦

As I come to the last chapter of this book, I fear sounding like the dog in this story when actually I have most often been the mouse. I recognize the daily struggle of ministry in a poor country. What defines day-to-day realities for many involved in health and healing ministry in Africa? A clinician faces dozens of people lined up before the outpatient clinic; a church hospital administrator wonders how to avoid a strike among the nursing staff while searching for funds to purchase essential medicines and supplies; a community health leader is interrupted while writing a new funding proposal by a delegation of community members who demand more services.

I recognize that any suggestions I can make in this chapter confront almost overwhelming realities. Yet I truly believe we can and must make changes to minister more effectively, even in the face of difficult realities.

The goal of this book is the integration of health and healing ministry into the work of the church. Stuart Bate (1995), a South African theologian who has extensively studied the healing practices of independent and Pentecostal churches in his country, describes their ministry of healing as an integral expression of the biblical mission of the church. Using a model of ministry from Aberich (cited in Bate 1995, 237), he describes a five-fold expression of the church's mission; *martyria* (witness), *koinonia* (community), *diakonia* (service), *kerygma* (proclamation), and *leitourgia* (celebration). In Table 13:1 I have modified his framework to summarize the goals of biblically integrated and holistic health ministry. Each expression of mission suggests practices that reflect the light of God's kingdom and also the dangers that lie hidden in the shadows of traditional practice and belief. In the remainder of this chapter, I present a number of strategies that promote progress toward the goals of Table 13:1.

For health and healing ministries in Africa to become biblically holistic expressions of the Church's mission, they:
• Must be Christocentric
• Must recognize the reality of the spirit world but not use it
• Must make reconciliation a central part of healing practice

Table 13:1

Health and Healing as an Expression of the Church's Ministry

Work of the church	Expression in Health and Healing Ministry	
	Bringing Light	Avoiding Shadow
Witness to the Kingdom of God in the World	• Affirmation that the kingdom of God is present in the healing power of Christ • Affirmation of faith in Christ • Evangelism – people respond to healing by commitment to the Healer • Models the giving of self	• Maintaining focus upon the power of Christ rather than the healer, the practice or the ritual • Promoting faith in God rather than faith in faith • Building a mature understanding that preserves faith in the power of God even in the face of continued illness or incomplete healing
Community as an Expression of the Family of God	• Encouraging the expression of all of the spiritual gifts to build a community of healing • Reconciling broken relationships • Providing a safe, supportive retreat for sick and wounded people • Modeling of Christian community among staff	• Avoiding the creation of closed insular communities that fail to interact positively outside themselves • Promoting transcendence, not division • Within an institutional setting, refusing to use appeals to Christian community as a manipulative device to maintain the leader's power or to avoid confronting problems or uncomfortable change

Service to Others as an Expression of God's Compassion and Grace	• Compassionately identifying with the suffering of others • Maintaining gentleness of touch, tone, and expression • Modeling an organizational culture of grace and service to one another • Maintaining focus upon the needs of the poor	• Continuing to confront issues and concerns that may cause discomfort to others • Maintaining personal balance in service • Maintaining accountability
Proclamation of God's Message to the World	• Proclamation of the gospel of Christ in the context of his compassion and healing power • Using health teaching to challenge false belief with God's revealed truth • Restoration of relationship to God as an expression of shalom	• Building recognition that true faith in God is not always linked with individual health and wealth; avoiding "faith" as a means to an end • Avoiding the temptation to blame the person who is sick or injured for his or her condition • Valuing health and healing ministry as a integral part of proclamation rather than just a means to an evangelistic end
Celebration of God	• Incorporating individual and group expressions of worship into healing ministry • Bathing health and healing ministry with prayer • Incorporating Christian symbols and rituals as authentic expressions of repentance, petition, reconciliation, thanksgiving, and worship	• Avoiding both of these perceptions—that prayer, ritual, and symbol are "magical" manipulation of God or the spirit world, and that they are customary Christian expressions unrelated to the power of healing

Modified from Bate 1995, 269–274

- Must make prayer an integral part of the healing process
- Must make biomedicine the servant of healing ministry and not the master
- Must develop new approaches to health promotion and education that shape and challenge basic beliefs
- Must continue to address health at community and environmental levels
- Must promote a growing partnership between churches in the North and South
- Must prepare pastors and Christian health workers in a biblical theology of healing
- Must engage African churches in a biblical process of contextualization of healing practice.

CHRISTIAN HEALTH AND HEALING MINISTRY IN AFRICA MUST BE CHRISTOCENTRIC

Accepting Christ as 'our Saviour' always involves making Him at home in our spiritual universe and in terms of our religious needs and longings. So an understanding of Christ in relation to spirit-power in the African context is not necessarily less accurate than in any other perception of Jesus (Bediako 1990, 9–10).

The spiritual and physical worlds converge in the healing encounter in Africa. Christ stands in the middle of the crossroads. In many Christian health ministries, however, we seem either not to see him or are not quite sure how to explain his presence. In either case our proclamation is incomplete.

Essential Proclamations concerning Jesus the Healer

Proclamation One: Christ fulfills the role of the ancestors[1] in healing.
Africans turn to their ancestors for healing. The ancestors share kinship with the one who is sick and therefore are most likely to help in times of need. Because they live as spirits they are closer to the high god and more able to influence him. Jesus, however, is the perfect mediator. "We can find in Him all that we as Africans are looking for in our ancestors" (Milingo 1984, 78). Though not related to Jesus by racial lineage, Africans of any tribe share a common link to Jesus. They, like Jesus, bear the

image of the Creator God. They may choose to identify with an "adaptive past" by accepting membership into the family of God. They then have two stories. One is the story of their kinship group; the other is the story of the gospel, no longer a foreign teaching but a story that belongs to them. By their choice then, Jesus can become a member of their family who inhabits the spiritual realm (Bediako 1990). Unlike their genetic ancestors, however, who may or may not have influence with higher spirits and divinities, Christ is the perfect and sinless representation of his Father, the One High Creator God. As the true Elder Brother, Jesus "displaces the mediational function of the natural 'spirit-fathers'"(Bediako 1990, 18).

Proclamation Two: Jesus brings the distant High God near.

Christ is the only member of the Godhead who has ever been sick, tired, or injured – the only one who ever experienced the need for healing. Through the mediation of Jesus then, who suffered and is also one with the Creator God, God must be moved by the suffering Christians who are Jesus' brothers and sisters.

Proclamation Three: Jesus commands the power to heal.

Jesus certainly demonstrated that power during his ministry in Palestine and through his followers since then. He also empowers scientific medicine as the Creator and Sustainer (see Chapter 11). These messages should be part of our proclamation. Jesus also is the most powerful of the spirits and voids claims of earthly authorities to divine power.

When Jesus entered the realm of the spirits after his death and resurrection, he entered as Lord. Because he is one with God, He is the most powerful of spirits including those who were once human. "He is supreme over all 'gods' and authorities in the realm of the spirits. So He sums up in Himself all their powers and cancels any terrorizing influence they might be assumed to have upon us" (Bediako 1990, 19). To proclaim to people who are ill and living in fear of spirits that they may be adopted into the lineage of the living Christ who is the most powerful of the spirits is to promote their healing.

Because of his victory over the cross and the power of death, Jesus centers all power in himself. He therefore "de-sacralizes all the powers, institutions, and structures which rule human existence and history – family, nation, social class, race, law, politics, economy, religion, culture, tradition, custom, ancestors – stripping them all of any pretensions to ultimacy" (Bediako 1995c). Traditionally, the power of leaders and traditional healers among many peoples in Africa was rooted in their relationship to the ancestors. Because there was no distinction between secular and sacred power, to oppose a leader was to oppose all the spiritual powers sustaining the people or nation. Because all power now is given to Jesus, this claim can no longer stand. There are two main applications for health and healing.

First, on an individual level, traditional healers who derive their power from their relationship to ancestral or ruling spirits are eclipsed by the power of Jesus. Many traditional healers claim that their insight for diagnosis and treatment is derived from their being "ensouled" by a Spirit-Being with greater power and knowledge. Jesus, who commands all power and who is one with his Father, is "ensouled" by God as an essential characteristic of his Being. He therefore supersedes not only the role of the ancestors and spirits but also the role of the healers who derive their power from the ancestors (Pobee 1979). Additionally, as further evidence that Jesus is the Lord in the spirit realm, he has sent us his own spirit, the Holy Spirit, who empowers all who belong to God's family (Bediako 1990). The message to the individual who is sick or oppressed is therefore one of freedom from fear.

Second, all other human leaders command only the power delegated to them by God. Because the power is delegated to them by One above them and does not reside in them by the nature of their identity, they are accountable to the laws and principles of the One who rules over them. Their word, therefore, may be challenged on the basis of the principles of God's kingdom. The church therefore should challenge evil (even when it has the approbation of political authority), serve as a prophetic voice, and represent the welfare of those who have no power. Because many health problems are rooted in patterns of social injustice, this proclamation frees the church to act on behalf of the powerless (Bediako 1995c).

At the beginning of World Relief's maternal and child health project in rural Cambodia, I challenged the nurse who leads the program to represent the concerns of the poor rural women and children to political leaders and to those who exercise authority in the ministry of health. She had embraced her role as a servant and teacher but had never considered the power and authority that she commanded as a function of her position and the access she had to those in power. Advocacy for the poor, powerless, and marginal within a society needs to be done wisely and with sensitivity, but Christian health workers have Christ's authority to promote justice.

Proclamation Four: Jesus Christ forgives sin and bears our curse.

In the tradition of many African peoples, sin is the disruption of essential relationships. Sin may result in sickness or misfortune. Being reconciled to those who are estranged is therefore an essential part of the healing process.

Any sin is a personal affront to the Creator God and to his Son, Jesus. All sins therefore (even those sins that are finessed so that they appear not to affect the covenant of family and community relationships) are personal offenses and must be forgiven and reconciled. Because any sin is a personal offense against God, we are all guilty before him, and because of our disobedience, he has pronounced a curse upon us. Apart from Jesus we are powerless to escape God's curse or to reconcile the sin.

Jesus has borne our sin and suffered the full weight of God's curse against us for the offense that we have caused him. Through his mediation and sacrifice, we can find forgiveness, reconciliation, and freedom from the power of God's curse. Sometimes, people are unable to be reconciled to the person against whom they have sinned or to appease those who have placed a curse upon them. It may be that the person has already died or that the person (or his or her ancestral spirit) refuses to be reconciled or to remove the curse. In those times, Jesus pronounces God's forgiveness for the personal offense against him, but also delivers from the power of the person who refuses or who is no longer able to be reconciled. In suffering God's curse for our disobedience and freeing us from it, Jesus also is able to free us from the power of lesser curses. He can remove not only the guilt, bitterness, and resentment that are the natural effects of unforgiven sin but also the fear of curses. A person who is bound by these emotions cannot be whole either spiritually or physically (Ram 1995).

Dangers of Proclamation

Syncretism

The most apparent danger is that of so mixing the Christian message with African traditions that the two become inseparable.[2] Christianity is not an *African* religion any more than it is a Chinese or American religion.

Christianity is, however, an *African's* religion because "the African experience of the Christian faith can be seen to be fully coherent with the religious quests in African life" (Bediako 1995a, 60). The danger of syncretism is particularly great in health and healing activities because they are central to the religious quests of many Africans and encompass a broad range of expressions within biblical Christian traditions.

Failed healing

Independent African churches demonstrate great growth through their emphasis on healing. People will shift their allegiances to whichever person or group is successful in healing each new illness. Are we sure that we want to put Christ's credibility to the test by identifying him so closely with healing when, in fact, sooner or later, healing will fail and the person will die? As long as we attribute the success or failure in physical healing to medicine, we can presumably still introduce Jesus as a last resort. We can prevent Jesus from "failing" (at least in the perception of the person who turned to him unsuccessfully for healing). What about illnesses that we recognize as incurable such as AIDS or advanced cancer?

Among people whose religious expression is very practical, this becomes a critical question of witness. One destructive way out of the dilemma is to blame the victim, a scapegoat, or the healer. The failure may be attributed to the sick person's lack of faith, to continued evil behavior, or to the evil or unbelieving influence of another (Bate 1995). Failure may come also because the healer was not sufficiently skilled, was cut off from his or her source of power, or was confronting forces greater than he or she could handle.

For the Christian worker, the situation in which healing apparently fails must be answered on two levels. On the first level, the Christian health worker may choose to give the physical reason for death or continued illness or disability. On a second level, however, rather than trying to attribute reasons for the failure of Jesus' power or will to heal, the person must be answered positively in continuity with the character of Christ.

- When we join God's adoptive family we recognize that he will eventually invite us to return home. Death is the doorway.
- Healing cannot be complete in this life. God can complete his restoring work only among the 'living-dead' who must die in order to fully live with him.
- God, who is eternal, has the names of his children inscribed on his

hands and therefore can never forget them. There is no danger of being forgotten and passing into the unknown realm of nameless spirits. God preserves not only the individual but also his family and people eternally.

We must answer these questions with the truth of the Christian's hope. We cannot ignore truth to better fit the belief that healing will always happen. Nor can we ignore truth by trying to separate the Lord of healing from the process in order to "protect" his reputation.

Rejection of medical care and preventative interventions based upon science as not being of Christ

To reject scientific medicine as a demonstration of faith in Christ does not honor him but limits the expression of his power. It is not outside his dominion but a part of it. In the same way, to uncritically reject all non-scientific expressions of Christ's healing power as wrong does not honor him but limits the expression of his power.

Defining exclusive communities with only one healer

A man once gave a gift of land to his three sons and asked them to farm it and make it productive. He also instructed each son on how to be a good farmer. Through the years, each of the three sons focused on one of his instructions and began to forget the others. One remembered what his father had taught him about the preparation of the land to receive the crop and became an expert in it. Another remembered what he had learned about how to select what seed to plant and the precise time to plant it. A third remembered what his father had taught about the importance of selecting the right tools and became an expert in evaluating new farming tools and picking those that were best suited to his crop.

At first as the three sons discussed what they remembered, they did it in a good-natured way. However, one day one of them said, "What our father told us about preparing the land is the most important part of his teaching. Unless you follow what I am doing you are not honoring him."

Each son then said the same about what he had remembered. In time the sons and their families drew away from one another. They each proclaimed their own area of knowledge to their friends and slowly not only the three families but the entire village became divided. People spoke only to those who agreed with them. Even while the sons became more powerful as community leaders, the productivity of their fields began to decrease. One day the father returned.

"Not one of you honors me," he said, "because you have turned against one another. Are not all of you my sons? Also, you have not made good use of the gifts I have given you– the land is not productive and you have hoarded your knowledge instead of sharing it with one another." He grieved over his sons' foolishness.

When people center their practice upon the teaching of one person, they may come to identify what they teach and practice as the *only* true expression of the person they claim to follow. When Christian leaders use partial knowledge about health and healing to create exclusive and competitive communities or to build their own power, they dishonor Christ.

PROCLAIMING JESUS IN THE CONTEXT OF HEALTH AND HEALING MINISTRY

How is this to be done? The remaining portion of this chapter helps to answer that question, but one principle is so crucial I want to highlight it here. *Only those who are insiders to the particular culture may effectively proclaim these truths and only in the culture's mother tongue.* While visiting a Christian health and development project in urban Johannesburg, I was invited to address a group of men and women from the poorer communities of the city. Because some of these truths were fresh in my mind (and though I should have known better), I tried to share them through a translator. By the end I had little idea of what I had actually communicated. These truths must be presented by those who know the traditions of a particular people *in their language*. Language and traditional belief are so intertwined in this area that outsiders thinking in patterns of thought and language shaped by their own culture are unlikely to communicate God's truth accurately.

The following additional factors are also important to effective Christian health and healing ministries in Africa.

RECOGNIZE THE REALITY OF THE SPIRIT WORLD BUT DO NOT CALL UPON SPIRITS AS ALLIES IN HEALING

Refusing to recognize the reality of the spirit world or ignoring its influence within the health care setting in Africa is neither biblical nor does it coincide with the experience of many Africans. Certainly spirits do not lie behind everything attributed to them nor is every supposed spirit possession authentic. Nevertheless the weight of biblical and historical evidence confirms their existence. Many African Christians including Milingo (1984) have maintained that they have freedom to call upon good or neutral spirits for help if it is done in the name of Christ.

However, no biblical teaching supports this position. God forbids communicating with spirits – angels as well as demons or ancestors (Moreau 1990). While angels certainly protect Christians, they do not act independently but only under God's authority. Christian health programs in Africa must have a person on the health team who knows how to discern and confront spirits. Interventions should also include preventative education within communities. Jesus' instruction in Luke 11, for example, about the evil spirit who returns to the person from whom he was cast, bringing along seven even more evil than himself, is a preventative message.

MAKE RECONCILIATION A CENTRAL PART OF HEALING

"The Bible uses the word 'reconcile' to describe a process of bringing peace to different kinds of situations. Different passages in the Bible actually describe those situations. We can see that reconciliation means that a person must restore peace:
with God
with their brother (family)
with their neighbor
with different ethnic groups
with an enemy" (TEE Manual 1996, 1).

Without reconciliation there can be no true healing. How may reconciliation be introduced into Christian health and healing ministries?

Only God can enable and complete reconciliation.

As I listened to stories of horror among survivors of the ethnic conflicts in Rwanda, I soon realized that wounds so deep cannot be healed apart from the power of God. Reconciliation is not simply conflict mediation. Though people may be trained in skills and insights related to reconciliation, it is, at its core, not a rational-technical skill but the work of God (Schreiter 1992). This is true not only of the spiritual, emotional, and physical trauma of hatred but of other conditions as well. "According to the African view of healing ... the fear of death from AIDS is indeed not the primary concern to be addressed; of primary concern is the balance which has been disturbed ... It is primarily the relationships between people which are affected, and where balance has to be restored ... Relations among human beings are most fully restored where we share with Jesus, in the community of His followers and of His creation, the fullness of liberations which he brings" (Saayman 1992, 53).

True reconciliation requires that victims discover God's grace and power to forgive those who have offended them (Schreiter 1992). Punishing the perpetrator cannot bring about reconciliation, a truth that the South African Truth and Justice Commission has recognized in examining the abuses and crimes during apartheid. Punishment cannot bring healing but will only contribute to continuing separation.

Churches must be involved in reconciliation.

Rev. Michael Cassidy, who was quietly involved over many years in key elements of the peaceful transition of power in South Africa and the end of apartheid, remembers vividly his time in Rwanda only weeks before the massacres began. He preached in the stadium in Kigali and met many of the top political and church leaders as well as envoys from many western countries. At the end of the meetings, however, the churches of Rwanda remained silent, divided by the same legacies of ethnic conflict that were soon to explode in hellish violence (Cassidy 1995). A church that mirrors or contributes to the divisions within a society, family, or community cannot be a reconciling force (Schreiter 1992). When invited to participate in a reconciliation process by those who have been affected by conflict, however, churches may become not only a healing force within a society, as in South Africa, but a community of healing for estranged individuals and families.

Churches that transcend the divisions of their congregations, communities, and nations promote healing and prevent violence. After a study of biblical passages concerning relationships between the tribes of Israel, Kenyan university students developed the following biblical principles that describe churches that are reconciling forces within a divided society.

- The churches must be led by one who represents the interests of all and not just the group to which he or she belongs.

- Church members must ascribe to a transcendent set of biblical values and laws that define ethnic, family, and individual relationships.
- Whenever possible, church disputes must be handled at the level at which they occur by those who are wise, upright, and hate bribery.
- When disputes cannot be handled at the level at which they occur, or involve people from divisions within the dominant society, they must be handled by men and women who are wise, upright, hate bribes, and place justice above individual or "party" interests.
- Each unique group should be permitted to retain its separate cultural identity within the church.
- Each group must share in the support and work of the church and participate in important church institutions.
- Each group must share equitably in the benefits and services of the church.
- All groups should be represented in church decision-making.
- When the nature of a decision to be made might favor one group above another, the decision should be made by consensus of representatives from each group (Long 1994).

The process of reconciliation must be surrounded by prayer.

Prayer is the vehicle of repentance and healing. Praying individually and together not only brings people together before God but also places God at the center of the reconciling process and releases his healing power. "Divine power comes to us as service and solidarity: power as self-emptying, utterly trusting; power as deciding to stand firm with those who suffer when flight would seem to be the better strategy. It is only this kind of power that can prevail. It is the power of the stripped and tortured One on the cross who has chosen not to come down from that cross, but to stay with the victims of violence even into the maws of death ... That is the kind of God who offers us reconciliation" (Schreiter 1992, 79).

On an individual level, reconciliation must involve "whole-person history taking, diagnostic formulations, and treatment" (Allen 1995, 30).

For those with serious injury or chronic or life threatening disease, diagnosticians must examine the illness or injury as well as the web of relationships surrounding the patient.[3] This must be done by one who knows the mother tongue of the patient and who understands the nature of kinship patterns for the ethnic group. Few doctors or clinicians are able (or have the time) to examine relationships in that much detail. A trained chaplain, pastor, or gifted lay person must be integrated into the healing team.

The process of reconciliation should build upon the traditions of the culture and the rituals, stories, and symbols of the church.

Churches and individual Christian peacemakers in Africa should use cultural traditions as powerful symbols of reconciliation, just as Christians in North America may symbolize reconciliation in a handshake or hug. These traditions may include eating together in a meal symbolizing the return of peace, the exchange of gifts, or symbolic or substantive compensation to the one who was harmed.

Ritual gives concrete expression to suffering and healing and bridges the gap between unique individual experience and the meaning of the gospel story (Schreiter 1992). For churches that follow a sacramental system, confession, penance, baptism, and anointing may powerfully symbolize reconciliation (Taylor 1963). For Christians from other traditions, sharing of the Lord's Supper, and church traditions such as foot washing may also provide concrete expression to an inner process of healing. Shared prayer has concrete, ritual dimensions that bring healing to those who pray together.

Christian symbols and stories are powerful, concrete representations of the reconciling process. The gospel story is at the heart of reconciliation. The story of the prodigal son and the historical accounts of conflict resolution in Israel and the early church are powerful examples of reconciliation. Paul freely uses the symbols and metaphors of blood, death, and the cross to represent the reconciling process (Schreiter 1992). These Christian symbols may also become bridges of understanding to the many peoples in Africa for whom blood sacrifice remains an important vehicle of reconciliation.

PRAYER MUST BECOME AN INTEGRAL PART OF THE HEALING PROCESS

On the eve of her return to Africa, a missionary nurse with more than twenty-five years of health ministry at hospital and community level described the struggle of her mission in identifying roles for short-term teams. She had suggested that they should go and pray with those who are sick, with pastors and with families and congregations. Most North Americans, however, wanted to go and "do" something. After many years of health ministry in Africa, however, this nurse recognized that prayer *is* "doing" something.

Prayer:

- Releases the power of God in the life of the one who is praying and in the lives of others
- Brings or hastens healing
- Acknowledges God's power and sovereignty without attendant helplessness or fatalism
- Expresses repentance, forgiveness, petition, praise and thanksgiving
- Allows the person who is praying to hear from God
- Reconstructs meaning in life
- Builds spiritual unity

The act of praying may:

- Strengthen the immune response
- Calm the person who is praying
- Build hope
- Provide reflective insight
- Give strength to those who are weak
- Build a sense of efficacy and maintain a sense of community with others
- Motivate healthy changes in behavioral patterns
- Build an emotional bond between those who pray together

Prayer is the thread that holds together the very fabric of Christian health programs. Prayer should not, therefore, be a specialty. Every member of a health team can pray. It is as important a part of a healing culture as medicine.

Health programs must promote corporate as well as individual prayer. Corporate prayer is a vital expression of Christian community and is therefore even more powerful within an African context.

Many patients are able to pray for other patients as well as themselves, both individually and in groups. In doing this, patients not only break through the passivity often nurtured in a health care setting but, in caring for others, they enhance their own healing.

Each Christian, whether a patient, volunteer, or worker in a health and healing ministry may bless fellow patients and staff. Until I lived in Kenya, I never really understood the importance of blessings and curses. I cannot recall ever having heard a sermon on blessing as I grew up. In my study since that time, I discovered that Christians have been given the privilege to bless one another.

A Christian's authority to bless comes from God. Therefore the content of the blessing must be in accordance with God's will, best revealed in the Bible. Content for blessings may be found in biblical blessings and prayers and in the Psalms and other poetic passages.

Though blessings should be expressed in the language and cultural forms of the people, I have given some examples in English that could be particularly meaningful in the context of Africa.

> May the Lord bless you and keep you;
> May he make his face shine upon you and be gracious to you;
> May the Lord turn his face toward you and give you peace.
> Numbers 6:24–26

> May the God of hope
> Fill you with joy and peace
> As you trust in him.
> May you overflow with hope
> In the power of the Holy Spirit.
> Romans 15:13

> May God make all grace abound to you.
> In all things at all times
> May you have all that you need.
> 2 Corinthians 9:8

> May God soften your fields with showers
> And crown your year with bounty;
> May your carts overflow with abundance.
> May you be clothed in gladness
> As your meadows are covered with flocks
> And your valley mantled with grain;
> May you shout with joy and sing.
> Psalm 65:10–13

> May God show you the wonder of his great love;
> May he keep you as the apple of his eye

And may He hide you in the shelter of His wings.
Psalm 17:7–8

May God arm you with strength
And make your way perfect.
May he give you the feet of a deer
So that you can stand on the heights.
Psalm 18:32–33

May God give you the desire of your heart
And make all your plans succeed.
May we rejoice when you are victorious.
May the Lord grant all your requests.
Psalm 20:4–5

May God clothe you with strength and dignity;
May you laugh at the days to come.
May your children bless you
And your husband/wife praise you.
Proverbs 31:25, 28

May you be strong and very courageous.
May you be neither discouraged nor terrified
For the Lord your God will be with you
Wherever you go.
Joshua 1:9

BIOMEDICINE THE SERVANT, NOT THE MASTER

The organizational culture of most Christian health programs and institutions is centered upon biomedicine. Biomedicine shapes our vocabulary, structure, and processes. Patient treatment and care is dominated by the practice of medicine. To change the culture to one of healing with a better fit to the African context presents several challenges.

The culture of healing must begin to shift from an individual to community focus.

The biomedical model fits awkwardly to a culture in which health, sickness, injury, and healing are interwoven with relationships. There are some ways to achieve a better fit, however.

Include family and community members in certain aspects of the diagnostic practice.

While family members may not participate in the physical examination of the sick person, they may participate in at least part of the diagnostic interview and history, not only as information providers but also as diagnosticians. Though the diagnosis given by family members from a traditional perspective is often wrong, their participation provides the clinician with important details of the sick person's context that could reflect the etiology of the disease and affect the course of recovery. Additionally, it provides a bridge to the integration of biblical teaching that relates to traditional beliefs. Finally, the presence of family members may ease the fears of sick people who are coming into an unknown culture with little understanding of either medical procedures or the hospital culture in which they take place.

Integrate family and community members into treatment.

Many clinicians think about the participation of family members in only three aspects of treatment; administering medicines and other procedures that may be required on an outpatient basis, providing food (if the hospital has no food service) and personal items required by the sick person, and helping to meet the costs of treatment. Families often do not limit their involvement to those areas but do other things that encourage the sick person and promote healing.

In the broader context of healing, however, the family members may be assigned specific interventions by the clinician. These could include reading certain preselected portions of the Bible, regularly scheduled times of prayer at the bedside of the sick person, bathing, touching or massage, and, in some instances, becoming intermediaries to other family and community members who may be estranged from the patient. These interventions have an intrinsic healing effect likely to be enhanced even more if they are done at the instruction of the clinician. The clinician's word validates the interventions as important to the healing process and also gives them the added power of his or her own credibility and influence. Finally, many interventions such as prayer and Bible reading may be performed by Christians and non-Christians alike. Though there is a danger that they may assign a magical significance to the interventions themselves, their openness to the power of God and of his Word will have the greatest effect upon the patient and among the patient's friends and family.

Build a greater sense of community among the patients themselves.

Most hospitals isolate even ambulatory and non-infectious patients in their beds and rooms. Though adequate sleep and rest promote healing, loneliness does not. Patients need to build a greater sense of community among themselves. They should be encouraged to worship, pray, and perhaps even eat together in small groups. Staff may invite some patients to work with one another in tasks appropriate to their condition, perhaps in return for some credit toward their bill. These suggestions carry some additional risk of exposure to infection or injury but that again must be weighed against the potential healing power of participation in a hospital community.

Explore a bioethical model based not upon individual privacy but group responsibility.

Most bioethical models are based upon an individual's right to privacy. Confidentiality of the doctor-patient relationship is carefully guarded and any breach of that relationship must be justified. Bioethics in Africa, however, requires further exploration from a biblical basis. Within a communal culture, what balance does there need to be between an individual's right to privacy and the good of the family and community? Hiding a disease behind an individual's right to confidentiality may contribute to the spread of infection, particularly in HIV/AIDS, may slow the supportive response of the community to the needs of the sick person, or may subject the sick person to relational obligations that he or she is no longer able to carry out or that aggravate the sickness. Additionally, things that are hidden may build suspicion, accusations, and fear in the community. The answer is not an easy one nor is it likely to be constructed by non-Africans. It must be addressed, however, at the practical level of a church or mission health program and also among biblical scholars from Africa.

The culture of healing must fit every aspect of healing ministry into a mosaic of practice.

Many Christian hospitals and health programs follow some of the suggestions in this chapter but relatively few have developed a comprehensive picture that blends them into a mosaic of healing. How can that be done?

Develop a new vocabulary.

As I write this book, I realize that I will offend some people by the words that I use. The word *holistic*, for instance, carries a connotation of new age philosophy and alternative medicine. To avoid that problem, I have used the term *biblically holistic* to indicate that the source of my holism is the Bible and not African tradition or Eastern thought. Additionally, English as a language has dualism built into it. When that is overlaid with the scientific jargon of medicine, Christians committed to biblically holistic health are left with very few ways to express what they would like to say.

Some Christians in medicine have chosen to reject the term *alternative medicine* for the less inflammatory term of *complementary medicine* (Thomas 1997). Dr. Anthony Allen faced this problem in describing the biblical holism of his health program. "In asserting that semantics is praxis, I have pointed to the confusion that has abounded in Western-influenced health care systems and within the church about the meanings of the words health and salvation ... Christian health professionals have experienced problems of identity. We have tended to be living contradictions or split personalities" (Allen 1995, 33). Though it may seem tedious, the staff of Christian health programs need to explore what meanings the words *health* and *healing* have for them. It may uncover some basic differences in the understanding of these words that could impede progress toward a more integrative model.

As an Appendix, I have included a series of inductive Bible studies that medical and health workers in Africa, Asia, and the United States have used to help build greater shared understanding of health and healing from a Christian perspective. You may find these useful for individual or group reflection.

Change patterns of attribution in healing ministry.

Most Christian health workers attribute physical healing to medical intervention and spiritual healing to Christ. This pattern of attribution presents a mixed message to people who draw little distinction between the two. We often use scientific healing as a doorway to understanding about Christ. We must be sensitive to those times when we can use the message of Christ and his power as a gateway to understanding the efficacy of medical interventions.

Develop multidisciplinary teams.

Several times throughout this chapter I have referred to members of a healing team as if this team existed. In some health programs it does, but in many it does not. People bring different gifts, skills, and training to the healing ministry. No one person is likely to possess all the gifts and skills needed for comprehensive ministry, even at the level of a curative care institution. When the practice model is expanded to include primary health care at community level, it certainly exceeds the capacities of a single discipline. While the nature of the teams will vary from one place to another, they need to share some things in common. First, they must include those who speak the local language(s) and understand the traditional belief and practice. Secondly, they must be teams not only on paper but they must talk to one another. Organizational systems and policies need to support the work of the team rather than constructing barriers to be overcome. Mature, spiritually gifted, culturally attuned men and women trained as chaplains are essential members of the healing teams in Christian hospitals.

The culture of medicine is built upon a high differentiation of task and role reflected in the ever increasing specialization of medical care. The experience of working in Christian health care in Africa normally begins to erode specialization simply by the demands of the job. A team approach erodes it further because team members are chosen not only on the basis of their training but also their spiritual gifts. Team members may often serve in more than one role (Allen 1995).

Develop policies that allow each staff member to minister in areas of his or her gifts outside their given role.

A nursing assistant or even a cleaner may be gifted with healing gifts of prayer or faith. Systems need to be in place that not only lead to the discovery of these gifts but also encourage the staff member in exercising them (Allen 1995).

The church must be an integral part of the culture of healing.

Most Christian health programs in Africa have institutional ties to a church structure but little participation from local congregations. Local congregations, however, may play a key role in a culture of healing.

Congregations provide linkages to the community for health education and community health programs. In Haiti, where, as in Africa, there is little sense of community among the urban poor, churches in Port au Prince have become the vehicle for community health interventions both for their own members and for poor areas surrounding the church. Many programs in African-American churches and in the growing parish nurse program throughout the world also reflect the healing community role of local congregations. Local congregations may also become healing communities for patients who have no family willing to provide assistance and visit and pray with patients throughout the health program (Granberg-Michaelson 1997).

In many parts of the world volunteers from churches provide important services to Christian health programs. Because church-related hospitals in Africa have often been viewed by congregational members and church leaders alike more as opportunities for employment income and low-cost services rather than opportunities for volunteer ministry, congregational assistance is minimal in most areas. It has rarely been pursued in intentional strategies, however, particularly those that offer some reciprocity. Unchurched or non-Christian patients, for instance, could be referred to local pastors for continued follow-up after their release.

DEVELOP NEW APPROACHES TO HEALTHY EDUCATION THAT SHAPES AND CHALLENGES BASIC BELIEFS

In *Health, Bible and the Church*, Dr. Dan Fountain (1989) presents a model of culture that challenges health educators. Most approaches to health education begin and end in the outer circle. Even experienced educators appeal either to their authority or to the scientific rationale for the desired behavioral change. Beliefs and values are often regarded as irrelevant or as barriers to be overcome. Rarely does health education penetrate to change (or to affirm) values and beliefs and even less often the core of faith on which these beliefs rest.

Models of health education that target behavioral change from the inside out are rare. In *Let's Build Our Lives*, Dan Fountain (1990) accepts his own challenge and demonstrates how African pastors, working inductively from the values and beliefs of their friends, can use the Bible to bring about changed health behaviors. In the Jamkhet Community Health Program, Dr. Raj and Dr. Mabelle Arole used their village health worker training to challenge and change deep cultural beliefs about caste

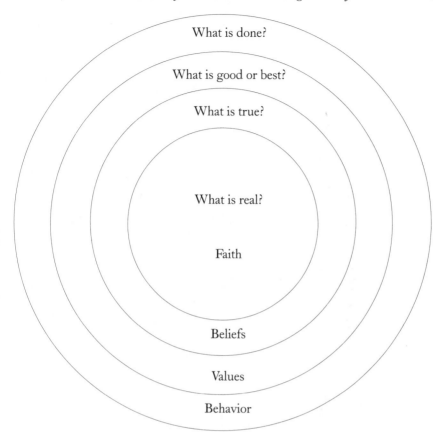

THE ELEMENTS OF CULTURE
(Adapted from Kwast)

roles and the behaviors that spring from them (Long 1997).

In Table 13:2, I present an analytic tool that can be used by health educators to analyze their educational approaches from a broader perspective so that they may discern if they can start from basic beliefs and move toward behavior change. It is not a lesson plan; an educator should not try to explain everything that might go on the chart.

Table 13:2

Integration of Biblical Perspectives into Health Teaching

Desired Practice	Scientific Justification	Traditional Practice	Traditional Values and Justification	Relevant Biblical Teaching and Values
Exclusive breast feeding of children to six months.	Breast food is the best for the child, given in a context that promotes bonding; with balanced nutrition and immunological properties; delays new pregnancies; prevents diarrhea from dirty water in formula.	Generally supportive but withholds colostrum. Some perception that formula may be better because it is "modern."	Colostrum is "old milk" and not good for the child. Modern methods must be better than old ones.	If God were to make a perfect food, what would it be like? Plentiful, free, in a context of relationship, gives strength, protects? If you had a perfect food from God, would you give it to your children? Would God try and trick you by making some of it good and some bad? Present breast milk as God's gift. Begin to build perception of God as loving Creator who is concerned about us. Present him as the one who created and knows us. Affirm most of the traditional beliefs but with a biblical rationale.

Complete childhood immunizations	Protection against preventable infectious diseases by creating an immune response. Need to expect side effects as possible response – it shows that the body is developing its defense.	Values the power of injections but often does not complete series because of unexplained side effects.	Probably tied to method of transmission rather than knowledge of the medicine itself. Wrapped up with concept of injections as powerful agents. Therefore may increase fear of side effects as being more powerful when in response to injection rather than pill (?). Is concept of power tied to traditional healing practices that involve the breaking of the skin or other invasive procedures?	God has equipped our bodies with His healing power—Psalms that speak of our creation. Idea of power that grows in opposition to another power—that the power of good is seen most easily in its response to evil. Why would they oppose a witch in their village? Because they have experienced the evil. The body must experience some discomfort in the present to prepare itself to fight off evil in the future. Healing is brought about through suffering—Christ as the wounded healer. Side effects of immunization involve suffering that brings healing? God has created us to exercise dominion. Part of this dominion is found in prevention. Farmers "inoculate" their fields to protect against infestation in the future. So we inoculate our children to show that we can control some aspects of their future.

CONTINUE TO ADDRESS HEALTH ISSUES
AT COMMUNITY AND ENVIRONMENTAL LEVELS

Most men and women who experience the healing touch of Christ's grace will experience it at home in the villages and poor urban areas of Africa. The reasons that led to the emergence of primary health care are no less compelling today. Churches are being increasingly recognized by donor agencies and governments as essential partners in community health efforts. Churches represent the most widespread presence in non-Islamic Africa. Together churches represent the largest force in Africa committed to behavior change; volunteers teach in thousands of villages every week. When all other institutions fall apart the churches remain.

NURTURE PARTNERSHIPS BETWEEN CHURCHES
IN THE NORTH AND SOUTH

Any hospital administrator in Africa who has persisted through this chapter to this point has almost without doubt grasped some of the financial implications of these suggestions. Three strategic elements essential to renewed ministry all require money. First, the poor must be an integral part of the ministry. Health problems cluster among the poor and the poor are given a central place in God's kingdom, but the poor are poor and often cannot pay for even basic services. To insist that Christian health programs must minister to the poor and also achieve financial sustainability is to place upon these programs a burden that has never been shouldered successfully. Health ministries to the poor are always subsidized in cash or in kind even to maintain basic services. Secondly, preventative services and health promotion in Africa will not be sustained on a fee for service basis. Finally, this approach requires additional investments in staff and lengthens the average time spent with each person.

Church-related hospitals are already pushing the limits of creativity in making ends meet. Beyond the careful use (and re-use when safe) of supplies and tiered approaches to patient charges, some, such as Chogoria Hospital in Kenya, are also subsidizing their work through agricultural production on hospital land and complementary business income.

Many hospitals collaborate with one another to form organizations such as the Mission for Essential Drugs and Supplies (MEDS) in Kenya to allow for quantities of scale in obtaining materials. Some receive funding, supplies, or personnel from the ministries of health or programs such as the Expanded Program of Immunizations (EPI) supported by bilateral and multilateral agencies. Many receive project grants from non-African governments, private foundations, and Christian relief and development agencies. Finally, many still depend upon the volunteer services of missionaries and short-term expatriate medical workers.

Even with this assistance most Christian hospitals and health programs in Africa cannot maintain themselves at minimally adequate levels. While I do not wish to underestimate the positive changes that churches and their health programs can make under present constraints, I am convinced that significant progress will demand a renewal of a healing vision not only in Africa but in the churches of more wealthy countries as well. Christian health and healing ministry needs to move beyond the narrowly defined sense of nationalism among citizens of African countries and the usually well intentioned but often paternalistic (or at worse, condescending) benevolence of expatriates. I am convinced that the way ahead will involve international teams under national leadership. Additionally it will involve long-term partnerships in ministry with churches or Christian agencies with greater access to resources.

PREPARE PASTORS AND CHRISTIAN HEALTH WORKERS IN A BIBLICAL THEOLOGY OF HEALING

The entire village had gathered to welcome back one of its sons. After nine and a half years of study in Europe he had finally obtained his Doctorate in Theology from a highly respected university. Fluent in four spoken languages as well as Greek, Latin, and Hebrew, most of his luggage consisted of the books that he had studied. Suddenly in the midst of the family and friends who have gathered to celebrate his return there was a disturbance.

Someone has fallen to the ground. It is his older sister…he rushes to her. People make room for him and watch him. "Let's take her to the hospital," he calls urgently. They are stunned. He becomes quiet. They all look at him bending over her. Why doesn't someone respond to his advice? Finally a schoolboy says, "Sir, the nearest hospital is 50 miles away, and there are few buses that go there." Someone else says, "She is possessed. Hospitals will not cure her!" The Chief says to him, "You have been studying theology for 10 years. Now help your sister. She is troubled by the spirit of her great aunt." He looks around. Suddenly he goes to Bultmann, looks at the index, finds what he wants, and reads again about spirit possession in the New Testament. Of course he gets the answer. Bultmann has demythologized it. He insists that his sister is not possessed. The people shout, "Help your sister, she is possessed!" He shouts back, "But Bultmann has demythologized demon possession" (Mbiti, cited in Bediako 1995, 135–136).

Few African seminaries help their pastoral students learn insights and skills that prepare them for the problems they will face among their congregation. They are uncertain of what they believe and how their beliefs interact with their day-to-day ministry. Like the new graduate in this story they look helplessly into the face of those who are suffering, unsure of what to do besides seeking medical care. Finally it is important that seminaries and Bible schools begin to develop training programs for hospital chaplaincy as a pastoral area unique from congregational and teaching ministries.

In order to provide this teaching it is essential that Christian scholars, pastors, and health workers in Africa give greater attention to defining the essential components of Christian health and healing within their own setting. In this book, I have provided a challenge and some biblical reflection, but as an outsider. African Christians who are mature in their faith and biblical knowledge and who know themselves and their peoples from the inside out must take up this discussion. Developing indigenous biblical approaches and understandings of health and healing has an immediate practical impact in areas that lie close to the heart of African religious practice and also serves as a gateway to the development of indigenous theology. Health and healing ministry touches upon the great doctrines of Christianity such as the person of Christ, the nature of God and his creation, sin, salvation, spiritual warfare, the nature and role of the church, and the nature of worship and prayer.

BIBLICALLY TRANSFORM
TRADITIONAL HEALING PRACTICES

Which traditional healing and health related practices may be used within a Christian health care setting? Ritual, symbol, and story powerfully influence health and promote or retard healing. What church traditions or health practices are interpreted by a particular culture so that they no longer carry the intended meaning? Answering these questions is not simple but it is essential to the transformation of Christian health ministries.

One book of the Bible, Hebrews, bridges the teachings between the person of Christ and patterns of Jewish belief and practice – belief and practice that share strong similarities to African thought and practice. Bediako (1990) suggests that Hebrews is therefore a key book in enabling a biblical contextualization of biblical teachings and practices within Africa.

Essential Components to the Process

How should these judgements be made? Each group must define its own process but there are some principles that should be common to them all.

- The judgements should be made by men and women who are mature in their Christian faith, are commissioned by their churches, who have agreed on some basic biblical principles concerning health and healing, and who value their own culture and traditions, but not uncritically. The group should include not only theologians and church leaders but also health workers and local pastors.
- The judgements must be specific to a particular cultural and church tradition. There will never be a single set of solutions that fits the wide variety of people groups and church traditions in Africa.
- Debate must be conducted in the vernacular of the people group and the judgements publicized in that language as well (with translation to other languages if required).
- Others may be brought into the group to present alternative points of view or to provide historical or technical perspectives. One group of mature church leaders in Cote d'Ivoire, for instance, invited early missionaries to return and give their perspective on how some church practices were established. The purpose was not to dishonor the early missionaries but rather to honor their work by carefully listening to the rationale behind practices. These African church leaders reserved the decision-making to themselves, however, as they should.

Judging Traditional Practices

Tables 13:3 and 13:4 help to conceptualize the nature of the judgements that must be made. Table 13:3 focuses upon two dimensions of traditional

Table 13:3

Adapting Traditional Practices for Christian Health and Healing Ministries

	Strength of Linkage between Traditional Practice and Its Meaning		
Meaning of Traditional Practice within the Culture	Strong	May be transformed	Weak
Incompatible with biblical truth	Reject as practice in Christian ministry	If possible, transform to Christian meaning; If not, discourage	Try to transform to Christian meaning
Neutral	Use if appropriate to need	If practice is effective, consider giving it a Christian meaning	
Compatible with biblical truth	If effective, try to use and reinforce	If effective, strengthen the Christian meaning	

practices; the meaning given to the practice by the particular culture and the strength of the linkage between the practice (form) and its traditional meaning. All traditional practices intrinsically harmful to physical health fall into the category of practice that is contrary to scripture. Here are some examples of practices that might generate greater debate.[4]

Example One: Trances

A council of mature Christians selected by their church must decide if diagnoses involving a trance-like state of a healer should be permitted as part of Christian healing practice. First they determine that the meaning given to that practice is that the healer is acting as a medium for ancestral or other spirits. After discussion, they conclude that possession by spirits to aid in healing is contrary to biblical teaching. Finally they examine how strongly that practice is linked to the meaning. After discussion they determine that trances are so strongly linked to spirit possession in the minds of their people that they could never be used without that association. They therefore forbid that practice within the setting of Christian healing.

Example Two: Anointing

Council members conclude that many of their people regard anointing with oil or water as magical; that is, the substance itself is imbued with power by the healer. They also determine that this meaning is contrary to biblical teaching. With further consideration, however, they also conclude that the practice, also taught in Scripture, has links to the traditional meaning that might be transformed by teaching. They decide to modify the practice and require that it always be performed by a group of Christians, rather than a single healer, in the strong context of prayer and confession. They then permit the modified practice to be used in the course of Christian healing ministry.

Example Three: Sacrifice

The council then considers the question of offering a blood sacrifice as part of the healing process. They determine that the sacrifice carries two meanings. Most of their people regard sacrifice first as appeasement of offended spirits. Secondly, however, the council notes that in some ceremonies the families that had been enemies also eat the sacrificed animal together to mark their reconciliation. In this instance, they determine that

Table 13:4

Evaluating Church and Medical Practices Regarding Their Cultural Meaning

Meaning Given to Church Practice or Medical Practice by the Culture	Importance of Church Practice or Medical Practice		
	Essential	Very Important	Of Some Importance
Incompatible with biblical truth	Instruct intensively to change meaning; consider small changes that might alter meaning	Consider alternative practice or give instruction to change meaning	Search for alternative practices
Neutral	Continue as required but look for opportunities to build understanding of health and biblical themes		
Compatible with biblical truth	Recognize those practices to which the culture assigns a different or deeper meaning and through disciplined reflection and instruction, use practice as a door to deeper biblical understanding of health, healing, and the gospel		

the first meaning is contrary to biblical teaching while the secondary meaning is compatible. They therefore look for a solution that preserves that second meaning while weakening the first. Finally they suggest that the offending family give an animal to the local congregation. Other church members kill the animal and prepare a meal for the two families as well as the church elders to eat together. At that meal, they might also celebrate communion, linking the sacrifice of Christ to the peace that has now been established between the two families.

Example Four: Neutral and Supportive Meanings

The council also determines that some health and healing practices, such as breast feeding or selected herbal remedies are neutral *from the perspective of their people*, as long as they do not cause intrinsic harm. They either permit their use when appropriate or look at the power of metaphor or symbol to introduce a specifically Christian meaning. Finally, they also determine that some practices have traditional meanings consistent with biblical messages that should be integrated into Christian health and healing ministries. If the linkage between the practice and the biblically consistent traditional meaning is weak, it should be strengthened to make the witness of the activity stronger.

Judging Church and Medical Practices

Table 13:4 examines the traditional meanings that may be given to medical and church practices. Again, examples help to illuminate the table.

Example One: Patient Warnings to Build Compliance

The council, now reinforced by mature Christians trained in health and medicine, decides to examine the practice of warning patients of the physical consequences of their lack of compliance with medical procedures. For instance, "If you do not continue this medicine four times a day, your child will probably die." They decide that many of their people may equate this warning with a curse or prediction. If the child subsequently dies or the illness is prolonged, the family of the child might attribute that to the powerful ill will of the clinician. Additionally, they decide that this cultural meaning is contrary to biblical teaching. They then conclude that while compliance with the timing and dosages of the medicines is essential, the practice of using warnings based upon possible consequences is not. They, together with the clinical staff, search for alternatives and decide, whenever possible, to base their instruction upon the limitations of the power of the medicine. As the power of the medicine wears down, it must be renewed, just as food eaten in the morning will not give power for work in the evening. Furthermore, they decide that, whenever possible, the instruction should be given to all of the family members who are present.

Example Two: Immunizations

The council then turns their attention to immunizations that must be given by injection. In looking at traditional belief, they discover that parents give two interpretations to the practice. First they attribute greater power to substances that are given through the breaking of the skin. Secondly, some attribute the power of the immunizations to spiritual power attained through ritual scarification. They immediately determine that there are no suitable alternatives to immunizations given through injections – they are truly essential. They then plan through teaching to change beliefs. They wish to have people understand the interaction between power and the method of administration. ("If I were to cut you open and put a piece of meat into your body, would that meat make you strong?" "No, some things that are powerful when taken into the body through the mouth are not powerful if given through the breaking of the skin. And the reverse is also true.")

Example Three: Baptism

This same approach may also be used to evaluate church practices. The council is concerned because their people assign a cleansing and cooling effect to baptism and therefore want it to be repeated. They decide that baptism is essential to the Christian faith, but the popular understanding of the rite fits neither biblical teaching nor the interpretations given by their church. They therefore identify a need to provide additional teaching about its meaning and, perhaps, to develop a practice other than baptism that would symbolize cleansing from repeated sins.

Example Four: The Lord's Supper

The council then turns to the question of the Lord's Supper (Eucharist). They may find that the people assign two meanings to it. One symbolizes the sacrifice to satisfy a God who is holy and just and therefore offended

Table 13:5
Non-Medical Interventions of African Churches
for Disease and Injury

Prayer	Sacraments and Church Rituals Shared with Western Traditions	Rituals and Symbols from African Church Traditions
Petition for individual healing Prayer for inner healing Prayer of confession Prayer for forgiveness Prayer for healing of memories Prayer of blessing Prayer for justice Corporate prayer of peace by former opponents Prayer for prophetic insight Prayer for spiritual protection Prayer for deliverance from possessing or oppressing spirit	Anointing of sick Prayer for healing by church elders Laying on of hands Baptism Confession Penance Communion (Eucharist) Holy water Exorcism Speaking in tongues Ecstatic experiences (slain in the Spirit, holy laughter, etc.) Crucifix Icons	Prayer with culturally significant healing symbols by recognized healer of power Wearing clothing or other articles blessed by powerful healer Purgative substances Ash Staves Spirit possession (ancestors or Holy Spirit) Cleansing ceremonies Peace meals or ceremonies of reconciliation Physical manipulation of sick person by group or healer Sacrifices and libations Healing services and campaigns Period of residency in the healing village of a recognized prophet

Adapted from Bate 1995, 278–279

by sin. The second symbolizes a table of peace, a meaning that is implicit in the ceremony. They then decide to make a greater use of the Lord's Supper as part of the healing process when relationships must be made whole again.

SCOPE OF THE TASK

The task of biblical contextualization is broad in its scope. Table 13:5 lists only some of the non-medical interventions already used by churches in Africa in the context of health and healing ministries. The list is both a challenge and a reminder of the depth of resources that African churches are already bringing to the work of health and healing.[5]

♦ ♦ ♦

Chief who listens to the poor, humble King,
your words are precious jewels.
We don't buy them, we don't beg for them;
you give them to us freely!

Giver of good gifts, we are waiting for you,
And the sick are waiting for medicine.
O Jesus, you have swallowed death
and every kind of disease,
And have made us whole again.

(Kuma 1981, 11)

♦ ♦ ♦

May the church bring wholeness to the peoples and nations of Africa by the grace and power of her Lord, Jesus, who gives good gifts and who listens to the poor.

Notes

1   Throughout this chapter, I will refer to ancestral spirits from the perspective of those who believe in them. Though I believe that spirits exist and communicate, I believe it is impossible to determine biblically if they are ancestral

spirits under the command of Satan or demonic spirits who pose as ancestors. (See Chapter 2 for a more detailed discussion of ancestral spirits.)

2　Though I recognize that the practical applications I suggest in this chapter relate closely to the on-going missiological and theological debates concerning issues of continuity/ discontinuity, inculturation, contextualization, and questions of form and substance, I take the position of many evangelicals that Christianity is discontinuous with African traditional beliefs. I also believe however that God witnesses to Himself outside the special revelation of the Bible and that this general revelation is reflected in many non-Christian systems of belief and religious practice. I do not believe that African traditional religion is an incomplete, earlier, or alternative expression of Christianity. Rather I believe that Christianity may have authentic expressions in African cultures, necessarily differing from its expressions in other cultures. I refer my reader to those who have written extensively on these subjects and particularly encourage them to include African theologians such as Bediako, Pobee, Mbiti, and others.

3　In his book, *Primary Diagnosis and Treatment* (1992), Dr. Dan Fountain has included a series of questions (pages 46–50) that can help the diagnostician inquire into the context of relationships affecting the health of a patient in an African setting.

4　These examples largely reflect how I might respond and so I offer them as illustrations rather than as answers.

5　I do not personally agree with all of the interventions in this list. I believe that some of these practices carry meanings that many peoples in Africa would inextricably link to meanings contrary to the Bible. They do represent interventions that are currently being used in churches, however, and therefore need to be evaluated.

Appendix

Some Biblical Perspectives on Health and Healing Ministry

LESSON 1
DISEASE PREVENTION, HEALTH, AND THE LAW

Scripture References

God's Promises and Curses
- Exodus 15:26
- Deut. 7:15; 28:15, 21–23

Health from the Commandments
- Exodus 20:8–14; 23:10–12

Disease Prevention: Infection
- Lev. 13:1–17, 45–46; 14:8–9
- Deut. 23:12–13

Disease Prevention: Body Fluids
- Lev. 15:1–13, 25–27, 31

Disease Prevention: Food and Drink
- Lev. 11:29–40; 17:13–15

"Diseases of Poverty": Charity

- Deut. 24:19–22; 23:24–25; 26:12–13

"Diseases of Poverty": Social Justice

- Lev. 25:8–13, 23–31, 39–43
- Deut. 15:1-5, 7–11; 24:6, 10–15

The Law given to Moses and the People of Israel by the Lord contained many commandments which we now know are health related. We want to examine those commandments in this Bible study.

God's Promises and Curses

- List the health related promises and curses God made to the Israelites. On what condition were these promises and curses based?
- How are both prevention and cure part of the promises in this passage?
- The Israelites believed that disease was a personal punishment of God for sin. How does God in the Deuteronomy passage suggest that sin and disease may be related?
- Based on this passage, how would you respond to an accusation that a person with AIDS is being personally and individually punished by God for his or her sins?

Health from the Commandments

The principles of the Sabbath rest are carried throughout the Law in many ways. The commandment to honor your father and mother carries a specific promise of long life (and health) with it. Adultery is almost always associated in the Bible with ill health.

- In your experience, what differences have you found in the general health between those who follow these commandments and those who do not?
- What special significance do the principles underlying the Sabbath rest have for patients suffering from stress related disorders?
- In what ways do you observe or fail to observe the principles of the Sabbath rest in your own practice of medicine?

Disease Prevention: Infection, Body Fluids, Food, and Drink

Please answer the following questions for each of these sections. Do not try to read the passages aloud but first look at the questions and then at the passage with the question in mind.

- What preventive and treatment strategies do you find in these commandments that are in agreement with accepted medical practices today?
- Which of the infectious diseases you see most often among your patients would significantly decrease if these laws were followed?
- How was the role of the clergy (priests) in health care different from their roles today? In what ways do you think the separation of care with medical professionals caring for the body and the clergy caring for the soul and spirit result in better patient care than for the Israelites? What has been lost by the dividing of the person's care between several professionals?
- What more might you do to involve pastors as colleagues in patient care?

"Diseases of Poverty": Charity and Justice

- In your medical experience, what have you observed about the relationship of health, disease, and poverty to one another, beyond the inability of the poor to afford medical care?
- Examine the laws in regard to charity and justice. On what principles are they based?
- Think about our methods of showing charity today and the methods given by God. How are they different in the role and the dignity of the poor person?
- What problems of social justice did the laws address in regard to money-lending and the years of restoration and Jubilee? What parallels do you see in your own country?
- Based on these principles, what might you and your colleagues be able to do in your practices to care for the poor beyond providing care that is free or at reduced rates?
- How may you in your practice (and the health care institutions with which you are involved) practically address some of these same issues

today?

Summary Questions

- What have you learned about the nature and causes of disease and health?
- Who did God intend to be involved in health promotion and disease prevention?
- What principles in regard to healing ministries do you find here?
- What practical implications does this have to your practice?
- How might following through with some of the principles you have discovered affect your income?

LESSON 2
LESSONS FROM THE PSALMS

GUILT, REJECTION, AND GOD'S SILENCE; REPENTANCE; FORGIVENESS; STRENGTH; AND SECURITY

Scripture References

The Agony of God's Silence and Men's Scorn
- Psalm 6
- Psalm 22: Does God Care?

Guilt and Forgiveness
- Psalm 32: The Pain of Sin and Joy of Forgiveness
- Psalm 38: Guilt and the Abandonment of Friends

Security and Salvation
- Psalm 30: Wailing into Dancing
- Psalm 34: Security and Righteousness

Created for Now and Eternity
- Psalm 139: Known of God
- Psalm 103: Strength for Now and Hope for the Future

David writes more expressively about his mind and heart than any other biblical writer. Medical research of today is finding that a complex and powerful relationship exists between the state of a person's mind and his/her health. The efficacy of the immune system is linked with powerful emotions of hopelessness, despair, loneliness, and guilt in ways that we are just beginning to understand. David's experiences echo in our own souls.

Agony of God's Silence and Friends' Scorn

- How does David experience his relationship to God in these Psalms? How does it affect him?
- In Psalm 22, David remembers God's faithfulness to his fathers and his own heritage of trust in the Lord. Why does this fail to comfort him? What effect does it have?
- How does the response of the people to David affect him?
- Why is the anguish of soul similar to David's more likely to affect a person who is sick than one who is healthy? What hard questions about a time of illness is a Christian more likely to struggle with than a non-Christian?
- How do we normally respond to people experiencing what David felt here? What well intended things might make matters worse rather than better?

Guilt and Forgiveness

- If a patient came to you exhibiting the physical symptoms David mentions in Psalms 32 and 38, what would be your tentative clinical diagnosis? What therapy or diagnostic steps would you undertake?
- In Psalm 38:11, David writes that his friends now avoid him. In your experience, how have patients responded whose friends leave them?
- In your own setting, how may a patient's enemies contribute to his/her continued ill health? What was David's response to the freedom he found from guilt by God's forgiveness?
- If the root cause of your patient's illness was guilt about a specific relationship or event (not general sinfulness before God), how likely is it that the guilt would be "diagnosed" and adequately "treated"?

Security and Salvation

- In Psalms 30 and 34, how did David's experience with the Lord

contribute to his health?
- What do you think the "fear of the Lord" might have to do with health? (What other fears might "the fear of the Lord" displace?)
- What relationship does behavior as well as attitude have to health in Psalm 34? (See verses 12–14). How might security, the fear of the Lord, righteous living in regard to relationships with others, and good health all be interrelated?

Created for Now and Eternity

- In Psalm 139, describe the activities of God in relationship to David (and in relationship to patients today).
- In verses 13–16, God describes his activities in creating the "inmost being" of David at the same time as he describes the creation of his body. How do we fail (or succeed) to reflect the unity of the soul and body in God's eyes in our practice of medicine?
- What is David's response to his knowledge that "All the days ordained for me were written in your book before one of them came to be"? Why is it not a fatalistic response (i.e., There is nothing I can do. It is God's will)?
- From Psalm 103 list the benefits of the Lord (v. 2) that David urges his soul not to forget. Which of these benefits is related to health? How? How is the act of consciously remembering them and meditating upon them related to health?
- In Psalm 103, why is the knowledge of the certainty of death (13–17) not a depressing thought to David?
- What are the implications of these psalms to our ministry to the seriously ill and dying?

Summary Questions

- What have you learned about the nature and causes of disease and health?
- In what ways would David's experience of health and ill health reflect those of your patients?
- What principles in regard to healing ministries do you find here?
- What practical implications does this have for the work of a Christian health practitioner?

LESSON 3
LESSONS IN HEALTH FROM THE PROVERBS

Scripture References

Wisdom and Health
- Prov. 3:1–2, 5–8, 13–18; 4:20–23

Relationship of Health, Joy, and Hopelessness
- Prov. 12:25; 13:12; 14:30; 15:13; 15:30; 17:22; 18:14

The Healing of Relationships
- Prov. 12:18; 15:4; 16:24; 17:1

Wisdom and Health

- According to these passages, what is it that brings health?
- Solomon's concept of health seems to go beyond physical well being. What else seems to be included?
- In what way is the heart both physically and metaphorically the "well-spring of life"?
- In your practice, what characterizes a "good" patient? How is this related to a biblical concept of wisdom?

Health, Joy, and Hopelessness

- List the things from these passages that contribute to health.
- List the things that detract from health or bring sickness.
- How can you tell if a patient has a "crushed spirit"? How do they respond differently to treatment from one with a joyful heart? What can you do beyond what you do now to heal the "crushed spirit" as well as cure the diseased or injured body?
- A community, family, or institution can also have a crushed spirit. What can crush their collective spirit? How are their responses similar to those of the individual with a crushed spirit?
- What might you do in your diagnostic interview that would more closely fit a biblical perspective upon health and disease?

The Healing of Relationships

- What is the most effective "therapeutic instrument" for the treatment of a "crushed spirit?"
- What do you as a Christian physician say or do in your relationship to your patients that heals the spirit?
- How have you seen yourself or other health care professionals wound and crush the spirit of their patients without intending to do so?
- How may you build or crush the spirits of:
  - communities in which you work
  - your subordinates and your bosses
  - your colleagues?

Summary Questions

- What have you learned about the nature and causes of disease and health?
- What principles in regard to healing ministries do you find here?
- What practical implications does this have to your practice of medicine?
- How might following through with these principles affect your income?

LESSON 4
THE HEALING MINISTRY OF JESUS

Scripture References

- Luke 4:38–40   Peter's Mother-in-law
- Luke 5:12–16   Leprosy
- Luke 5:17–26   The Paralytic and His Friends
- Luke 7:2–10   The Centurion's Servant
- Luke 7:11–17   The Widow of Nain
- Luke 8:26–39   The Gerasene Demoniac
- Luke 8:40–56   A Bleeding Woman and a Dead Girl
- Luke 9:37–43a   The Young Demoniac
- Luke 17:11–19   The Ten Lepers
- Luke 18:35–43   The Blind Beggar
- Luke 22:47–51   The Last Healing Before Jesus' Death

In the Bible references, you have all eleven accounts of Jesus' healing ministry in the book of Luke. You will likely not have time to work with all eleven. Please include "The Paralytic and His Friends," "The Centurion's Servant," "The Gerasene Demoniac," and "The Bleeding Woman and a Dead Girl" in the analysis. If you have time remaining at the end, choose one or two more. For each account of healing, please do the following analysis:

Diagnosis

Jesus often did a diagnosis on three levels before he healed. The first and most simple was the physical problem. Secondly, he often looked beyond the physical problem to the more basic needs of the "patient." Lastly, he evaluated the condition of those around the patient and often took some action directed toward them as well.

Give the diagnosis of the problems Jesus was addressing in each of the accounts:
- Physical
- Deeper needs of the "patient"
- Others around him

You may not be able to have a "diagnosis" at each level for each account of healing.

Treatment

- What did Jesus do at each level of the problem to address it?
- What was the response to his "treatment"?

Summary Questions

- What have you learned about the nature and causes of disease and health?
- In what ways would Jesus' healing ministry closely match the needs and beliefs of your patients?
- How was Jesus' healing ministry more like that of a traditional practitioner than of a medical professional? How does the source and use of power differ between Jesus and a traditional practitioner?
- In what circumstances would your patients reject your attempts to broaden your healing practice?

- What principles in regard to healing ministries do you find here?
- What practical implications does this have for your practice?

LESSON 5
LESSONS IN HEALTH FROM THE EPISTLES

Scripture References

Relationships of Health or Destruction
- Gal. 5:13–15
- Eph. 4:25–32
- Col. 3:12–17
- James 3:3–12
- 1 Pet. 3:8–12

Restoration and Forgiveness
- 2 Cor. 2:5–8
- Gal. 6:1–5

Support and Comfort
- 2 Cor. 1:3–11
- 2 Cor. 8:7–15
- James 5:13–20

Joy and Peace
- Phil. 4:4–9

What effects do the quality of our personal relationships have upon health? Research has indicated that people who receive love and affection and who have extensive "social networks" of friends live longer and in better health than those without them. Social networks provide not only emotional and spiritual support but also "instrumental support," helping out in work, giving money, and providing advice at times of distress.

The church is a "social network" established by God for the care of his children and the accomplishment of his ministry. By looking at passages that teach about the mutual obligations of Christians one to another, we can also learn about health.

Relationships of Health or Destruction

- In the passages in this section, list the things we are to avoid in our relationships to one another. From your clinical experience, describe the health of those who themselves are bitter, angry, vindictive, etc., or who are the victims of another's anger or bitterness.
- Make a list of those things that are to characterize our relationships to one another. From your clinical experience, how has the recovery of patients who have these types of support been different from those who did not.
- With these positive qualities as goals, how would you characterize the relationship of you and your medical colleagues to patients and communities?
- How does the presence of these negative or positive qualities in: 1) subordinate/authority, 2) authority/subordinate, and 3) co-worker/co-worker relationships within the hospital affect the quality of ministry to patients and communities?
- We normally think of medicines, surgery, and therapy as "instruments of healing." What are the major "instruments of healing" in the area of relationships? What skills are necessary to use them? How are they integrated into your ministry of healing?

Restoration and Forgiveness

- What happens to the health of a person rejected by and/or isolated from family and community?
- If the root cause of your patient's illness was guilt about a specific relationship or event and the isolation from community associated with it, how likely is it that the disturbance in the relationship would be "diagnosed" and adequately "treated"?
- What role does confrontation play in the "therapy of restoration"?
- What is the effect upon hospital ministry of destructive relationships among staff that continue unchallenged and unresolved?

Support and Comfort

- In the three passages in this section, what areas of support and comfort are we commanded to offer?
- How would integrating these ministries into our treatment fit the

patient's concept of disease and health? How well would it fit the view of health and disease we receive in our professional medical training?

- What is necessary for the practice of prayer and comfort to be more than a routine ritual? (2 Cor. 1:3–6 and James 5:13, 16 provide a description of an experiential and relational context that makes these ministries effective.)
- What is the effect of "instrumental support" such as that encouraged in 2 Cor. 8:7–15 upon community and individual health?

Joy and Peace

- In your experience how has the clinical experience of patients whose patterns of thought are characterized by Phil. 4:8 differed from those who focus on other matters?

Summary Questions

- What have you learned about the nature and causes of disease and health?
- What principles in regard to healing ministries do you find here?
- What practical implications does this have for your practice?

References

Allen, E.A., 1995. *Caring for the Whole Person*. Monrovia, CA: MARC Publishers.

Ambe, J.B. 1992. *Meaningful Celebration of the Sacrament of Reconciliation in Africa*. Eldoret, Kenya: AMECEA Gaba Publications.

Amelemba, W., D. Dortzbach, N. Kiiti, W. Long, C. Mwal'wa, and P. Robinson. 1996. *Growing Together: A Guide for Parents and Youth*. Nairobi, Kenya: MAP International.

Atkins, T. 1990. "What is Health?" In *A New Agenda for Medical Missions*, ed. D.M. Ewert, 7–18. Brunswick, GA: MAP International.

Avalos, H. 1995. "Ancient Medicine: In Case of Emergency, Contact Your Local Prophet." *Bible Review* 11 (June): 26–32, 34–35, 48.

Backus, W. 1996. *The Healing Power of a Healthy Mind*. Minneapolis: Bethany House Publishers.

Balk, D.E. 1991. "Sibling Death, Adolescent Bereavement and Religion." *Death Studies* 15:1–20.

Balzer, K. 1989. "Music and Dance in Zionist Healing Ceremonies." In *Afro-Christian Religion and Healing in Southern Africa*, eds. G.C. Oosthuizen, S.D. Edwards, W.H. Wessels, and I Hexham, 172–183. Lewiston, NY: Edward Mellen Press.

Bate, S.C. 1995. *Inculturation and Healing*. Pietermaritzburg, South Africa: Cluster Publications.

Bediako, K. 1990. *Jesus in African Culture: A Ghanian Perspective*. Accra, Ghana: Asempa Publishers.

Bediako, K. 1995a. *Christianity in Africa: The Renewal of a Non-Western*

Religion. Maryknoll, NY: Edinburgh University Press/Orbis Books.

Bediako, K. 1995b. "Cry Jesus! Christian Theology and Presence in Modern Africa." *VOX Evangelica* 23: 7–26.

Bediako, K. 1995c. "De-sacralization and Democratization: Some Theological Reflections on Nation-building in Modern Africa." *Transformation* 12: 5–11.

Beg, M.A., and A.S. Zilli. 1982. "A Study of the Relationship of Death Anxiety and Religious Faith to Age Differentials." *Psychologia* 25: 121–125.

Bergin, A.E., K.S. Masters, and P.S. Richards. 1987. "Religiousness and Mental Health Reconsidered: A Study of an Intrinsically Religious Sample." *Journal of Counseling Psychology* 34 (2): 197–204.

Berkman, L.F., and S.L. Syme. 1979. "Social Networks, Host Resistance, and Mortality: A Nine-Year Follow-up Study of Alameda County Residents." *American Journal of Epidemiology* 109: 186–204.

Bledsoe, C.H., and K.M. Robey. 1986. "Arabic Literacy and Secrecy among the Mende of Sierre Leone." *Man* 21(2): 202–226.

Boman, T. 1960. *Hebrew Thought Compared with Greek*. New York: WW Norton.

Bond V., and P. Ndubani. 1997. "The Difficulties of Compiling a Glossary of Diseases Associated with Sexual Intercourse in Chiawa, Rural Zambia." *Social Science and Medicine* 44(8): 1211–1220.

Bosch, D.J. 1987. "The Problem of Evil in Africa: A Survey of African Views on Witchcraft and of the Response of the Christian Church." In *Like a Roaring Lion*, ed. P.G.R. de Villiers, 38–63. Pretoria: C.B. Powell Bible Center.

Brand, P. 1995. "The Laws of Health and Wholeness." In *Transforming Health: Christian Approaches to Healing and Wholeness*, ed. Eric Ram, 39–52. Monrovia, CA: MARC Publications.

Brichto, H.C. 1975. "The Case of *Sota* and a Reconsideration of Biblical 'Law.'" *Hebrew Union College Annual* 46: 55–70.

Broadhead, W.E., B.H. Kaplan, S.A. James, E.A. Wagner, V.J. Schoenbach, R. Grimson, S. Heyden, G. Tibblin, and S.H. Gehlbach. 1983. "The Epidemiologic Evidence for a Relationship between Social Support and Health." *American Journal of Epidemiology* 117(5): 521–536.

Brodeen, J. 1995. "The Unleashed Word: A Power to Create, a Power to

Destroy." Unpublished paper, Wheaton College Graduate School, Wheaton, IL.

Brown, M.L. 1995. *Israel's Divine Healer.* Grand Rapids, MI: Zondervan.

Brueggemann, W. 1976. *Living Toward a Vision: Biblical Reflections on Shalom*. Philadelphia, PA: United Church Press.

Busia, K.A. 1967. *Africa in Search of Democracy*. London: Routledge and Kegan Paul.

Byaruhanga-Akiiki, A.B.T., and O.N.O. Kealotswe. 1995. *African Theology of Healing*. Gaborone: Department of Theology/Religious Studies, University of Botswana.

Byrd, R.B. 1988. "Positive Therapeutic Effects of Intercessory Prayer in a Coronary Care Population." *Southern Medical Journal* 81(7): 826–829.

Carpentier, P., T. Prazuck, F. Vincent-Ballereau, L.T. Ouedraogo, and C. Laifaix. 1995. "Choice of Traditional or Modern Treatment in West Burkina Faso." *World Health Forum* (16): 198–202.

Carroll, J.T. 1995. "Sickness and Healing in the New Testament Gospels." *Interpretation* 49 (April): 130–132.

Cassidy, M. 1995. *A Witness Forever.* London: Hodder and Stoughton.

Chamberlain, K., and S. Zika. 1988. "Religiosity, Life Meaning and Wellbeing: Some Relationships in a Sample of Women." *Journal for the Scientific Study of Religion* 27(3): 411–420.

Chavunduka, G.L. 1995. "Traditional Medicine in Africa." *Transforming Health: Christian Approaches to Healing and Wholeness*, ed. Eric Ram, 289–298. Monrovia, CA: MARC Publications.

Cheetam, R.W.S, and J.A. Griffiths. 1989. "The Traditional Healer/Diviner as Psychotherapist." In *Afro-Christian Religion and Healing in Southern Africa*, eds. G.C. Oosthuizen, S.D. Edwards, W.H. Wessels, and I. Hexham, 305–312. Lewiston, NY: Edward Mellen Press.

Christensen, T.C. 1990. *An African Tree of Life*. Maryknoll, NY: Orbis Books.

Cook, J.A., and D.W. Wimberley. 1983. "If I Should Die Before I Wake: Religious Commitment and Adjustment to the Death of a Child." *Journal for the Scientific Study of Religion* 22(3): 222–238.

Daneel, M.L. 1970. *Zionism and Faith-Healing in Rhodesia: Aspects of African Independent Churches*. The Hague, Netherlands: Mouton and

Company.

Daneel, M.L. 1990. "Exorcism as a Means of Combating Wizardry: Liberation or Enslavement." *Missionalia* 18 (April): 220–247.

De Rosny, E. 1985. *Healers in the Night*. Maryknoll, NY: Orbis Books.

Dickson, K. 1984. *Theology in Africa*. Darton, London: Longman & Todd.

Dorff, E.N. 1996. "The Jewish Tradition." In *Caring and Curing*, eds. R.L. Numbers, and D.W. Amundsen. New York: MacMillan Publishing Company.

Dube, D. 1989. "A Search for Abundant Life: Health, Healing and Wholeness in the Zionist Churches." In *Afro-Christian Religion and Healing in Southern Africa*, eds. G.C. Oosthuizen, S.D. Edwards, W.H. Wessels, and I. Hexham, 109–136. Lewiston, NY: Edward Mellen Press.

Dudley, R.L., P.B. Mutch, and R.J. Cruise. 1987. "Religious Factors and Drug Usage Among Seventh-Day Adventist Youth in North America." *Journal for the Scientific Study of Religion* 26(2): 218–233.

Dumbrell, W.J. 1984. *Covenant and Creation*. Exeter, Devon, UK: Paternoster Press.

du Toit, B.M. 1981a. "The Isangoma: An Adaptive Agent among the Urban Zulu." In *African Healing Strategies*, eds. B.M. du Toit, and I.H. Abdalla, 82–95. New York: Trado-Medic Books.

du Toit, B.M. 1981b. "Religion, Ritual, and Healing among Urban Black South Africans." In *African Healing Strategies*, eds. B.M. du Toit, and I.H. Abdalla, 151–179. New York: Trado-Medic Books.

Edwards, F.S. 1989. "Amafufunyana Spirit Possessions: Treatment and Interpretation." In *Afro-Christian Religion and Healing in Southern Africa*, eds. G.C. Oosthuizen, S.D. Edwards, W.H. Wessels, and I. Hexham, 207–225. Lewiston, NY: Edward Mellen Press.

Fako, T.T. 1981. "The Dilemma of African Traditional Medicine: The Case of the Botswana." In *African Healing Strategies*, eds. B.M. du Toit, and I.H. Abdalla, 190–229. New York: Trado-Medic Books.

Ferraro, K.F., and C.M. Albrecht-Jensen. 1991. "Does Religion Influence Adult Health?" *Journal for the Scientific Study of Religion* 30(2): 193–202.

Folkman, S. 1997. "Positive Psychological States and Coping with Severe Stress." *Social Science and Medicine* 45(8): 1207–1221.

Fountain, D. 1989. *Health, the Bible and the Church*. Wheaton, IL: Billy

Graham Center, Wheaton College.

Fountain, D. 1990. *Let's Build Our Lives.* Brunswick, GA: MAP International.

Fountain, D. 1994. *Primary Diagnosis and Treatment.* London: MacMillan Press Ltd.

Fountain, D. 1996. "Why Africa's Transformation Waits." *Evangelical Missions Quarterly* 32(3) (July): 320–326.

Gass, K.A. 1987 "The Health of Conjugally Bereaved Older Widows: The Role of Appraisal, Coping and Resources." *Research in Nursing and Health* 10:39–47.

Gehman, R.J. 1985. *Ancestor Relations among Three African Societies in Biblical Perspective.* Dissertation, School of World Mission and Institute of Church Growth, Fuller Theological Seminary, Pasadena, CA.

Gehman, R.J. 1989. *African Traditional Religion in Biblical Perspective.* Kijabe, Kenya: Kijabe Printing Press.

Genia, V., and D.G. Shaw. 1991. "Religion, Intrinsic-Extrinsic Orientation and Depression." *Review of Religious Research* 32(30): 247–283.

Georgemiller, R.J., and S.H. Getsinger. 1987. "Reminiscence Therapy: Effect on More and Less Religious Elderly." *Journal of Religion and Aging* 4(2): 47–58.

Germond T., 1994. Private interview, Medical University of South Africa, Pretoria.

Gibbs, H.W., and J. Achterberg-Lawlis. 1978. "Spiritual Values and Death Anxiety: Implications for Counseling with Terminal Cancer Patients." *Journal of Counseling Psychology* 25(6): 563–569.

Goody, J. 1996. "Cognitive Contradictions and Universals: Creation and Evolution in Oral Cultures." *Social Anthropology* 4(1): 1–16.

Gottlieb, N.H., and L.W. Green. 1984. "Life Events, Social Network, Lifestyle, and Health: An Analysis of the 1979 National Survey of Personal Health Practices and Consequences." *Health Education Quarterly* 11(1): 91–105.

Granberg-Michaelson, K. 1997. "Staying Healthy: The Spiritual Dimension." *Contact* 155:3–5.

Granberg-Michaelson, K., and W. Granberg-Michaelson. 1995. "Healing, the Church's Birthright." In *Transforming Health: Christian Approaches to Healing and Wholeness,* ed. Eric Ram, 237–250. Monrovia, CA: MARC Publications.

Green, M. 1996. "Medicines and the Embodiment of Substances among

Pogoro Catholics, Southern Tanzania." *Journal of the Royal Anthropological Institute* 2(3): 485–498.

Griffith, E.E.H., and G.E. Mahy. 1984. "Psychological Benefits of Spiritual Baptist 'Mourning'." *American Journal of Psychiatry* 141(6): 769–773.

Haddon, W. "Advances in the Epidemiology of Injuries as a Basis for Public Policy." *Public Health Reports* 95: 411–421.

Hallgren, R. 1991. *The Good Things in Life*. Vol. 2, Lund Studies in African and Asian Religions. Malmo: Plus Ultra/Graphic Systems AB.

Hammond-Tooke, W.D. 1989. "The Aetiology of Spirit in Southern Africa." In *Afro-Christian Religion and Healing in Southern Africa*, eds. G.C. Oosthuizen, S.D. Edwards, W.H. Wessels, and I. Hexham, 43–65. Lewiston, NY: Edward Mellen Press.

Hanson, K., 1998. "Report on KPC Survey, Ponea Kriek District, Cambodia." World Relief, Wheaton, IL.

Harris, D.J. 1970. *Shalom! The Biblical Concept of Peace*. Grand Rapids, MI: Baker Book House.

Heibert, P.G. 1994. *Anthropological Reflections on Missiological Issues*. Grand Rapids, MI: Baker Books.

Hill, H. 1996. "Witchcraft and the Gospel: Insights from Africa." *Missiology: An International Review* 24(3): 323–344.

Hilton, D. 1996. "Curing, Healing, and Community." *Contact* 152 (December): 3–5.

"HIV/AIDS and Traditional Culture." 1996. A Declaration of the Organization of Africa Instituted Churches and the Bishops and Heads of Churches in Nyanza Province, 3–4. Ahero, Kenya.

House, J.S., K.R. Landis, and D. Umberson. 1988. "Social Relationships and Health." *Science* 214: 540–545.

Israel, B.A. 1985. "Social Networks and Social Support: Implications for Natural Helper and Community Level Interventions." *Health Education Quarterly* 12: 65–80.

Isralowitz, R.E., and T.H. Ong. 1990. "Religious Values and Beliefs and Place of Residence as Predictors of Alcohol Use among Chinese College Students in Singapore." *The International Journal of Addictions* 25(5): 515–29.

Jansen, G. 1973. *The Doctor-Patient Relationship in an African Tribal Village*. Assen, Netherlands: Van Gorcum and Company.

Jansen, J. 1981. "Changing Concepts of African Therapeutics: An

Historical Perspective." In *African Healing Strategies*, eds. B.M. du Toit, and I.H. Abdalla, 61–81. New York: Trado-Medic Books.

Jekel, J.F. 1995. "Biblical Foundations for Health and Healing." *Perspectives on Science and Christian Faith* 47 (Spring): 150–158.

Johnson, S.C., and B. Spilka. 1991. "Coping with Breast Cancer: the Roles of Clergy and Faith." *Journal of Religion and Health* 30 (1): 21-33.

Kagame, A. 1969. "La Place de Dieu et de l'Homme dans la Religion des Bantu." *Cahiers des Religions Africaines* 3(5): 1.

Kailing, J.B. 1994. "A New Solution to the African Christian Problem." *Missiology: An International Review* 23(4): 489–506.

Kaiser, W.C., Jr. 1982. *A Biblical Approach to Personal Suffering*. Chicago: Moody Press.

Kawachi, I., B.P. Kennedy, K. Lochner, and D. Prothrow-Stith. 1997. "Social Capital, Income Inequality, and Mortality." *American Journal of Public Health* 87(9): 1491–1498.

Kealotswe, O.N.O. 1989. Spiritual Healing and Traditional Medicine in Botswana. In *Afro-Christian Religion at the Grassroots in Southern Africa*, eds. G.C. Oosthuizen and Irving Hexham, 184–190. Lewiston, NY: Edward Mellen Press.

Kiernan, J.P. 1990. *The Production and Management of Therapeutic Power in Zionist Churches within a Zion City*. Vol. 4, Studies in African Health and Medicine. Lewiston, NY: Edward Mellen Press.

Kiiti, N., E. Gatua, E. Odira, D. Dortzbach, and M. Long. 1996. "Home Care for People with AIDS in Kenya: Mobilization for Action." Unpublished paper, MAP International, Nairobi, Kenya.

Kinoti, G. 1994. "African Christians and the Future of Africa." *Transformation* 11:24–32.

Kirwen, M.C. 1978. *The Missionary and the Diviner*. Maryknoll, NY: Orbis Books.

Koenig, H.G. 1988. "Religious Behavior and Death Anxiety in Later Life." *Hospice Journal* 4(1): 3–24.

Koenig, H.G., H.J. Cohen, D.G. Blazer, C. Pieper, K.G. Meador, S. Shelp, V. Goli, and B. DiPasquale. 1992. "Religious Coping and Depression Among Elderly Hospitalized Medically Ill Men." *American Journal of Psychiatry* 149(12): 1693–1700.

Koenig, H.G., S.M. Ford, L.K. George, D.G. Blazer, and K.G. Meador. 1993. "Religion and Anxiety Disorder." *Journal of Anxiety Disorders*

7: 321–342.

Koenig, H.G., L.K. George, K.G. Meador, D.G. Blazer, and S.M. Ford. 1994. "Religious Practices and Alcoholism in a Southern Adult Population." *Hospital and Community Psychiatry* 45(3): 225–231.

Kroll, J., and W. Sheehan. 1989. "Religious Beliefs and Practices Among 52 Psychiatric Inpatients in Minnesota." *American Journal of Psychiatry* 146: 67–72.

Kudadjie, J.N., and R.K. Aboagye-Mensah. 1992. *The Christian and Social Conduct*. Accra, Ghana: Asempa Publishers.

Kuma, A. 1981. *Jesus of the Deep Forest: Prayers and Praises of Afua Kuma*, trans. Jon Kirby. Accra, Ghana: Asempa Publishers.

Kwast, Lloyd E. 1981. "Understanding Culture." In *Perspectives on the World Christian Movement: A Reader*, eds. Ralph D. Winter and Steven C. Hawthorne. Pasadena, CA: William Carey Library.

Larson, D.B. 1993. *The Faith Factor: An Annotated Bibliography of Systematic Reviews and Clinical Research on Spiritual Subjects*. Volume Two (December). Rockville, MD: National Institute for Health Care Research.

Levin, J.S. 1996. "How Religion Influences Morbidity and Mortality and Health: Reflections on Natural History, Salutogenesis, and Host Resistance." *Social Science and Medicine* 43(5): 849–864.

Levy, S.M. 1986. "Behavior as a Biological Response Modifier: Psychological Variables and Cancer Prognosis." In *Women with Cancer* (289–305), ed. B.L. Anderson. New York: Sringer-Verlag.

Lewis, C.S. 1965. *Perelandra*, New York: Macmillan.

Long, H. 1997. Electronic mail to author, 7 June. Korhogo, Cote D'Ivoire.

Long, W.M. 1992. "Organizational Competence for the Facilitation of Community Participation in Three Community Based Health Care Projects in Kenya." Doctoral dissertation, School of Public Health, University of North Carolina, Chapel Hill.

Long, W.M. 1994. "God Sees Us in Our Tribes." *Seeing Ourselves Through God's Eyes*. Unpublished inductive Bible studies, Nairobi Chapel, Nairobi, Kenya.

Long, W.M. 1997. "Introducing Social Change through Community Health." *Evangelical Missions Quarterly* 33(1): 318–334.

Matthews, D.A., and D.B. Larson. 1995. *The Faith Factor: An Annotated Bibliography of Clinical Research on Spiritual Subjects*. Volume Three,

Enhancing Life Satisfaction (April). Rockville, MD: National Institute for Health Care Research.

Matthews, D.A., D.B. Larson, and C.P. Barry. 1993. *The Faith Factor: An Annotated Bibliography of Clinical Research on Spiritual Subjects* (July). Rockville, MD: National Institute for Health Care Research.

Mazrui, A. 1986. *The Africans.* Boston: Little, Brown.

Mbiti, J.S. 1975. *The Prayers of African Religion.* Maryknoll, NY: Orbis Books.

Mbiti, J.S. 1992. *African Religions and Philosophy.* Nairobi, Kenya: East African Educational Publishers.

McComiskey, T.E. 1985. *The Covenants of Promise: a Theology of the Old Testament Covenants.* Grand Rapids, MI: Baker Books.

Meyer, C.B., and S.E. Taylor. 1986. "Adjustment to Rape." *Journal of Personality and Social Psychology* 50(6): 1226–1234.

Milingo, E. 1984. *The World In Between.* Maryknoll, NY: Orbis Books.

Mkhwanazi, I. 1989. "The Isangoma as a Psychotherapist." In *Afro-Christian Religion and Healing in Southern Africa*, eds. G.C. Oosthuizen, S.D. Edwards, W.H. Wessels, and I. Hexham, 261–279. Lewiston, NY: Edward Mellen Press.

Moreau, A.S. 1990. *The World of the Spirits: A Biblical Study in the African Context.* Nairobi, Kenya: Evangel Publishing House.

Morris, B. 1995. "Woodland and Village: Reflections on the 'Animal Estate' in Rural Malawi." *Journal of the Royal Anthropological Institute* 1(2).

Moschella, V.D., K.R. Pressman, P. Pressman, and D.E. Weissman. 1997. "The Problem of Theodicy and Religious Response to Cancer." *Journal of Religion and Health* 36(1): 17–20.

National Institutes of Health. 1995. "Classification of Alternative Medical Practices." Rockville, MD: Office of Alternative Medicine.

National Institutes of Health. 1996. "OAM Grant Awards." Rockville, MD: Office of Alternative Medicine.

Ndeti, K. 1972. *Elements of Akamba Life.* Nairobi, Kenya: East African Publishing House.

Nel, Philip J. 1997. "Shalom." In *New International Dictionary of Old Testament Theology and Exegesis* Vol. 4, ed. Willem VanGemeren, 130–135. Grand Rapids, MI: Zondervan.

Nouwen, H.J.M., D.P. McNeil, and D.A. Morrison. 1982. *Compassion: A Reflection on the Christian Life.* New York: Doubleday.

Nussbaum, Stan, ed. 1996. *African Proverbs: Collections, Studies, Bibliographies.* Compact Disk #3, 20:21 Library. Colorado Springs, CO: Global Mapping International.

Nyansako-ni-Nku. 1981. "Traditional Healing and the Church in Africa." *Point* (2): 134–141.

Oosthuizen, G.C. 1989. "Indigenous Healing within the Context of the African Independent Churches." In *Afro-Christian Religion and Healing in Southern Africa*, eds. G.C. Oosthuizen, S.D. Edwards, W.H. Wessels, and I. Hexham, 71–90. Lewiston, NY: Edward Mellen Press.

Orchardson, I. 1961. *The Kipsigis.* Nairobi: Kenya Literature Bureau.

Orubuloye, I.O., J.C. Caldwell, and P. Caldwell. 1997. "Perceived Male Sexual Needs and Male Sexual Behavior in Southwest Nigeria." *Social Science and Medicine* 44(8): 1195–1207.

Pargament, K.I., D.S. Ensing, K. Falgout, B. Olsen, K. Van Haitsma, and R. Warren. 1990. "God Help Me (I): Religious Coping Efforts as Predictors of the Outcomes to Significant Negative Life Events." *American Journal of Community Psychology* 18(6): 793–824.

Patel, V. 1995. "Explanatory Models of Mental Illness in Sub-Saharan Africa." *Social Science and Medicine* 40(9): 1291–1298.

Perner, C. 1992. "Anyuak Religion and Language." *Journal of Religion in Africa* 22(2): 152–158.

Perrin-Jassy, M.F. 1973. *Basic Community in the African Churches*, trans. Sister Jeanne M Lyons. Maryknoll, NY: Orbis Books.

Peterson, C., and M.E.P. Seligman. 1987. "Explanatory Style and Illness." *Journal of Personality* 55(2): 237–265.

Pobee, J.S. 1979. *Toward an African Theology.* Nashville, TN: Abingdon.

"Policy Framework for Urgent Interim Reparation Measures." 1996. Johannesburg, Republic of South Africa: Truth and Justice Commission.

Poloma, M.M., and B.F. Pendleton. 1991. "The Effects of Prayer and Prayer Experiences on Measures of General Well-Being." *Journal of Psychology and Theology* 19(1): 71–83.

Putnam, R.D. 1993. *Making Democracy Work.* Princeton, NJ: Princeton University Press.

Rabins, P.V., M.D. Fitting, J. Eastham, and J. Fetting. 1990. "The Emotional Impact of Caring for the Chronically Ill." *Psychosomatics* 31(3): 331–336.

Rakotsoane, F.C.L. 1996/1997. "Jesus Christ as the Leader of the Ancestors." *Challenge* (39) (Dec./Jan.): 20–21.

Ram, E. 1995. "Healing of the Spirit." In *Transforming Health: Christian Approaches to Healing and Wholeness,* ed. Eric Ram, 79–101. Monrovia, CA: MARC Publications: .

Renne, E.P. 1997. "Local and Institutional Interpretations of IUDS in Southwestern Nigeria." *Social Science and Medicine* 44(8): 1141–1148.

Richardson, V., S. Berman, and M. Piwowarski. 1983. "Projective Assessment of the Relationships Between the Salience of Death, Religion, and Age Among Adults in America." *Journal of General Psychology* 109: 149–156.

Robertson, O.P. 1996. *Covenants.* Suwanee, GA: Great Commission Publications.

Robinson, P. 1994-1996. Private conversations in Kenya.

Roskies, E, and R.S. Lazarus. 1980. "Coping Theory and the Teaching of Coping Skills." In *Behavioral Medicine: Changing Health Life Styles,* eds. Park Davidson and SheenaDavidson. New York: Brunner/Mazel.

Saayman, W. 1992. "AIDS, Healing, and Culture in Africa." *Journal of Theology for South Africa* (78): 41–56.

Schreiter, R.J. 1992. *Reconciliation.* Maryknoll, NY: Orbis Books.

Schwab, R., and K.U. Peterson. 1990. "Religiousness: Its Relation to Loneliness, Neuroticism, and Subjective Well-Being." *Journal for the Scientific Study of Religion* 29(3): 335–345.

Shaw, M. 1996. *The Kingdom of God in Africa.* Grand Rapids, MI: Baker Books.

Shenk, D.W. 1983. *Peace and Reconciliation in Africa.* Nairobi, Kenya: Uzima Press Ltd.

Shorter, A. 1985. *Jesus and the Witchdoctor.* Maryknoll, NY: Orbis Books.

Silver, R.L., and C.B. Wortman. 1980. "Coping with Undesirable Life Events." In *Human Helplessness: Theory and Application,* eds. J. Garber, and M. Seligman. New York: Academic Press.

Simpson, J.W., Jr. 1988. "Spirit." *The International Standard Bible Encyclopedia,* gen. ed. G.W. Bromley, Vol. 4, 599–601. Grand Rapids, MI: Eerdmans Publishers.

Smith, D.K., A.M. Nehmkis, and R.A. Charter. 1983-84. "Fear of Death, Death Attitudes and Religious Conviction in the Terminally

Ill." *International Journal of Psychiatry in Medicine* 13(3): 221–232.

Spence, C., T.S. Danielson, and A.M. Kaunitz. 1984. "The Faith Assembly: A Study of Perinatal and Maternal Mortality." *Indiana Medicine*, March 1984: 180–183.

Spring, A. 1981. Health Care Systems in Northwest Zambia. In *African Healing Strategies*, eds. B. M. du Toit, and I.H. Abdalla, 135–150. New York: Trado-Medic Books.

Strawbridge, W.J., R.D. Cohen, S.J. Shema, and G.A. Kaplan. 1997. "Frequent Attendance at Religious Services and Mortality over 28 Years." *American Journal of Public Health* 87(6): 957–961.

Strecher, V.J., B.M. DeVellis, M.H. Becker, and I.M. Rosenstock. 1986. "The Role of Self-Efficacy in Achieving Health Behavior Change." *Health Education Quarterly* 13(1): 73–91.

Tamburrino, M.B., K.N. Franco, N.B. Campbell, J.E. Pentz, C.L. Evans, and S.G. Jurs. 1990. "Post-Abortion Dysphoria and Religion." *Southern Medical Journal* 83: 736–738.

Taylor, J.J. 1963. *The Primal Vision: Christian Presence amid African Religion*. Philadelphia, PA: Fortress Press.

"TEE Manual for Church Leaders." 1996. Unpublished manuscript for field testing, MAP International and New Sudan Council of Churches, Nairobi, Kenya.

Tennant-Clark, C.M., J.J. Fritz, and F. Beauvais. 1989. "Occult Participation: Its Impact on Adolescent Development." *Adolescence* 24(96): 752–772.

Thomas, G. 1997. "Doctors Who Pray." *Christianity Today* (Jan. 6, 1997): 20–30.

Thomas, J. 1989. "A Study of the Social and Spiritual Impact of Tenwek Community Health Program on Kipsigis Communities." Unpublished paper, HNGR program, Wheaton College, Wheaton, IL.

Thorson, J.A., and F.C. Powell. 1990. "Meanings of Death and Intrinsic Religiosity." *Journal of Clinical Psychology* 46(4): 379–391.

Tsey, K. 1997. "Traditional Medicine in Contemporary Ghana: A Public Policy Analysis." *Social Science and Medicine* 45(7): 1065–1074.

Twesigye, E.K. 1987. *Common Ground, African Religion, and Philosophy*. New York: Peter Lang Publishing.

Twumasi, P.A. 1975. *Medical Systems in Ghana*. Accra, Ghana: Ghana Publishing Company.

Vanderhoof, A.L. 1994. "Cursing and Blessing in Biblical and Cultural

Use." Unpublished paper, Wheaton College, Wheaton IL.

Verhoef, Pieter A. 1997. "Time and Eternity." In *New International Dictionary of Old Testament Theology and Exegesis*, Vol. 4, ed. Willem VanGemeren, 1252–1255. Grand Rapids, MI: Zondervan.

Walsh, A. 1980. "The Prophylactic Effect of Religion on Blood Pressure Levels among a Sample of Immigrants." *Social Science and Medicine* 14B: 59–63.

Walton, J.H. 1994. *Covenant: God's Purpose, God's Plan*. Grand Rapids, MI: Zondervan Publishing House.

Wessels, W.H. 1989. "Healing Practices in the African Independent Churches." In *Afro-Christian Religion and Healing in Southern Africa*, eds. G.C. Oosthuizen, S.D. Edwards, W.H. Wessels, and I. Hexham, 91–108. Lewiston, NY: Edward Mellen Press.

Whitaker, R.E., and J.E. Goehring, comps. 1988. *Eerdmans Analytic Concordance*. Grand Rapids, MI: Eerdmans Publishers.

Wind, J.P. 1995. "A Case for Theology in the Ministry of Healing." *Interpretation* 49 (April): 143–157.

Wolff, H.W. 1981. *Anthropology of the Old Testament*. Philadelphia, PA: Fortress Press.

Yoder, P.S. 1995. "Examining Ethnomedical Diagnoses and Treatment Choices for Diarrheal Disorders in Lubumbashi Swahili." *Medical Anthropology* 16: 211–247.

Zvanaka, S. 1997. African Independent Churches in Context. *Missiology: An International Review* 25(1): 69–75.

Index